Second Edition

Precision POOL

Gerry Kanov
Shari Stauch

Human Kinetics

Library of Congress Cataloging-in-Publication Data

Kanov, Gerry, 1949-
  Precision pool / Gerry Kanov and Shari Stauch. -- 2nd ed.
      p. cm.
  Includes bibliographical references and index.
  ISBN-13: 978-0-7360-7387-5 (soft cover)
  ISBN-10: 0-7360-7387-6 (soft cover)
  1. Pool (Game) I. Stauch, Shari, 1962- II. Title.
  GV891.K33 2008
  794.7'3--dc22

                                                              2007033448

  ISBN-10: 0-7360-7387-6
  ISBN-13: 978-0-7360-7387-5

The Web addresses cited in this text were current as of July 2007, unless otherwise noted.

Acquisitions Editor: Jana Hunter; **Developmental Editor:** Anne Hall; **Assistant Editor:** Cory Weber; **Copyeditor:** John Wentworth; **Proofreader:** Anne Rogers; **Indexer:** Dan Connolly; **Permission Manager:** Carly Breeding; **Graphic Designer:** Fred Starbird; **Graphic Artist:** Tara Welsch; **Cover Designer:** Keith Blomberg; **Photographer (cover):** Klaus Stemmler/Zefa/Corbis; **Photographer (interior):** Jason Zwiker, unless otherwise noted; **Photo Asset Manager:** Laura Fitch; **Visual Production Assistant:** Joyce Brumfield; **Photo Office Assistant:** Jason Allen; **Art Manager:** Kelly Hendren; **Associate Art Manager:** Alan L. Wilborn; **Illustrators:** Paul Harris and Gerry Kanov; **Printer:** Premier Print Group

We thank Pivotal Fitness of Summerville, South Carolina, and Ewa and Mitch Laurance for assistance in providing the photo shoot locations for this book.

Human Kinetics books are available at special discounts for bulk purchase. Special editions or book excerpts can also be created to specification. For details, contact the Special Sales Manager at Human Kinetics.

Printed in the United States of America   10   9   8   7   6   5   4   3

The paper in this book is certified under a sustainable forestry program.

Human Kinetics
Web site: www.HumanKinetics.com

United States: Human Kinetics
P.O. Box 5076
Champaign, IL 61825-5076
800-747-4457
e-mail: humank@hkusa.com

Canada: Human Kinetics
475 Devonshire Road, Unit 100
Windsor, ON N8Y 2L5
800-465-7301 (in Canada only)
e-mail: info@hkcanada.com

Europe: Human Kinetics
107 Bradford Road
Stanningley
Leeds LS28 6AT, United Kingdom
+44 (0)113 255 5665
e-mail: hk@hkeurope.com

Australia: Human Kinetics
57A Price Avenue
Lower Mitcham, South Australia 5062
08 8372 0999
e-mail: info@hkaustralia.com

New Zealand: Human Kinetics
P.O. Box 80
Torrens Park, South Australia 5062
0800 222 062
e-mail: info@hknewzealand.com

To our better halves, Laura and Jeff, who remind us that pool is FUN,
even when we miss . . .

Contents

Foreword

In *Precision Pool*, Gerry Kanov and Shari Stauch take you step by step through the great game of pocket billiards. As two of the most respected and well-known writers in the sport, they complement each other terrifically as they manage to entice the novice, educate the avid player, and fulfill the desires for perfection of the skilled professional. In a concise and easy-to-understand format that includes text, diagrams, and photos, they convey the wisdom and vast knowledge that come only from years of experience.

I wish a book like this had been available when I first started playing. I think of the hours I could have saved with a coach at my side, instructing me along the way. Sure, there was the occasional kind-hearted veteran who would lend advice as I was learning early on, and by virtue of watching great players I picked up a lot of knowledge, but generally I had to seek to improve using the trial-and-error method. The same is not true for you.

This book is so much more than your average book on the basics of pool. I have played for over 25 years and won all of the major championships in the sport, yet this book is a resource I can turn to even now. Whether I want a reminder of the fundamentals or an idea for a new practice drill, *Precision Pool* has it covered.

To sum it up, *Precision Pool* speaks to players at all levels of ability. The book is accessible to everyone, it's easy to understand, and it gives you the tools to take your game to the level you choose. What level that is will be your choice. Have fun, and good luck!

Ewa Laurance, "The Striking Viking"
World Champion
Member of the Billiard Congress of America Hall of Fame

Acknowledgments

First, a shout-out to our terrific editor, Anne Hall. Imagine all the work that goes into creating a second edition in color that includes new text, new photos, and even new diagrams. Anne, many thanks—you made it all painless.

For advice on the topics that required us to call out the experts, thanks to Cecilia C. Heiges, OD, for her in*sight*ful thoughts on eyesight and to physical trainers Alex Chumley and Christina Yates for offering up pool-specific exercises that won't require you to spend your first years' winnings to join a gym!

Next, big thank-yous to ace pool photographers Jerry Forsyth, Dale Shank, and Garry Hodges. Your photos of our sport's top professional pool players really are worth a thousand words. Thanks also to *Pool & Billiard Magazine* art director Paul Harris for kick-starting our color diagram templates. Thanks to photographer Jason Zwiker; models Natalie Spencer, Megan Stauch, Jake Stauch, and Mitch Laurance; and professional player and model Ewa Laurance, who also graciously hosted our photo shoot in her ultimate home billiard room! Thanks also to trainer and model Christina Yates and model Jake Stauch for volunteering to illustrate physical training techniques at the Pivotal Fitness training center.

And finally, as always, a huge thank-you to all the pool players who have come before us to grow our sport, to the champions who continue to make it great, and to the fans, who can appreciate the talent and finesse and sheer beauty of a well-struck shot.

Introduction

Whether you're a beginning player interested in learning more about pool . . .
An amateur who'd like to compete in local leagues and tournaments . . .
A dedicated semi-pro aspiring to break into the pro ranks . . .
An enthusiastic student of the cue sports . . .
Or a professional player seeking new insights . . .

We guarantee that *Precision Pool* will offer you ideas you've never had the opportunity to explore in any instruction book on the cue sports.

GETTING THE MOST OUT OF *Precision Pool*

Pool is a *sport*, recognized as sport by the International Olympic Committee. To truly enjoy playing this sport you'll want to learn more than just the rules of the game and how the balls move around the table. You want to know how to move, how to think, how to become mentally and physically tougher than your opponents. *Precision Pool* travels beyond the normal realm of available material written on the sport, opening a colorful new world in which to develop your knowledge and your skills. Our goal is for you to truly enjoy the learning process and to come to appreciate the artistry, sport, and sheer fun of pocket billiards.

One of the most engaging aspects of pool is the colorful surface and targets we become mesmerized by as we play. The first thing players learn is what color goes with what numbered ball, and which color cloth is the most common (green rules!). Yet, sadly, most pool instruction books offer up a black-and-white world. For the first time in a mainstream instruction book for pool, we're offering you lessons in living color—brightly colored diagrams and photos that make the sport and its intricacies come alive. We hope you enjoy the view as much as we've enjoyed adding the color.

Precision Pool assumes that you have a little working knowledge of the cue sports and the rules of your favorite among today's most popular games, be it Nine Ball, Eight Ball, Straight Pool (also known as 14.1 Continuous), or One Pocket. If you need a rules refresher, visit your local club or billiard supply store for a copy of the Billiard Congress of America's *Billiards: The Official Rules & Records Book*. This inexpensive guide is updated annually with new rules variations and professional sports records; it also includes rules for less popular games to amuse and inform you and your pool-playing friends.

Use the Keys

You'll quickly discover through your own practice and competition that there just isn't enough paper in this book, or a book 100 times its size, to diagram every shot you'll encounter on your path to great pool playing. Still, we felt the need to arm you with as much actual situation play as we could. The compromise has resulted in diagrams of key shot and game situations throughout the book—shots that you'll definitely encounter in your own game and that will serve as a guide for you to expand your knowledge. Along with teaching you new skills, we've accompanied our lessons with practical applications of the skills in game situations. After all, power tools are only useful if you know how to use them.

With a full-color book comes the added luxury of being able to make each diagram more user-friendly. In our diagrams, the path of the cue ball to the object ball is depicted with a solid line, and the paths of the object balls are depicted with solid arrows. The resulting path of the cue ball after it has made contact with the object ball is depicted with a dashed arrow. For clarity, color has been added to these lines and arrows when necessary. Lastly, certain figures include cue ball illustrations next to the main diagram to indicate the optimal spot of impact for your cue tip.

Where applicable, we've described situations for each of the most popular cue games, but as any pro knows, you can learn something in every pool game, and plenty of the situations illustrated intermingle between common games. Even if you're strictly a Nine Ball player, take the time to read about Eight Ball, Straight Pool, and One Pocket. In most cases, a concept that's relevant in one game carries over to another. Because of the nature of the sport, its confines and concepts, and its dual offensive and defensive characteristics, there will be many similarities in the skills required, as different as the format and rules may appear at first glance.

Take It in Order

The text has been prepared in the order most players take to develop their skills. This means if you start with chapter 7, you'll learn safeties that you won't yet have developed the physical skills to execute. Likewise, it's impossible to learn speed control in chapter 3 if you haven't taken the time to develop sound fundamentals in chapter 1. Take the time to read the book at least once from beginning to end before skipping to those areas that most interest you.

This expanded full-color edition of *Precision Pool* is organized into 12 chapters, two more than the original edition. We have also added material that focuses on development of the "whole" player. We have included exercises that offer hands-on practice for the many techniques and skills you'll learn.

We begin with chapter 1, The Shooter's Checklist, which tells you about the various kinds of equipment you'll encounter, how to choose and maintain your own equipment, and the fundamental skills you'll need to master first: proper handling of the cue, proper stance, stroke, approaching the table, and establishing your rhythm of play. Of the thousands of people we encounter in billiard clubs across the country, the vast majority could improve their games 100 percent just by learning proper fundamentals. These comprise your foundation; build it strong!

Chapter 2, Aim and Vision, lets you in on the secrets of aiming, beginning with a unique section on finding the pocket center and adjusting for pocket movement. Perhaps the most often-asked question from our readers and fans is how to aim, and we've suggested the best and most popular options available. Then, in a special section unique to pocket billiard instruction, you'll learn how to improve your aiming accuracy with information on how your eyes work, optical illusions, perception, focus, and eye dominance—factors that can affect your aim and your choice of aiming methods.

In chapter 3, Cue Ball Control, we focus on the techniques and optimal results of using center ball, follow, draw, and left and right english as you learn to maneuver your cue ball around the table.

Chapter 4 then delves into Game Breaks—you'll learn how to develop a powerful break. The break is one of the most important shots of the game; a well-built break can win you the game. We offer up the best breaks for each of the most popular cue games, including difficult defensive breaks.

The more advanced concepts of pool are discussed in chapter 5, Critical Shots. You'll learn to execute bank shots, combinations, and carom shots, along with critical (yet often overlooked) stop, stun, and drag shots. We also show you the advanced skills of executing kicks, jump shots, and massés—the real crowd pleasers.

In chapter 6, Position Play, you'll be able to use all your newfound skills in real game strategy, beginning with position and pattern play. Basic pattern types are discussed and diagrammed for the most popular games. Chapter 7, Pattern Play, then integrates the rules into sound advice on how to look for patterns, how to find natural paths around the pool table, and when to travel toward or away from the object ball—all keys to honing your own skills. Equally important, you'll learn in chapter 8, Safety Play, when to recognize that a good pattern doesn't exist, making a safety option your best bet. Many sample safeties are shown, and you'll learn how to create effective safeties that use the cue ball, object ball, or both balls.

Chapter 9, Situation-Specific Shots, integrates the knowledge from pattern and safety play into dozens of key shot situations, offering considered options for all those times at the table when you're just not sure which way to go. Learning the decision-making process in real game situations will increase your skills in making the right choice when you step to the table. That's followed by chapter 10, Match Strategy and Tactics, with a natural progression into advanced game situations, including taking intentional fouls, winning games via the three-foul rule, and using an opponent's strengths and weaknesses to your advantage. You'll discover secrets of team strategy and learn how to find, enter, and compete in lucrative leagues and tournaments.

Chapter 11, Mind–Body Toughness, transports you into that brave new world of billiard instruction that serious players have sought for years. Incredibly important to your high-performance pool game is heightening your mental awareness. The first part of this chapter addresses the most practical methods of building concentration in your pool sessions, practicing mental imaging for run-outs and pinpoint position play, building confidence in your skills, and playing pool effortlessly. We continue with your physical game, including exercises, stretching, and warm-ups to maximize your playing ability. Pool, like golf, tennis, or bowling, is a sport, and these additional skills will furnish you with immediate improvement in your physical performance by targeting areas specific to pool. It's well known that most pros go back to the basics when they're having problems with their own skills, so we've also included a unique trouble-shooting section that offers quick fixes for typical problems you might be experiencing in your game as a result of poor physical habits.

Finally, we put it all together in chapter 12, Practice Made Fun. Included are several fun games to maximize your practice sessions without the dull repetition and monotony associated with practice drills. No individual can practice everything we've suggested every day, so you'll want to target certain areas of your game on certain days as you develop your skills. We provide you with a sample one-week program, allowing you to target areas of your game, continue a regular practice regimen, and avoid the boredom that can stagnate your progress.

Over 100 million men and women worldwide have picked up a cue in the last year and played pool, and most of you are still looking for ways to improve your game. No matter what your current level of ability, no matter how far you wish to take your skills, *Precision Pool* will take you there faster.

Above all, pool is about having fun. This is a sport, a game, a form of recreation enjoyed by millions of people. But it can be a difficult and frustrating sport for untold millions—and you—if you're not enjoying it. Accept the challenges, embrace the difficulties, and revel in the mastery of each new skill, no matter how trivial at first glance. There's not a professional player in all the pool circuit who will tell you they've mastered the art of the cue sports. What they *have* mastered is the love of pool, and the thrill of discovery in a sport that will endlessly challenge them for as long as they wield a cue. We wish the same for each of you.

Gerry "The Ghost"

Shari "The Shark"

CHAPTER 1

The Shooter's Checklist

Let's get started. First, you'll want to find the best places to play, practice, and improve your cue skills. The right place for you to play depends on your skill level, geographical location, and budget. Once you've established your main base of billiard operations, you can determine the equipment you'll need. Armed and ready to attack your pool game, we'll begin by building a strong physical foundation with fundamental skills such as stance, various bridges, the stroke (or swing), and timing. Even if you're already an accomplished player, a quick cross-check of your fundamental skills against the information in this section will enhance your cueing ability.

THE RIGHT PLACE TO PLAY

Pool is a unique sport. It doesn't require a field or a gymnasium, a course or a track. Although it's played indoors like bowling or basketball, the minimal area required for competition allows the sport access to a variety of venues. This flexibility has made the cue sports one of the most popular recreational activities in the United States. It has also made for some confusion about table sizes, games, and rules and where it's best to play, compete, and improve your game.

Though there are many choices of where to play, your preference most often depends on your level of skill. This is not unlike golfers who begin on municipal courses, and, as their games progress, seek the greater challenges offered by championship-caliber courses. In pool, however, the jump to playing on better equipment in better clubs won't cost you an arm and a leg. Billiard club rates remain highly competitive, especially considering the escalating costs of other recreational activities—just compare the cost of a couple of hours of pool to the price of a movie ticket and a bag of popcorn.

Players today are usually first exposed to the game on a relative's or friend's home table. Naturally, as a player's environment expands, so do the choices of where to play pool, and from those first experiences at home, occasional games are played in a local bar or lounge. This is typically the first avenue for organized competition. Not surprising, it's this atmosphere that transforms the person who plays pool on occasion into a pool player. Players begin to engage in weekly league play at their local bars and, soon after, many of them seek better equipment, bigger tables, and the open space and social climate of a billiard club, participating in club leagues and tournaments. A few will even advance to the professional arena.

Many players, after a few years of regular visits to the billiard club, will come full circle and begin playing at home again after the purchase of their own table. This offers them the flexibility of playing as often as they'd like without waiting for a table. They also get the enjoyment of owning equipment purchased and maintained to their own specifications.

Other venues where pool has become quite popular are recreation centers, senior centers, and college campuses. In fact, wherever people congregate these days, there's likely to be a pool table. This makes for tremendous variances in the equipment and playing conditions you'll encounter, but you'll soon find the ideal place with equipment that best suits your own tastes.

EQUIPMENT

Specific equipment is essential to the game of pool. Without a pool table, proper lighting, cloth and balls, a pool cue, and some accessories, you can't play the game. A pool table will be provided, of course. From there, cues, cases and an assortment of accessories offer you the chance to personalize equipment to your game.

Pool Table

The primary piece of equipment required for playing pocket billiards is a pool table. Pool table sizes come in 7-, 8-, 9-, and 10-foot (2.1, 2.4, 2.7, and 3.0 m) models, plus a hybrid called the oversized 8, 8.5, or big 8 (a model that now accounts for less than 1 percent of manufacturer sales). Snooker tables, gaining popularity in some areas of the United States, are a standard 12 feet (3.7 m); however, 10-foot models are becoming more available.

The purchase of a pool table today is easily the best buy in the recreation marketplace. A table costing a few thousand dollars 20 years ago sells for virtually the same price today, despite increased material and labor costs. And if you're in the market for a home table purchase, this is one piece of furniture that will grace your home for a lifetime.

The most popular size for a home table is 4 by 8 feet (1.2 by 2.4 m), which fits well in most large recreation rooms or basements. Remember that it's not just the size of the table you should consider but the space you must have on all four sides—typically a minimum of 60 inches (152 cm), which is the length of a cue from the table edge. This allows extra space for the player to pull the cue back on the backswing, even when executing rail shots, while avoiding any obstacle such as a wall, post, or piece of furniture. Smaller tables were invented to accommodate smaller playing areas, and if your available space won't allow an 8-foot model, the 7-foot option is available, most often tagged with the nickname "bar table" or "bar box." Actual bar tables are typically 7 feet long but come equipped with coin-operated mechanisms, an option you won't need unless you're trying to make your money back.

Most billiard clubs have a selection of competition-size tables that are 4.5 by 9 feet (1.4 by 2.7 m), though 8-foot models are popular in the southern United States. Older rooms, or upscale rooms with a selection of antique tables, might feature some tables that are 5 by 10 feet (1.5 by 3.0 m)—which was the commercial standard until the early 1950s—along with carom tables (no pockets), and even the massive snooker table, which is 6 by 12 feet (1.8 by 3.6 m). If you frequent such an establishment, you'll undoubtedly have an excellent opportunity to watch and learn the carom and snooker games from local aficionados of those disciplines.

A good pool table will have a slate bed, and no matter what people might try to tell you, there's no substitute. Slate provides the most consistent table surface; plus it's heavy, durable, and elastic, and it will last forever. Most slate used in pool tables is imported from the Liguria region of Italy and bears an OIS (Original Italian Slate) mark. A few manufacturers have experimented with other materials. Brazilian and Chinese slate are more economical options for manufacturers, but pocket billiards is laden with tradition, and the desire for Italian slate is no exception.

Table cushions are made of rubber, which, along with the slate, is covered with billiard fabric. Materials for the rest of the table vary depending on the manufacturer's preference of construction, stability, design, and decor.

Beyond the basics, there's a table to satisfy every person's tastes, from traditional to contemporary, designed in every color of the rainbow, with billiard fabrics to match. Today, the average price in US dollars that customers pay for a pool table is $3,400 for a 9-foot model, $2,300 for an 8-footer, and $950 for a 7-footer.

A billiard dealer can steer you in the best direction toward the purchase of a pool table. It's safe to say that such a purchase is still one of the best values around—a well-constructed table will outlast all of us.

Billiard Lighting

Proper lighting over your billiard table, though an often-overlooked feature, ensures the maximum use of your equipment by preventing troublesome shadows and painful eyestrain. For the best lighting for your pool table, use fluorescent bulbs rather than incandescent light bulbs. Fluorescent lighting is easier on the eyes, and frankly, more economical and environmentally friendly. Because they'll last much longer, fluorescent bulbs are definitely worth the initial cost difference you'll pay. Many manufacturers now offer fluorescent light bulbs for regular incandescent sockets. To prevent shadows on the balls, especially near the short rails of the table, billiard lights should extend the length of the table. This makes for clearer visibility of balls and angles. Some billiard clubs have tried to cut costs with inferior lighting; try to choose a club with lighting that allows you to play comfortably for the longest time. Also avoid clubs where the lighting is recessed in the ceiling. You can trust that club owners who don't know enough to place the lights closer to the table probably don't have a reasonable amount of knowledge about your other equipment needs, either.

Cloth and Balls

Once commonly called *felt*, billiard fabric is really a worsted or nonworsted wool or wool–nylon blend. Worsted wools (more expensive) consist of combed fibers and result in the most consistent playing surface with the least *pilling*. Pilling occurs when fibers loosen from the wool strands and form small cloth bits, or pills, on the surface of the table.

You can purchase billiard fabric in virtually any color to match your decor, but we caution against anything that tends to quickly become harsh on the eyes. Reds, purples, and other bright colors might be pretty to look at for a few minutes, but eye fatigue soon sets in, and you won't be enjoying your game as much or as often. The same can be said of bold patterns. At first glance they might seem like fun, but they often aren't practical over the long haul. Some home table owners have found compromise in using a patterned cloth covering the cushions only. Also growing in popularity is actual artwork in the cloth, such as a favorite painting or photograph.

These actually tend to be less distracting than a repeating pattern, but, depending on the image used, they can create optical illusions on anything from angles to distance to the pocket. Decorated billiard fabric is an appealing option for the family game room, but think twice if you're a serious player. Pool's tough enough without the added distractions.

If you're playing in a club or lounge, cloth types and color choices will already be made for you. Because cloth must be changed more often, chances are that billiard fabric in public venues will be more durable but less ideal for playing. Don't worry about this; it's best to learn to play in all sorts of conditions. And the cloth that's playing poorly today because of excessive heat or humidity might play great tomorrow. This is just one of those variables we have to live with. Look on the bright side—unless you're competing on an outdoor table, your pool game will never be rained out!

Most billiard balls distributed and sold in the United States are from a single company, Saluc, located in Belgium, best known for balls manufactured under the Aramith name. Saluc produces more than 900 kinds of balls and exports them across the globe. Balls used to be made of ivory, but composite material and clay, today's durable alternatives, are predominantly made of phenolic resins. Balls from Asia are made from polyester resins, making them less expensive to produce; the quality of these is geared toward limited use on your home table.

Because phenolic resins are photosensitive, white portions of billiard balls often yellow with age, but that won't affect their playability. Balls should be cleaned to avoid buildup of chalk, dirt, and hand oils. Many people wax their billiard balls, and although this makes them look great, it can also cause some skidding because the smooth finish eliminates friction. Clean but not too slippery is what discerning players desire. Various cleaning products are on the market for your equipment; consult your local billiard supply store for their recommendations. Be sure you use a product that won't leave residue on the balls that can transfer to the cloth surface of your table.

The standard size of a pocket billiard ball is 2.25 inches in diameter (5.7 cm); it weights 6 ounces (170 g). Manufacturers take great pains to keep a close watch on variances in weight, size, roundness, and balance so that you won't have to. You will, of course, run into unusual cue balls on coin-operated tables. These balls are heavier and larger, or they contain a magnet inside to keep the cue ball from arriving in the same spot as the object balls (allowing you to retrieve the cue ball on a scratch without inserting more coins). New technology also allows for recognition of a cue ball based on its color so that a cue ball can now match the set; look for such innovations at clubs near you.

The Pool Cue

Not so many years ago, a good custom cue could cost as little as $100. That was then, this is now. American-made, wood, two-piece custom pool cues have become all the rage, and the collectors' market has forced prices up and up. Graphite and composite-material cues were introduced to the market in the 1980s and have become popular, both on their own and used in combination with wood materials.

The beauty and quality of today's custom cues are more sought after than at any time in history. Pro shops, billiard supply stores, and magazine ads offer an amazing number of choices, and most cues are the best built and best playing available to any generation of pool players. Players with one cue are becoming rare; most add to their personal collection as they continue to progress. Also more popular than ever now are specific cue companies making shafts for many different brands of cues. These special shafts offer less deflection or more durability, depending on what you're looking for, than your traditional maker might offer. Add to this the new bevy of break cues, jump cues, and break–jump combinations, and you'll find that cue cases are quickly becoming close cousins to golf bags.

It's the limitless variety that makes cue buying and pool playing so exciting. A single manufacturer might produce a dozen lines, with half a dozen models in each line, all varying in color, wrap, inlay, joint, and so on. Some players are under the impression that the larger manufacturers won't make a custom cue, but all the large cue makers we know are willing to create to a customer's specs. Custom cue makers number in the hundreds in the United States alone, and several dozen are featured each year in booths at consumer shows, tournaments, and even art galleries.

The following list and figure 1.1 cover some of the terms and specifications you'll need to know regarding your cue:

- *Length*: The standard length of a cue stick is 58 inches (147.3 cm). Most cue makers provide choices in length, with a range of 56 to 60 inches (142.2 to 152.4 cm). The player's height is not as much of a factor as limb length, though height and limb length tend to correspond. If you're short, a long cue might feel cumbersome and unbalanced. If you're tall or have long arms, you'll tend to run out of cue with a shorter model. That is, you'll have to hold the cue too far back to achieve a proper stroking motion. If you have this problem, seek a longer weapon.

- *Weight*: The most common weight range for cue sticks is 18 to 21 ounces (510 to 595 g); the standard settles in at 19 to 19.25 ounces (539 to 546 g). Players are divided over the desirable weight of the break cue. Some lean toward a heavier cue with the idea of putting more weight behind the stroke, whereas others prefer a lighter cue, claiming this allows more speed and flexibility in the stroke, resulting in more power. Many players still prefer to break with cues similar in weight to their regular playing cues.

- *Balance*: When speaking of the weight of cues, many players also talk about the balance point—which refers to where the weight is on the cue. To test the balance point, hold the cue on one hand, palm up and flat, until it doesn't tip toward either side. Most manufacturers advertise a balance point 1 to 2 inches (2.5 to 5 cm) above the wrap or 8 inches (20 cm) above the butt. This is partially a matter of personal preference, but a cue that's properly balanced will always feel natural to you, never awkward or butt-heavy. If you hold your cue farther up, you'll want a balance point that corresponds.

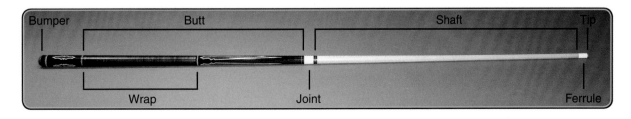

Figure 1.1 Parts of a pool cue.

- *Tips and tapers*: 13 millimeters is the most common tip size, with ranges from 10 millimeters (predominantly snooker cues) to 14 millimeters. Too small a tip can result in a loss of control; too large a tip won't allow you to put as much spin on the cue ball. Cue tips are made of leather or one of the new varieties of synthetic materials on the market. The synthetics retain their shape better, but traditionalists prefer leather. Another option is the layered tip, which offers the best of both worlds—leather glued in layers to offer the qualities of leather but better preserve the shape and playability of the tip. These tend to be more expensive, but many top players agree they more than make up for the added cost in what they offer toward consistency. Taper, without getting too technical, is the amount of size gradation of the shaft from the tip back toward the joint of the cue. These will vary depending on the manufacturer, but they settle into the 9- to 12-inch (23 to 30 cm) range; the 10-inch (25 cm) pro taper is the most common.

- *Joints and ferrules*: You'll often find ivory in the ferrule and joint construction in older cues and in the artistic cues produced by some of today's custom cue makers. Though considered a prized material in cue construction, ivory is also more delicate. The newer plastics are more common, and usually more durable. Joint materials vary even more, from steel to plastic to various animal horns or tusks, including ivory. Each will feel slightly different to you, but we have cues in our collection with steel joints, plastic, and even buffalo horn—and they all play well. Again, it boils down to personal preference and your desire for the product of a certain cue maker. Then, you'll hear about joint screws. There are big screws, short ones, wood-to-wood, quick release joints, metal–wood combinations that will again all be part of your selection process. A cuemaker's goal is to build a cue that feels as much like a one-piece cue as possible, allowing the energy of the shot to travel from the cue tip through the cue to your stroking arm.

Bottom line—does the cue feel good? Does it offer a solid hit? Do you feel comfortable shooting with it? These are the questions that should concern you.

Accessories

Billiard accessories are designed to help you play better, or make playing easier. Your local retailer or a billiard club with a retail section can offer you a selection of cue cases to shelter your cue; pocket liners to make the pockets on your pool table smaller and more difficult; mechanical bridges and bridge heads for hard-to-reach shots; cue papers, burnishers, and cleaners to keep your cue clean and smooth; chalk and talcs; gloves to eliminate the need for messy talcs; tip tappers, shapers, and scuffers to maintain your cue tip; jump cues that make jumping the cue ball over impeding balls easier; break cues designed to improve your breaking ability; and so on. The list is seemingly endless.

Then there's the proliferation of instructional materials available in today's marketplace, on everything from building cues to playing One Pocket. In the recent past, knowledge of these skills was a closely kept secret, passed on to the fraternity of players and select manufacturers. But you can now benefit from the pool boom of the 1980s that caused a tremendous increase in retail sales and an ever-increasing demand for educational materials. Many books and tapes now exist on the cue sports, and most have something of value to offer the aspiring player. Your best

Developing Your Preshot Routine

A consistent preshot routine is a simple yet critical part of any successful player's game. It's so simple, in fact, that players often skip over it in favor of the more tangible, and supposedly more challenging, aspects of the game.

But imagine this. You're playing a match against a talented opponent who has just run the last three racks. He or she finally misses a combination shot and leaves you a look at the next ball. Your first instinct is to jump out of your chair and shoot, just so you feel you're back in the game. But wait. Before the urge to shoot overwhelms you, step back and take a deep breath. This is where your preshot routine should kick in. Your routine brings comfort to your body and confidence to your mind, promoting familiarity and consistency.

Your preshot routine begins in your mind. Analyze the table and the situation. Playing pocket billiards is like playing chess; you can't think about just one move at a time. A successful strategy is a well thought-out coordination of moves. Before stepping into your stance, have a plan. Indecision is a formula for disaster.

Your thinking will depend on which of the cue sports you're playing. Take Nine Ball as an example. Your opponent has just missed the 3-ball, and you have a decent shot. The questions to ask yourself are, Where are the 4-ball and the 5-ball? and Do I have the skill to make the 3-ball and place the cue ball in good position to make the 4-ball? Will it be at a good angle to get on the 5-ball?

In your mind, you follow the rack all the way to the 9-ball. Think through at least three balls before you shoot the first ball. When you can't, a safety play should come to mind. Now, and this is critical, before you shoot that second ball (4-ball), you must have again thought through at least three balls. If this sounds burdensome or difficult, you'll find it becomes easier with practice.

Strategy in Nine Ball is in some respects easier than in other cue games because the table dictates your next shot. Other games don't afford such a luxury; the patterns are virtually limitless, and some patterns are better than others. That's where experience and knowledge of the different games come into play.

These steps can guarantee you a successful preshot routine:

1. Step to the table and chalk up.
2. Review the pattern and options dictated by the lay of the balls.
3. Decide where to put the object ball and where to put the cue ball.
4. Visualize the shot happening with all its related table activity.
5. Step into the shot.
6. Put all your focus on pocketing the ball, knowing your cue ball will arrive in the exact spot you have visualized.
7. Shoot the shot with confidence.

Naturally these steps work best after you've learned the proper fundamentals. Your stance, grip, bridge selection, rhythm, and timing should all be determined before you begin your preshot routine.

bet in selecting instructional materials is to check with better players in your area, talk to your local club owner (many show videos in their clubs to get players more involved and even rent instructional videos to patrons), or consult book and video reviews in billiard publications.

Many Web sites are devoted solely to pool players. The Pool & Billiard Online Expo (www.poolmag.com/expo.cfm) boasts a dozen showrooms packed with Web sites that offer everything from tables to cues to accessories to supply stores and billiard clubs. If you enjoy surfing the Internet, this is an ideal place to begin learning more about the sport and its equipment. The site also includes live tournament coverage and instruction tidbits, including the popular "tip of the day."

FUNDAMENTAL SKILLS

So you've chosen your equipment and you're ready to play pool. You know the object of the sport is to make balls (if you want to continue shooting). You also need to play *shape* for the next shot. However, before we go too far, there's no substitute for good fundamental skills. If your body doesn't feel comfortable, nothing else will either. These fundamentals, including stance, grip, bridges, swing, follow-through, and rhythm and timing will turn your body into a solid foundation from which to manipulate the cue stick.

Stance

One of the most important keys to playing well begins with how players plant their feet, or rather, the back foot. The placement of the back foot—right foot for right-handed players, and left foot for left-handed players—is key. If your back foot is too close to the table, your body becomes cramped and can't swing the cue freely. This often results in a crossover stroke or jumping up on the shot to get your body out of the way. If your foot is too far back, your body is bent too far forward. This too puts you in an awkward position and restricts cue movement.

Here are 10 easy steps to find the proper placement for your back foot:

1. Stand up straight behind a shot at the table.
2. Line up the little toe of your back foot with the cue ball and object ball.
3. Hold the cue stick with your back hand (not your bridge hand).
4. Let your arms hang naturally down at your sides.
5. Place the tip of the cue stick about an inch (2.5 cm) behind the cue ball (see figure 1.2).
6. Pivot your back foot—that is, swing your heel in toward your body.
7. Step your front foot to a comfortable position.
8. Bend at the waist.
9. Lock or slightly bend the back leg.
10. Allow your front leg to bend slightly and be relaxed (see figure 1.3).

Different body types dictate different positions for comfort. Players with short legs might have a closer foot position than players with long legs or wide shoulders. It's most important that you listen to your body to find your comfort zone. Shorter players tend to lock the back leg. Taller or long-legged players must often bend both legs or end up with sore backs. Weight distribution also depends on what's most

Figure 1.2 Approaching your pool stance.

Figure 1.3 Bending into a relaxed stance.

comfortable for you. Famed legend Willie Mosconi believed weight should be evenly distributed on both feet. Joe Davis, a legendary snooker champion, thought the forward leg and foot should bear more of weight, and yet another legend, Michael Cochran, believed weight should be on the back leg and foot.

Why do we stress comfort so much? Because pool is often played over long stretches of time. Start out uncomfortable and you'll finish downright sore. Again, a stance that keeps you balanced and sturdy through your entire shot and feels good too is what works for you.

These guidelines should put you in position to deliver the cue smoothly and deliberately. In fact, it's a process you'll want to return to often during each playing session. Check your body position regularly until it becomes second nature. Spacing yourself properly behind your shot prevents many bad habits in your game. A relaxed leg position allows you to make subtle subconscious adjustments in your aim (more on aiming in chapter 2).

Once you've established a comfortable stance, check the following:

- Are you balanced? A friend or partner can help you with this. If you lose your balance or move your stance when nudged from either side, you're not balanced. Remember that you're laying a foundation; it's got to start out sturdy.

- Can you easily see the shot on the table? Check your head position. Your chin should be directly over the cue stick and everything—cue, chin, and swinging arm—should be in line behind the shot (see figure 1.4).

- Does your cue stick have room to swing freely through your shot? If your cue is hitting any part of your body in your follow-through, you'll need to adjust.

Figure 1.4   Front view of ideal stance. Notice that the chin is directly over the cue.

photo by Garry Hodges

Pro Vivian Villarreal is able to deliver a powerful swing by keeping her chin higher than is typical for women players.

- How low are you bent over? Bending too much will, in most cases, restrict movement of your swinging arm. We've observed in many players that a lower head position equates to aiming accuracy. But it's also true that standing up a bit more offers more power in your delivery. Watch professionals play. Notice any stance differences between the two sexes? Nine out of 10 men play with their heads up higher in their stance, whereas women tend to play with their chins on, or nearly on, the cue. One exception on the women's pro tour is Vivian Villarreal, the Texas Tornado. She's also known for having one of the most powerful strokes among pro female players. If you're running out of room to execute with the power you need, try raising your body a few inches to give yourself more room to deliver that perfect swing.
- Is your swinging arm hanging naturally? Make sure your back arm is not turned inward or outward from the elbow and can deliver a smooth swing naturally, as shown in figure 1.5. Again, giving yourself enough room should eliminate poor arm position.

You're going to notice, especially among better players in your area and pros playing on television, many variances from the physical outlines we're describing here. Let's get one thing straight from the outset. Many professionals have physical quirks that might not look right or pretty or be by the book. They might vary a great deal from what we're telling you to go for. You'll see very low stances, sideways stances, cockeyed head positions, sidearm swings, forward grips, and so on. Remember, though, in most cases they've been playing that way for 10 or more years, 6 to 10 hours a day. In other words, bad habits that were perhaps never corrected in the early years of play were overcome over time. Unless you plan to invest as much time into your pool game as they have, learn proper body placement from the beginning.

Figure 1.5   Keeping the back arm in line with the elbow ensures a smooth swing.

Now that you've developed your basic stance, one quick note: You won't always be able to use it. Certain shots in which the cue ball is difficult to reach require a few variations, including stretching one leg behind you or putting a leg on the table. The rules are less strict here because different body types find different comfort zones for stretch shots. See figures 1.6 and 1.7 for classic examples, and then do some experimenting on your own. Later we'll discuss altered stance positions for your break and for unusual critical shots such as swerve, jump, and massé shots.

Grip or Hold

Very little has been written about the grip hand, perhaps because it's almost always behind your body, your line of aim, and the spot where most people assume the game is being played—on the table. Nevertheless, even tiny problems with your back hand and arm can translate to critical errors up front. Consider bowling. So much depends on the movement and proper coordination of the back arm as it swings back from the body and then comes forward to release the bowling ball. Now visualize your swinging arm in the same way, holding a cue instead of a ball. Your back arm and hand are what really control your cue on every shot.

Unfortunately, when players do realize that control lies with the back hand, they tend to start overcontrolling, which becomes problematic. The solution is compromise. Develop solid fundamental skills in handling your cue properly, then let the cue stick do the work. This means, first and foremost, ease up on your grip. Frankly, we prefer not to use the word "grip." People picture a death grip or vice grip and feel they need to strangle their cue. Wrong. A better word than "grip" is "hold."

Much has been written on where to hold the cue, mostly focusing on finding the balance point of your cue stick, then moving the hand back 5 to 6 inches (about 12 to 15 cm) or more if you're a taller player. Shorter players with long arms will tell

Figure 1.6 Stretching to reach a shot with one leg behind you provides a comfortable alternative stance for hard-to-reach shots.

Figure 1.7 Another stance alternative is one leg on the table. (But remember, in the rules of pool, the other foot must always be touching the floor.)

Figure 1.8   The ideal swinging position of the arm.

you this hold doesn't work. In fact, there's no steadfast rule for a spot to hold your cue behind the balance point. Instead, focus on the placement of your swinging arm in relation to the cue and the floor. The upper part of your arm, from your shoulder to your elbow, should be parallel to the floor. The lower part of your arm should be perpendicular to the floor when in a relaxed position (see figure 1.8).

If you need to move your arm back farther, or up closer to the balance point, go ahead. If you don't know where the balance point of your cue is and feel that you need a reference point to start with, you can find the point a few inches from the bottom of the wrap or 8 inches (20 cm) above the butt. Hold the cue lightly with your index finger and thumb until, like a scale, the cue stick tips neither to one side nor the other.

On finesse shots, or shots in which the cue ball and object ball are very close together, you'll be using a shorter bridge, in which case you'll need to move your grip hand closer to the joint of the cue to maintain your parallel position. In contrast, when your bridge hand is farther from the cue tip, your back hand moves backward, accordingly (see figure 1.9).

To hold the cue properly, use your two middle fingers and your thumb. Then wrap your index and little fingers around the cue. Your cue should rest gently in your grip hand, and your hand should turn neither inward nor outward but rather hang relaxed and in line with your arm from your elbow down. Imagine you're holding a cream puff that, if squeezed too hard, will ooze out filling. A light hold on the cue is crucial for a straight, smooth follow-through; this point can't be emphasized enough. Just check out the pro golf tour, where you'll see few calluses on players' hands despite the rigors of swinging a club at 120 miles per hour. A loose hold gives the professional golfer incredible results. What does that tell you? In the same way, a relaxed hold on your cue can give you the best results.

Here's a test to check if you're holding your cue stick too tightly. Lay your bridge hand down in an open bridge on the table. If you can lift the front of the cue stick off of your bridge hand, using your grip hand, you're gripping too tight. Figure 1.10 (page 16) demonstrates this exercise. It might not be easy to stay loose initially, especially in difficult or tense shot and game situations. But remain steadfast in your resolve and work toward a loose grip.

A simple way to practice loosening your grip is to hold a couple of pieces of chalk along with your cue stick. Shoot several shots holding both the cue and the chalk and you'll soon realize that holding onto the chalk with the cue in your hand forces you to relax your grip hand more. You still have control over your cue with the relaxed hold (see figure 1.11, page 16).

Figure 1.9 *(a)* Player is using a shorter bridge with the grip hand closer to the joint of the cue. *(b)* When the bridge hand moves farther from the cue ball, the grip hand moves back accordingly.

Often, the fingers and thumb surrounding the cue aren't the only problem areas in a player's grip. The wrist should also be relaxed. In other words, your entire arm, from elbow to fingers, should move freely and naturally. If you're forcing your arm to move, or forcing everything into a straight line, you're exerting force that just isn't needed, and that actually works against the power of your stroke.

Figure 1.10 Is your grip too tight? If you can lift your cue off the table in this position, you need to loosen your hold on your cue.

Figure 1.11 Use chalk cubes to determine just how loose your grip should be.

All that said, there's increasing evidence that top players do vary their grip pressure slightly, depending on the shot they're taking. Different grip pressures can be applied strategically to shots to elicit different responses from the cue ball. If, for example, you intend to move the cue ball a short distance after contacting an object ball, slightly tighten your grip on the cue. This restricts wrist action and kills some of the roll of the cue ball. But be careful. Gripping too tight can make you anxious about the shot. Experiment with varying your grip pressure until you're comfortable with it, and watch the different cue ball reactions available to you from the same arm swing with just a slight variance in grip pressure.

The key to using grip pressure is to maintain the same pressure on the cue throughout the shot. If you tighten up more on your follow-through, you're in essence regripping the cue and changing the kinetics of the small muscles in your hand and wrist. This allows anxiety to enter the shot sequence. It also has a tendency to affect timing, preventing you from hitting the cue ball at precisely the right time, which can have a profound effect on your shot.

Bridges

Your bridge hand serves as a foundation on which to guide and support the front end of your cue stick. Most miscues are caused by a faulty bridge (or lack of chalk) so don't neglect building a bridge you can depend on to keep your cue moving straight through each shot.

Traditionally, the first bridge taught to students by instructors has been the closed bridge, with variations of the open bridge reserved strictly for cue ball positions on, or close to, the table rail. New theories have replaced tradition in recent years, and many professional players are leaning toward the open bridge for more of their shots (see figure 1.12).

The reasons for this choice are few but convincing. First, it's easier to sight the shot without the distraction of an impeding knuckle, which is raised in the closed bridge. Second, when a player reaches a certain skill level, the closed bridge is no longer needed as a guide; rather, the emphasis in aiming and delivery is placed on the swinging arm. In the past, players typically first made an open bridge before they learned the closed bridge from a local pro or teacher. Today's players learn the closed bridge, often switching to the open bridge when they're comfortable with their swing and delivery of the cue through the shot. Snooker players, who are shooting with smaller millimeter shafts at smaller balls into smaller pockets, almost always use the open bridge. (This makes a good case for the open bridge because the game of snooker requires great control and accuracy.)

Closed bridges might still be preferred in tight situations, when the cue ball and object ball are close together, or in certain finesse shots requiring extreme spin. A closed bridge is useful in teaching amateurs to stay down if they're having problems following through. On the other hand, a new player can begin to rely heavily on the closed bridge, and in fact will often move the hand during execution of a shot in a feeble attempt to steer the cue stick from the front. This bad habit is more easily avoided and corrected with an open bridge. By not allowing so much control in front, you won't attempt to steer your cue with your bridge hand. Your best bet? Learn to execute shots with all of bridges we show you here, then experiment with which works best for each of your typical shot situations. Being able to bridge in each of the ways shown gives you the most flexibility for executing any shot.

Figure 1.12   In the open bridge, the cue stick rests on top of the bridge hand, guided by the thumb and forefinger.

The Open Bridge

Place your bridge hand flat on the table. Putting pressure on the palm of your hand, slowly raise your knuckles above the bed of the table by sliding your fingertips back toward your palm (so pressure is now equally distributed between your fingertips and the palm of your hand). Spread your fingers as far apart as they'll go without discomfort. Keeping your thumb next to your index finger, allow the cue stick to rest between your thumb and first knuckle of your index finger. You can raise or lower the center of your hand to keep the cue level for draw (bringing the cue ball backward) or follow shots. Figures 1.13 and 1.14 indicate optional lower and higher hand positions with the open bridge.

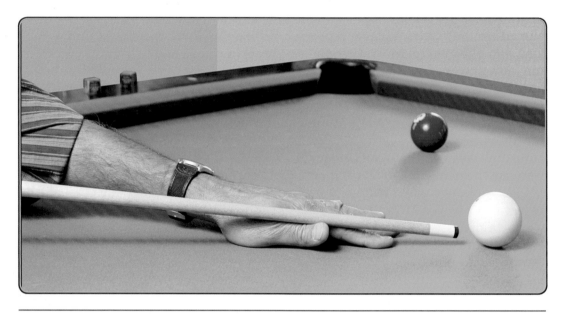

Figure 1.13   Lower your hand to achieve draw with a level stroke.

Figure 1.14   Raise your hand position for a level follow stroke.

The Closed Bridge

To form a closed bridge, place your hand flat on the table and spread your fingers, as in the open bridge. Then form a loop with your thumb and index finger through which your cue slides. When you form this loop, your hand naturally raises up on its side. The heel of your hand and your remaining three fingers rest on the table for support (see figure 1.15). This bridge, too, can be lowered or raised by extending the fingers or bringing them in closer to the heel of the hand. The bridge hand should only be tight enough to guide the cue; avoid holding it in a death grip. The cue should slide through your fingers freely, with no restrictions on your follow-through.

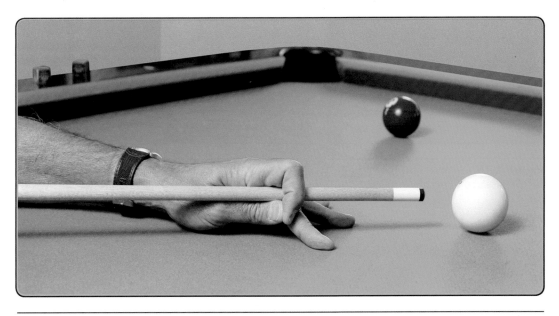

Figure 1.15   A closed bridge is formed by looping the forefinger and thumb around the cue.

Bridging Near the Rail

With a table bed surrounded by elevated rails, you'll be shooting many shots in which the cue ball is on or near the rail, in which case you won't have room on the table surface to make a normal bridge. You have several options for bridging on or near a rail, as shown in figures 1.16 through 1.20 (pages 20-21). Note that your choice depends on the cue ball's distance from the rail and on whether you need to draw the cue ball. Also note that in figures 1.19 and 1.20 the cue stick is elevated above rather than parallel to the bed to hit lower on the cue ball. If you must elevate the butt end of the cue, your follow-through is very important so that you do not dig under the cue ball or miscue.

As shown in figure 1.16, holding the cue between the first two fingers allows good control but can't be used if the cue ball is too close (and can impede your view of the shot). The closed bridge can also be used in bridging alongside the rail, as shown in figure 1.17. As shown in figure 1.18, if the cue ball is too close to the rail, use the rail itself to support your hand and bridge with an open hand. The open bridge on the rail shown in figure 1.19 may also be used if you need to elevate the butt end of your cue to impart draw on the cue ball.

Figure 1.16 A closed bridge formed by the forefinger and index finger.

Figure 1.17 This closed bridge can also be used alongside the rail.

Figure 1.18 Using the rail to support an open bridge.

You'll sometimes find yourself in a position in which object balls obstruct the cue, making the use of a normal bridge impossible. In such a case you'll need to elevate your bridge. Figure 1.20 shows an example of an elevated bridge. Again, the back end of your cue stick is elevated. For better control try to keep your cue as close to center ball as possible with a short but smooth stroke.

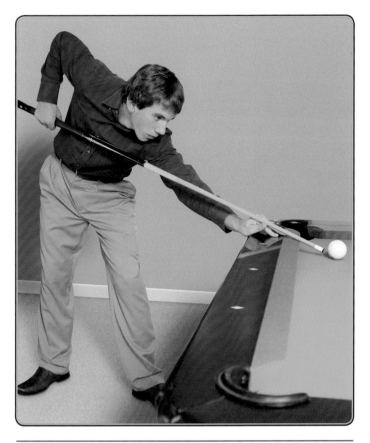

Figure 1.19   Using an open bridge on the rail for a draw shot.

Figure 1.20   This elevated bridge allows you to bridge over impeding balls.

Figure 1.21 The mechanical bridge is best used with an adjusted body stance.

The Mechanical Bridge

The mechanical bridge is sometimes called "the rake" but most often simply "the bridge." Knowing how to correctly use this piece of equipment is crucial for an all-around game. If a player isn't ambidextrous—that is, can't shoot pool just as well with both hands—this tool comes in very handy to shoot those shots that can't be reached with a conventional stroke. Because you're giving up control of the front end of your cue stick with your bridge hand, you might feel uncomfortable with this equipment at first. But with a little time invested in perfecting the proper technique, it's not that tough.

When you need to use the mechanical bridge, simply place the head of the bridge about where you would normally place your bridge hand on the table for a standard shot. With your normal bridge hand, hold the butt end of the mechanical bridge firmly on the table. (If impeding balls force you to hold the bridge aloft, try to keep the arm holding the bridge braced; moving the bridgehead alters your shot). Place your feet at least shoulder-width apart and square to the shot; in other words, line up your belly button with the shot.

Pro Tony Robles reaches a shot with the mechanical bridge.

photo by Jerry Forsyth

Place the tip end of your cue on the bridge head. With your normal swinging hand, hold the very end of your cue stick with the back of your hand facing the ceiling. Use a very light hold, using only your thumb, index finger, and middle finger—just enough to control the cue stick. Place the butt end of the cue stick in the middle of your chest, and then raise the elbow of your swinging arm about 90 degrees, or to shoulder height. When using the bridge, you're actually swinging your hand directly away from the middle of your chest. Figure 1.21 shows perfect body position when using the mechanical bridge.

To begin practicing with the mechanical bridge, start by hitting only the middle of the cue ball. As your skill with the bridge increases, try hitting above and below center. This will be more or less difficult depending on the type of bridge you're working with. Bridges with lower grooves offer more control, but bridges in most clubs and lounges have higher grooves for the cue and force you to elevate the back of your cue stick more, preventing ideal execution of draw shots. If this becomes a problem for you, speak to your local dealer or pro shop about a portable bridgehead you can slip on to your own break cue or house cue. Many pros carry their own in their cue cases. It's a minor investment that allows you the most level swing on a shot that can't be reached.

The Stroke or Swing

One definition of stroke is "to hit or propel a ball with a smoothly regulated swing." Because we want to focus on the movement of the arm, from here on we'll call the stroke in pool and billiards the "swing."

You'll find the swing is a big topic of discussion among pros and amateurs alike. People are always dissecting the strokes of top players, pointing out the grace or criticizing the irregularities. Again, trite as it sounds, there really are different strokes for different folks. But they all have the same goal. Perhaps the most irregular strokes can be seen in many of the top Filipino players, most notably top guns such as Efren Reyes and Dennis Orcollo. So, you might ask, with these strokes how can they be top players? In their case, what appears to be an irregular stroke is in fact their version of warming up the swinging arm. The arm and wrist are moved in a more dramatic fashion to loosen up the muscles in these areas—but on their final stroke, and through contact, they hit exactly where they want to hit the cue ball and stay loose to accomplish the ideal follow-through.

We're not telling you to imitate anyone's stroke. Again, the pros have played this way for years. What you can take from this is that developing a regulated but relaxed swing increases your performance level at the table.

How do you develop a smooth, relaxed swing? There are several key elements. First, the movement of the cue stick must be as level as possible; keep your swing parallel to the table. Any upward or downward hit on the cue ball translates to unwanted spin or bounce on the cue ball, which hurts your accuracy.

Here are some steps to use to find that parallel position:

1. Put your bridge hand on the table 18 inches (46 cm) in front of the end rail.
2. Securely make a closed bridge.
3. Let go of the stick with your back hand and allow the cue stick to come to rest on the end rail (see figure 1.22).

Figure 1.22   Find your parallel position with this simple exercise.

4. Your cue stick is now parallel to the table.

5. Resume your hold on the butt end of the stick without moving the cue out of its parallel position. You're now in position to deliver a level swing.

Next, be sure you're not losing control of the cue during your backswing. For better control and accuracy, limit your backswing to 5 or 6 inches (13 to 15 cm). Once you've mastered this, you might want to increase this gradually up to about 10 inches (26 cm), depending on how much power you need to execute a particular shot. Any more than this is analogous to golfer John Daly's past-parallel backswing—it might add to your game, but your timing must be perfect.

Right before you start your forward swing into the shot, allow a slight hesitation in your stroke. While hesitating, you should be looking at the object ball. This is where your timing comes into play. Hesitating allows you that extra moment to zero in and look at the object ball before you pull the trigger on your forward swing.

In your forward swing, visualize letting the cue stick stop by itself. Follow through, dropping your elbow as you do, and let the cue do the rest of the work. Your elbow drops naturally. There's no set rule for this—much depends on where you grip the cue, the length of your swing, and so on. This keeps you relaxed through execution of the shot and prevents you from overcontrolling your stroke.

Follow-Through

Here's a cliché that applies so well to pool—it ain't over 'til it's over. That goes for every single shot you execute. The most common mistake for amateurs is jumping up off a shot, perhaps in anxiety or, in most cases, to watch the result of their shot. Or a lack of confidence in your ability to execute a shot might cause you to jab at the ball, disallowing a proper follow-through and lowering your chance for success.

One of the most difficult things to learn is not to anticipate the hit. Anticipation of the hit can create anxiety and doubt in your swing. You won't get a true hit unless you swing *through* the ball. Pretend the ball isn't even there. As you practice, note how far the cue stick travels after contacting the cue ball. If it's stopping at or just a few inches past where the cue ball was on contact, you need to work on your follow-through. Figure 1.23 shows the proper distance range of follow-through after contact.

Here's an excellent practice technique for your swing—play a few racks with your eyes closed. This might sound difficult, but it's really quite simple. Just get down on the shot, take your practice swing, close your eyes, then shoot through the ball. You'll be amazed at the shots you can make with your eyes closed. This practice eliminates the hit anticipation and forces you to stay level rather than twist or make any unnecessary physical movements as you swing through the ball. This will not only help your swing but also will help you visualize each shot and boost your confidence in your ability.

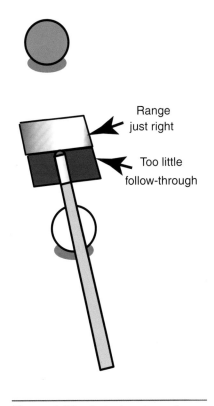

Range just right

Too little follow-through

Figure 1.23 Swinging through the ball requires a proper follow-through.

Remember not to move anything but your swinging arm. Any movement of your head is going to distort your perception of the shot, and your subconscious might try to adjust your body's position or its action through the shot, which can result in steering the cue stick and missing. Any movement of your body makes it more difficult to hit the cue ball where you had originally intended. Picture your body as a statue and your swinging arm as the only moving part.

Have confidence that you've made the ball and that your cue ball is heading in the desired direction. Don't get up until you've followed through completely. You'll get a lot of instant feedback this way and muscle memory to boot.

Rhythm and Timing

You've learned how to stand and bridge correctly depending on your shot situation. You've learned the importance of a relaxed grip and swing. Once you have mastered these fundamentals, they need to work in concert to produce effortless performance in your shot making and position play. This is where rhythm and timing come in.

Players of many sports—Michael Jordan in basketball, Tiger Woods in golf, and Albert Pujols in baseball, to name a few—can perform what seem to us to be superhuman feats. Each might attribute their abilities to near-perfect timing and rhythm. *Timing* in your pool game refers to the actual steps you take in execution of the shot: your warm-up strokes, swing, hesitation at the backstroke, and so on. *Rhythm* refers to the overall cadence of your game as you move from shot to shot.

Each of us also has our own personal rhythm. Some people think faster, jumping from one idea to another. Their eyes tend to focus quickly on the object ball and get out of focus quickly as well. They have a quicker internal pace. Some of us maintain

Etiquette at the Pool Table

Webster's defines *etiquette* as: "the manners and ceremonies established by convention as acceptable or required in social relations." In other words, every form of human interaction has unofficial rules to live by. Pool is no exception.

Let's first talk about your space around the pool table. When you head into the billiard club to play pool, you're actually renting the table and the space around it for a set period of time. By space we mean the area around the table a player needs to comfortably examine or execute any shot. Nothing is more irritating than to be looking over a critical table situation when suddenly someone walks between you and the table. A close second is when you're down on a shot and someone decides to walk by or bump the table just as you're ready to shoot. Give your fellow players a break by giving them space and courtesy. They're paying for it.

Play with a friend or practice partner? Here are a few golden rules:

- Don't grab the chalk as you leave the table. Your partner might need it before you do. If you feel the need to chalk your cue while sitting in your chair, keep a piece there, or, if you must, attach it to one of those chalk-on-a-rope things you can still find in your local pro shop.

- When you use chalk, don't place it face down on the table. The residue is left on the table to be wiped up by your and your partner's clothing.

- This applies to more serious match-ups: When a player makes a great shot, you don't need to make an immediate loud announcement of the fact. Chances are they're focused and preparing for the next shot; don't interrupt their preshot routine. Either wait until the end of their turn at the table and say, "Nice shot on the seven," or tap the butt of your cue lightly on the floor a few times in the time-honored tradition of the legendary players.

Years ago they called sharking "gamesmanship." Today there's no place for either term in our sport. Sharking is a bush league tactic, plain and simple. There are many forms of sharking: blowing your nose, roughing your tip with your cue tip shaper or scuffer, yawning loudly, standing in front of the shot, talking to a friend while your opponent is shooting, dropping your cue on the floor, moving around in your opponent's line of sight, chomping on ice cubes—the list goes on and on. In short, any sudden movement or noise—or constant subtle moves and noises—are sharking techniques when done intentionally. Those committing them unintentionally will catch on soon enough when they run out of practice partners.

If you must resort to sharking to gain advantage, we suggest you practice more or just concentrate on *your* game. If you try to shark your opponent and it doesn't work, it will only hurt your game and your reputation.

Be a good sport. For instance, players know when they touch the cue ball by accident. Be honest; call the foul on yourself. It's amazing how good karma comes back around your way. You also know when you make a bad hit on an object ball. Admit it. Otherwise, the short-term gain you might enjoy will cost you in the long run.

A little honesty and integrity goes a long way on the pool table. When a situation arises and you're not sure of the most sportsmanlike response, use your common sense. Ask yourself how you would like to be treated as a player, and then act accordingly.

a slower pace, waiting for the object ball to come into focus, or waiting for that last shred of doubt to leave us. Don't worry if you're geared toward one extreme or the other, or if you're in the middle. It makes no difference in the quality of your play whether your personal rhythm is fast or slow. What does make a difference is that you remain consistent and that you're true to your natural rhythm.

We've seen great players with no practice swings. They simply put a hand on the table and pull the trigger. On the other side of the spectrum, legendary players have used as many as 10 warm-up swings. What these players have in common is that *they did the same thing every time.*

Here are some steps to use to find your own rhythm and create good timing:

1. Line up as many balls as possible along the headstring.
2. Get into your stance to shoot the balls one by one into the corner pocket.
3. First, look at your target (the corner pocket); then take three practice swings before you shoot the ball directly into the pocket.
4. If three swings feel uncomfortable, try two or four.
5. If those swings still don't feel comfortable, try one or five, and so on, until you feel natural in your approach and neither rushed nor slowed in your attempt to pocket the balls.

After you've established your rhythm using these steps, set up shots on the pool table and practice maintaining the same pace on every shot. If you discover you're taking more time on more difficult shots, you need to scrutinize your shot before you're in your stance and swinging at the ball.

When you're looking for your rhythm, you might find that you're influenced by music playing in the background. To learn the purest sense of your rhythm, it's best to first find it without music. Once you've found your rhythm, you'll quickly learn what kind of music augments your game and what interferes.

Of course you won't always have a choice of music playing in the background, especially in billiard clubs. Some professional players have favorite tunes that match their rhythm to combat this problem. When they're playing in a match, they hum the tune (to themselves, of course) to maintain their own sense of rhythm, no matter what's going on around them. This has also proven to be helpful when you're playing someone whose rhythm is vastly different from your own. For instance, if you tend to play at a brisk pace, and you're playing an extremely slow, methodical player, when it finally becomes your turn at the table, you'll likely jump up and shoot too quickly, as if counteracting the effects of the slower pace. Others tend to match the pace of their opponent, playing slower, which can be equally damaging. Keeping your own rhythm in your head, even while sitting in your chair, prepares you for your turn at the table.

Once you have found your rhythm, timing comes into play. As Forrest Gump was so wisely told before he picked up a table tennis paddle, "The key to this game is to never take your eye off the ball."

Lucky for them, table tennis players need only to look at the ball and where it's being directed. Pool players have it a little tougher. You have a cue ball, an object ball, a target pocket, and a target area of position at which you want your cue ball to arrive. This gives you more items that can distract your attention from the task at hand. For proper timing, look at the object ball and its intended path *before* you get down on the ball. Also decide where your cue ball will go before you get down on your shot. Once in your stance, you might need to look briefly at where your cue stick is approaching the cue ball, especially in situations requiring extreme english. Now it's time for you to use your own personal number of warm-up swings before you execute the shot. (For more advanced players, this step is second nature, requiring no thinking at all.) Take a slight hesitation on your final backswing to help your final focus on the object ball.

The only time we recommend looking at the cue ball last instead of the object ball is when you're developing your power break, which we'll discuss at length in chapter 4. Looking at the cue ball last in any other shot situation often results in lost sight of your target, a poor follow-through, and difficulty in controlling the speed of the cue ball.

You've found a place to play, selected your equipment, and learned the fundamental skills you need to manipulate your cue stick. Your shooter's checklist of these fundamental skills is worth checking back on regularly; they are at the core of your success as a player. But for now you're ready to move on to the fun stuff—pocketing balls with deadly accuracy!

Aim and Vision

Once you have worked on mastering the solid physical fundamentals, you're ready to begin pocketing balls. This is where the sport gets really fun. For pool players, there's nothing quite like that satisfying *thunk* of a ball falling into a pocket. It's a feeling you'll enjoy each time you pocket a ball for as long as you play the game.

Pocketing balls with consistency relies on a few factors beyond your fundamental skills. First, you must know how to find the center of the pocket, depending on which pocket you're shooting at. Surprisingly, some players time and again shoot for the wrong side of the pocket. They come to believe their aiming skills are in question when in fact they just aren't aiming at the correct part of the pocket.

Second, you must learn to aim. We'll show you a few basic methods and visualization techniques used at some point by virtually every player who has learned the game. Few professional players can tell you exactly what they look at when they pocket a ball, but they'll all tell you how they learned to aim when they were starting out. Once you reach a consistent playing level, you'll come to rely less on aiming techniques and more on memory and feel for the shot, just as the pros do. Your visualization skills will extend beyond the pocketing of the ball to include the entire shot, including the resulting position of the cue ball.

Finally, to maximize your aiming efficiency, you need to understand how your eyes see the game. Many players question their ability to aim, but their problem usually lies not in their aiming technique but in their own eyes. So we'll take some time to discuss perception, focus, and eye dominance—factors that affect a player's aim and choice of aiming method. We've even included a few exercises to improve table vision and aiming ability.

FINDING THE POCKET CENTER

There are six pockets on a pool table, one in each corner and one in the center of each long rail. This much you know. But as simple as it seems, you might be amazed to discover how many players don't understand where the ball must enter a pocket if it's going to fall in. When you're shooting a ball that's 2.25 inches (5.7 cm) in diameter, and aiming at a pocket that's usually little more than twice that size, it's in your best interest to learn this lesson, and quickly. There's no point in cheating yourself out of space to pocket a ball by aiming at the wrong location.

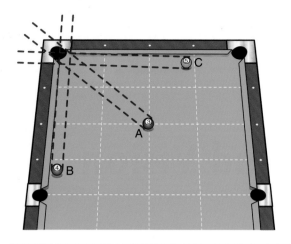

Figure 2.1   The pocket opening is not always the back of the pocket.

When finding the pocket from a location on the table, look at the opening from point to point. These points are defined as the extreme ends of each piece of cushion, as shown in figure 2.1. You can cheat yourself out of a much bigger pocket by aiming at the back of the pocket when it's not in your best interest to do so. That is, the *back* of the pocket is not necessarily the *middle* of the pocket. Rather, the pocket center depends on where you're shooting from on the pool table.

As you can see, we've also illustrated three examples of object ball position and where the center of the pocket is for each. Position A shows that when the object ball is sitting on the foot spot, for instance, the extreme back of the corner pocket is the target for the object ball. As the object ball sits on the table left of this spot, as shown in position B, the opening of the pocket moves to the right. The left point closes up and the right point opens so that you can more clearly see the cushion inside that point. You can no longer shoot the ball at the back of the pocket, as described earlier. If you do, you'll hit the cushion to the left of the pocket, and the object ball will bounce back out onto the table, rather like a basketball rebounding off the backboard. You must instead shoot the ball at the cushion inside the point, or where the cushion meets the pocket on the right side. As the ball moves farther left, you can see more of the cushion inside the points. Similarly, if you move the object ball to the right, as shown in position C, the optimal pocket opening shifts to the left. Thus, although the size of the opening is constant, the opening of the pocket "moves," and you must adjust your aim accordingly.

This same principle applies to the side pockets. If the object ball is straight in from side to side, the back of the pocket is the target. The difference with the side pocket is that, as the angle of attack becomes steeper, the opening gets smaller, as shown in figure 2.2.

Once you discover exactly where the pocket is in relation to the object ball, it's time to aim the cue ball at the object ball to send it into the correct opening of the pocket. Don't worry—it's less complicated than it sounds.

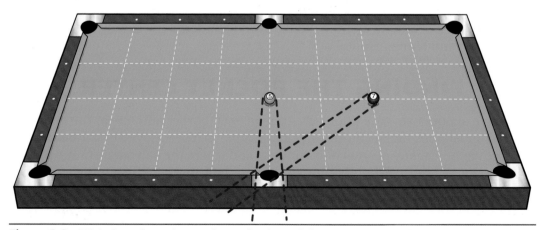

Figure 2.2   With the side pocket, as the angle of attack becomes steeper, the pocketing opening becomes smaller.

AIMING TECHNIQUES

There are several ways of aiming, including the ghost ball theory, measuring your aim with your own cue, and using of one of a variety of aiming practice techniques. Try not to get too caught up in methodology. Pick a system (or two) that works best for you. You might find that different aiming techniques work better under different circumstances or shots, so don't think you need to limit yourself to just one. Each of the aiming techniques we'll share with you involves some form of visualization, and the ones you choose will be a matter of personal preference.

The Ghost Ball

This is the most common—and usually easiest to comprehend—method of aim training in pool. To employ the ghost ball method, you simply visualize a line through the middle of the object ball to the pocket center. Then you place an imaginary (ghost) cue ball at the spot where the actual cue ball must arrive behind the object ball in order to pocket it, as shown in figure 2.3. If you use this method, it won't be long before you can automatically line up correctly without having to consciously visualize the ghost ball. Your memory takes over, knowing that the cue ball must arrive in that exact spot.

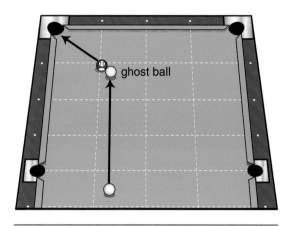

Figure 2.3 Visualize a ghost ball to improve your aim.

Parallel Aiming

A method of aiming popular long ago was to aim with parallel lines, a system that instantly taught players that because both the cue ball and the object balls are round, you cannot aim directly at the contact point. To learn this system, set up two striped balls, as shown in figure 2.4. Set up the striped object ball with the stripe facing the center of the intended pocket. Then place your striped cue ball virtually anywhere on the table that the shot can be made from. If you draw an imaginary line from the center of the cue ball parallel to the line from the center of the

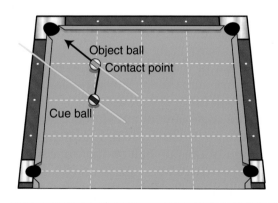

Figure 2.4 Parallel aiming is best learned using striped balls for both the object ball and the cue ball.

object ball to the pocket, you'll see the exact spot on the cue ball that must contact the spot on the object ball in order for the ball to be pocketed.

Once you have practiced this technique using a striped ball as your cue ball, replace the striped ball with the real cue ball. You'll find it's not at all difficult to see this line, and it will give you an immediate sense of where the cue ball actually must be aimed to hit the object ball at its contact point.

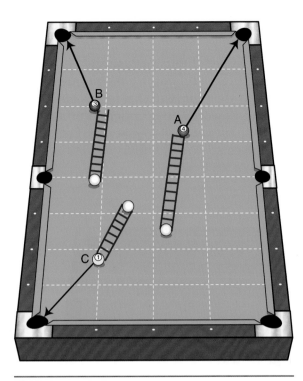

Figure 2.5 Using the railroad track technique. Shot A: cutting a ball to the right; shot B: shooting a ball to the left; shot C: shooting a straight shot.

Railroad Track

Some players prefer to visualize the entire path of the cue ball to the object ball rather than only the final spot where the cue ball must arrive. This aiming method is known as the railroad track system. Here, you line up the middle of the object ball with the pocket center, and then visualize a track running from the cue ball to the correct point on the object ball. As shown in figure 2.5, to cut a ball to the right, you simply line up the right side of the track with the contact point on the object ball, shown in shot A. For a shot to the left, line up the left-side track to the contact point, as shown in shot B. If the shot is straight in, as in shot C, you split the tracks down the middle and aim that point at the contact point.

Fraction Theory

The fraction method of aiming is a bit harder to explain but is quite effective for many players, including some professionals, who swear by its accuracy. Figure 2.6 shows aiming points resulting from various hits.

Say, for example, you have a straight-in shot. This shot requires a full-ball hit on the object ball. The middle of the cue ball should contact the middle of the object ball. Now let's look at what should happen if you have a 45-degree cut shot to your left, as shown in figure 2.7. To locate the fraction on your aiming point, look at the right half of the object ball and find the center of that half. That's your contact point. You aim the middle of the left half of the cue ball at that spot to accomplish a half-ball hit.

If the angle of your cut shot is greater than 45 degrees, you simply find the angle into the pocket and, looking straight on from the back of the cue ball, aim an equal amount of the cue ball on the opposite side. If you have a very thin cut shot, let's say somewhere between 80 and 90 degrees, you aim at the right edge of the object ball with the left edge of the cue ball to the point shown in position E. A three-quarter-ball hit, as shown in position B, applies to lesser angle shots (but not straight-in shots). You can also visualize this method as covering a fraction of the object ball with the cue ball, rather like an eclipse of the sun. With a full-ball hit your cue ball covers the entire surface of the object ball, whereas with a half-ball hit the cue ball covers only half of the object ball. Whatever fraction of the object ball is required to pocket the ball, you'll use that same fraction on the opposite side of the cue ball.

Although this technique can be difficult to understand initially, this particular aiming method gives beginners a great reference point to begin pocketing balls, after which it becomes easier to simply line up to the proper angle.

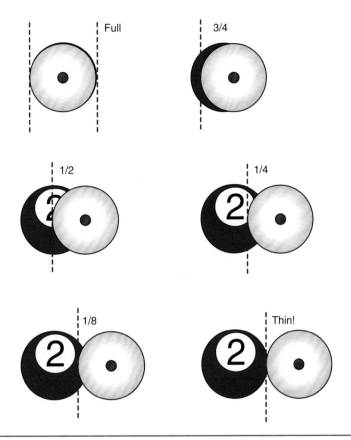

Figure 2.6 The fraction method of aiming shows aiming points resulting from various hits on the object ball, from a full-ball hit to a very thin cut.

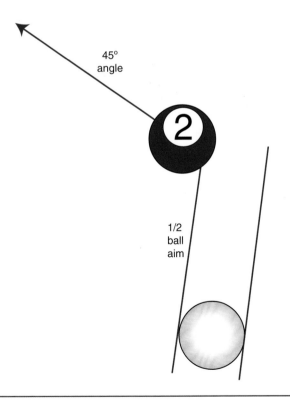

Figure 2.7 A 45-degree cut shot requires a half-ball hit.

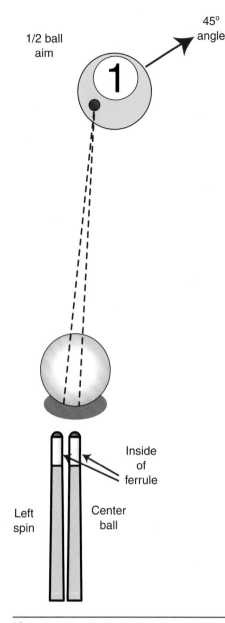

45°
angle

1/2 ball
aim

Inside
of
ferrule

Left
spin

Center
ball

Figure 2.8 Adding your cue stick as a measuring device to the fraction aiming method.

Measuring With Your Ferrule

Once accustomed to using the fraction theory of aiming, you can add another technique—namely, adding the variable of your own cue stick to make it easier to see your aiming point on the shot. Here, after you find the fraction on the object ball, you line up the inside of your ferrule to your aiming point on the object ball. For example, see figure 2.8 for a shot with a half-ball hit to the right. First you find the half-ball hit on the left side of the object ball that will send it to the right. Then, as you look down the shaft and ferrule of the cue stick as it contacts the cue ball, you aim the right side, or inside (going into the hit on the object ball), of the ferrule to the half-ball hit, cutting the ball to your right. If you're attempting a half-ball hit to your left, you find the halfway distance and line up the left side of your ferrule to that point on the object ball.

This method works well on longer shots, can work wonders on thin cuts, and can also help your aim when using english. As we've shown in figure 2.8, even with left english on the cue ball you'll keep the inside of the ferrule to the half-ball aiming point on the object ball.

Advanced Tips and Tricks

The aiming techniques so far described should help set you on your way to more consistent shot making. As we've mentioned, over time you won't consciously employ a particular aiming method but will come to rely on muscle memory. That said, even the pros resort to little tricks to keep them focused on their contact point, especially in situations in which a tough shot demands total focus on making the shot, regardless of resulting position. In pool lingo this is called *cinching the ball.*

Most of these techniques involve extended visualization. For example, you don't just visualize the contact point on the object ball, or ghost ball, or the railroad track to the object ball; instead you visualize a track all the way to the pocket. Or, as shown in figure 2.9, you visualize the tip of your cue extending to a reference point all the way to the rail beyond the shot, forcing you to follow through in a straight line to the contact point.

Many players, once they've learned a bit about shot making and have built up a memory for their aiming points of reference, will check their stroke and follow

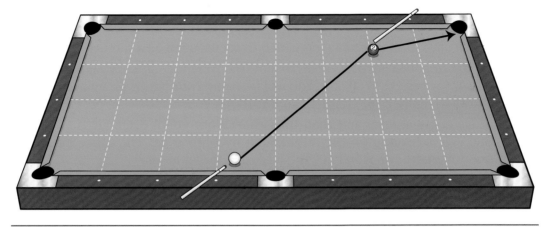

Figure 2.9 Visualizing the tip of your cue extending to a point beyond the shot helps you to follow through straighter.

through by playing with their eyes closed. Not all the time, mind you. We don't want you groping your way around the table. But you can check your aim and swing by lining up a shot, taking a few warm-up swings, and closing your eyes before you let the cue stick swing through the shot. The results of this exercise might astound you; if you trust in your ability, you'll make these shots without using your eyes in the final swing.

Another test for your aiming ability is one of the aiming devices offered on the billiard market. You'd be surprised (we were) to discover that where you think you're pointing that cue ball isn't always where it arrives. This is a great self-check method for your aiming and your body position. After all, you can aim perfectly, but if your arm isn't delivering that perfect swing, your cue won't be sending the cue ball where you think it needs to go.

HOW VISION AFFECTS YOUR AIM

Knowing how your eyes work—how they perceive and interpret visual images—can be fascinating and quite useful to you as a pool player. Not being optometrists ourselves, we sought the assistance of an expert, Cecilia C. Heiges, OD, who has long been fascinated with vision as it applies to sports performance. She answered our questions about how our eyes function and explained how to use an understanding of the eyes to enhance our pool games.

Many myths promulgated by players throughout the years can quickly be dispelled after a little explanation. Once you have a foundation of knowledge about how your eyes work, you can troubleshoot for many visual problems and thereby help your game.

Dominant Eye Theory

Spend more than a month or two at your local pool room and you're bound to hear someone mention the dominant eye theory. Do you have a dominant eye? If so, how do you find it? Can it hurt your game? According to Dr. Heiges, everyone does indeed have a dominant eye. "We're asymmetrical beings, and not everything is in perfect balance. At age 7 and beyond, most everyone has established a dominant eye."

How do you find your dominant eye? As it turns out, the test is quite simple:

1. Pick a spot in the distance on which to focus, such as a picture on a wall.

2. Hold your hands up to this spot, keeping them in the center of your body, about 6 to 12 inches (15 to 30 cm). You will be using your hands as a viewfinder, as shown in figure 2.10. View this spot through your hands with *both* eyes.

3. Close one eye first, and then the other. What you'll discover is that only one eye is fixating on the target seen by both eyes. The other eye, your nondominant eye, won't see the intended target at all.

Dr. Heiges negates the common misconception among pool players that eye dominance affects a player's aim or focus on a target, at least to the point that any conscious decision regarding your aim needs be made. She explained that only in the very early stages of childhood play might eye dominance affect action:

There are so many activities that force us to make a choice about how we use our eyes. You don't realize it because we're not aware of each subtle movement we make, what eye we may use, right or left. We just do the job, whatever that might be. A classic example is taking photos. You're at a family party and you automatically put that viewfinder up to your dominant eye. You're not thinking about that body decision. It will just happen. Your body figures it out for you and makes the necessary adjustment.

This can explain why some players with otherwise perfect form might have their head tilted to one side or the other, yet nearly never miss a ball. Their bodies have made subtle adjustments to making aiming techniques work for them.

Figure 2.10   Use your hands as a viewfinder to determine your dominant eye.

Vision Particular to Pool Players

The vision demands in our sport turn out to be very particular. According to Dr. Heiges:

> With pool you don't have the challenges of equilibrium and dynamic vision because the table is not moving and the player is not moving during the shot. However, pool players are utilizing a very unusual head posture (as compared to other sports) and resulting eye posture. Volleyball is one of the few other sports that I can think of where the eyes are turned up so often, and yet, unlike pool, their head position is up so that the eyes do not have to move so much. In pool the eye and head position are very unusual—you are working in a visual field that is very unusual—a superior hemifield.

The *superior hemifield* refers to the use of the upper half of your visual field. Picture yourself at the table for a moment. Your head is down, but your eyes must focus through this upper half to see the shot. Because we are an information society, most of what we do, explains Dr. Heiges, involves the use of the lower portions of our visual field—in reading, writing, working on computers, and so on. When forced to look up, our heads move to accommodate that.

What does all this mean to your pool game? First, if you don't play often, and then expect to play an all-night session, your eyes might tire before the rest of you. This portion of your eyes hasn't been used or exercised as often and so might be prone to earlier fatigue. Second, if you are too low on your shots, you could be putting undue stress on your eye muscles, resulting in poor or slow focus. Indeed, you might be causing yourself other physical maladies because your neck and head will have a tendency to crane in order to compensate. Position your body to keep it comfortable for your back, neck, arms, and legs and to allow the easiest use of your eyes.

What Should You Look at When You Shoot?

Here's another popular pool room topic: What do you, or should you, look at when you shoot? Answers range from the cue ball, to the object ball, to the pocket. Peripherally, you might see the other end of the table, someone walking by beyond the table, the wall beyond that. But what's most important? Can you look at everything at once? Should you?

According to Dr. Heiges, you're best off maintaining focus on the object ball.

> If you're trying to see anything else, or worse, everything at once, you're getting too central. You need to get global. Your peripheral retina is what tells you features of an object's location and its relative position in space with other objects. When you're looking at that ball (the object ball), you really want to be just feeling everything else. You don't even need to be looking at your cue stick or the cue ball; everything else falls into place.

Heiges says that this can be illustrated through a classic vision therapy exercise:

1. Hold your thumbs out in front of you with one arm fully extended and the other arm only halfway extended between your eyes and the farther thumb, as shown in figure 2.11.

Figure 2.11   Check your focus with this simple exercise.

2. Focus first on the thumb closest to you. While keeping your focus on this thumb, your distant thumb should appear (in your peripheral vision) to be blurry (not focused) and doubled. In other words, there will appear to be two blurry thumbs in the distance. You should simply be aware of this.

3. Shift your attention to the background thumb. It will appear clear and single. Now you should be aware that your near thumb is blurry and doubled.

This exercise is called physiological diplopia. This is the normal vision process when the target that you're not looking at falls off center. This technique gives you biofeedback and lets you know your eyes are working. The implications for the pool player are obvious. Try to focus on everything at once, and you'll quickly wear out your eyes. Instead, as Dr. Heiges advises, look at the various parts of the shot before you settle into your stance, but once you're down and ready to pull the trigger, allow your body and mind to *feel* rather than see all these spatial relationships, keeping your focus on the object ball.

CLEARER VISION POCKETS MORE BALLS

Several factors can alter your vision skills, many of which can be improved or corrected with knowledge; in other cases, professional vision therapy might be necessary. The following sections should help you gauge whether you want to seek professional advice and aid you in achieving optimal vision at the pool table.

Stress and Anxiety

Two of the questions we posed to Dr. Heiges involved how stress might affect vision, and if exercise and relaxation exercises can improve vision as much as other areas of the body. "When people are under stress they tighten up, and this really does affect your processing of visual information," explained Heiges. "The fight-or-flight syndrome kicks in, and the functional field of vision actually becomes tunneled."

As a result, focus might be heightened for execution of a shot, but the player could lose sight of the big picture. The remedy—exercises that relax the entire body, affecting the amount of adrenaline produced, and eye-specific exercises that both relax and strengthen the eyes.

Range of Motion

If your head and neck have limited range of motion caused by inflexibility, injury, arthritis, or even a great deal of tension in your neck and shoulders, the ability to keep your head up and eyes focused can also be limited. Correcting or minimizing the problem depends on the physical source or cause of your limitations. Tension, stress, and inflexibility caused by lack of exercise and relaxation can be easily corrected through stretching and relaxation exercises. Prior physical injury or arthritis in this area requires professional counseling and therapy.

Nearsightedness and Farsightedness

Dr. Heiges has theories about the correlation between nearsightedness and farsightedness as these conditions relate to the pool player:

> There are two types of vision: what is called your central vision, composed of roughly the central 5 percent, and the rest, which is called your *peripheral* or what I refer to as *global vision*. I've found that nearsighted people tend to focus on the central vision, and have a more difficult time integrating central vision with the global. They may be more perceptually central and thus can have more difficulty seeing the big picture. Farsighted people may be less detail oriented, seeing the big picture, but having less of a propensity for central focus.

Heiges stresses that there's no hard data supporting these theories, but they sound plausible to us and might be of value in identifying and monitoring problem areas in your game.

Weak Eye Muscles

Known to eye professionals as *strabismus*, weak eye muscles or eye muscles that work independently of each other, for whatever reason, can and will affect your game. If your eyes are not working together, you'll experience double vision and a lack of depth perception, which is critical to the cue sports. Dr. Heiges explains that people often compensate for this lack of depth perception, completing an incomplete spatial relationship in their minds through discerning such factors as light differentiation, shadow, color, tonality, and so on.

If your eyes don't work together, a variety of corrective measures might help—from exercise (reading is a great way to make your eyes work together) to vision therapy to surgery on the eye muscles themselves.

Effects of Aging

We can all expect our vision and perception to change as we grow older. But can eye–hand coordination be improved at any age? Great news! In fact, both vision and eye–hand coordination can be enhanced through vision therapy, which is just starting to catch on with the general public. So much of what was once regarded

Enhance Your Vision

When people feel tension in the body or are placed in tense situations, the eyes are the first body part to be affected. Not surprisingly, tension is the main culprit for the deterioration of one's vision. If you have any eye problems at all, first seek the advice of an optometrist. Many doctors now prescribe various forms of vision therapy, including exercise regimens, to optimize visual performance in sport activities.

The medical community has realized in recent years that the eye muscles, like other muscles in the body, tend to deteriorate not from age but from lack of exercise and proper care. Your vision and eye–hand coordination can be improved at any age, if you're willing to take a few minutes a day for your eyes only.

For relaxation, first take a few quick deep breaths, and then massage your eyebrows in a circular motion. You can also place your thumbs on your temples and, with your index and middle fingers placed between your eyebrows, pull them toward your thumbs and gently rub your eyebrow line from the center out to the sides of your head. This light massaging relaxes the eyes enough to start an exercise routine. Focus on the eyebrow area, and *don't* rub your eyes directly.

Next, release tension in your neck. Simply massage the base of your neck, or try stretching your neck, back, and then forward, chin to your chest. Do this slowly; sharp, jerky movements tend to increase tightness and tension. By relieving tension from your neck, you also relax your eyes. You might be pleasantly surprised at the results.

We've chosen a couple of exercises that require only widely available household items as tools. In the first exercise, use an ordinary pencil. Straighten out your arm while holding the pencil straight up in the air. Focus your eyes on the eraser of the pencil. While keeping your eyes focused on the eraser, slowly pull the pencil toward your nose until it touches. Reverse the process by slowly moving the pencil away from your face until your arm is fully extended. Don't lose focus on the eraser. Try 10 to 20 repetitions, once or twice a day. This exercise strengthens your eye muscles and helps your eyes work together.

This next exercise helps strengthen your muscular control. You'll need about a yard of string. Hold one end of a string against the end of your nose. Stretch the string out before you about 36 inches (91 cm) and attach the other end to a doorknob. At first you will see only one string, but continue looking at the far end of the string and suddenly you will see two strings.

As long as you're actually seeing with both eyes, you'll see the two strings coming to a V point, regardless of where you look along the one string. At the V point, two strings appear to cross, forming an X. By closing either eye, you will find that the illusory string you thought you were seeing with your left eye is actually seen by the right eye, and vice versa. Place your fingers on the string at a point closer to the nose. See the two strings.

See how close to your nose you can move your fingers along the string and still see two strings (optimally 3 to 4 inches [7.5 to 10 cm]). Resist the temptation to close one eye during any part of this exercise; this defeats the purpose. Continued daily practice strengthens eye muscles and rests the eyes.

Another activity that aids in eye–hand coordination is juggling. Several books are available on the subject. We suggest starting with balls or beanbags rather than knives.

Regular relaxation techniques and eye exercises will help you stay focused and prepare your endurance game for those longer sessions at the table. Aside from the obvious benefits to your pool game, these techniques will bring you a lifetime of healthier vision.

as naturally deteriorating function caused by age can in fact be slowed through proper care, knowledge, and exercise. What medical doctors in all specialties are discovering is that many of what were once considered symptoms of aging are in fact indicators of a sedentary lifestyle and physical inactivity. Unfortunately, much of medicine is still closely tied to the pharmaceutical and surgical industries. Although functional therapies are considered suspect or unscientific by some MDs, the benefits of these therapies are hard to deny. We offer a detailed discussion of eye therapy techniques in the following section.

For pool players, exercise is recommended for every body part involved in the sport, including your eyes. Don't hesitate to ask your doctor for advice about maintenance and preventive measures to take in caring for your eyes. Don't believe that drugs and surgery are your only alternatives.

Smoking

Smoking is very bad for the eyes, especially for contact lens wearers. Particles can get trapped between the lenses and the eye surface, thereby damaging this very sensitive area. Smoke can cause excess tearing, rubbing, and early eye fatigue. Worse still, smoking results in constriction of the blood vessels, and many of these tiny vessels at the back of the eye contribute to optimal vision. If you're a smoker who puts off quitting because you imagine the damage being long term and something to worry about later in life, think about the damaging effect it's having on your vision right now.

Color Discrimination

Perhaps you miss the same color ball all the time, such as the 7-ball or 3-ball in variations of red, or the 6-ball (green) on green cloth. This could suggest a color perception deficit or a lack of color discrimination, what many call *color blindness*.

There is a remedy. Color discrimination can be checked easily at the eye doctor's office. Today there are contact lenses that can improve the discrimination of color, which is really the way to go. Though color discrimination lenses for glasses have been and still are available, they've not been popular for vanity reasons. The contact lens also has the advantage of being close enough to the eye so as not to interfere with light transmission. These colored contact lenses don't cure color vision problems, but they do help people better discriminate between colors. Regardless, pool has a built-in backup system for the color blind—the balls are numbered!

Glare Caused by Lighting

Light reflects off round, shiny surfaces such as object and cue balls. The glare caused by the reflection can be misleading or bothersome and can quickly tire the eyes. Players who wear glasses have it even worse. Dr. Heiges informed us that there is a coating available for your glasses that reduces this glare. Again, contacts are better because they are too close to the lens of the eye to allow this distortion.

As we discussed in chapter 1, proper lighting ensures the maximum use of your equipment by preventing troublesome shadows and painful eyestrain. Fluorescent lighting is easier on your eyes, and to prevent shadows on the balls, lights should extend the length of the table. One long fluorescent light is better than three small bulbs because additional glare and light spots will reflect off the surface of the balls. Daylight-balanced fluorescent bulbs are much less fatiguing to the eyes than standard fluorescents. (Dura-Test in Fairfield, New Jersey, is one source for daylight-balanced fluorescent bulbs.)

Seeing Your Game Through Rose-Colored Glasses?

If you've seen photos or video of the flamboyant Hall of Fame player Earl Strickland, chances are you've seen the Oakley eyewear he sports at the table, too. Earl's eyewear isn't just to protect from dirt, dust, and glare. Color psychology might one day play an important role in the cue sports.

The field of color psychology studies the effects of color on human behavior and feeling. Color consultants claim hues in the red area of color are typically viewed as warm, whereas blues and greens are usually viewed as cool. Reds are also viewed as exciting, whereas blues and greens are viewed as soothing. Red-hued lenses might increase one's aggression at the table (it works for the bull, right?), but then again, we know that bright green cloth can feel anything but soothing after a long session. (Gold cloth seems the mildest compromise, but blue is becoming popular both on TV and for aficionados seeking a cooler experience.)

As far as tinted eyewear goes, the American Optometric Association says that gray offers a glare-free solution that won't modify colors. Yellow or gold might reduce glare (less important in the poolroom than under TV lights) but can intensify the green of the table.

Physiological tests have revealed similar responses to back up the claims of the color psychology field. It's claimed that red hues increase body tension and stimulate the autonomic nervous system, whereas cool hues actually release tension. An increasing number of studies link colors to specific responses. One study found that weightlifters perform better in blue rooms; another found that babies cry more frequently in yellow rooms. A third study suggested that the color pink calms prisoners.

If wearing eyewear to improve your performance appeals to you, experiment with a variety of lenses. Try it in practice first to see if you can discern any differences in your performance and to check if any tints either make your eyes tire more quickly or give you clearer eyes at the table.

photo by Jerry Forsyth

BCA Hall of Famer Earl Strickland sports Oakley M shades in a soothing shade of blue.

Use Your Common Sense

Finally, as you practice your aiming techniques and work to enhance your vision, don't overdo it. Becoming fixated on an object and staring for long periods of time can produce unnecessary eyestrain, and it won't help your game anyway. Glance at your shot, your cue ball, your cue stick, and the object ball rather than taking long, hard stares. As you've probably already discovered, staring at anything too long actually disturbs your focus; the object of your scrutiny might even seem to move or waver in your vision. Perhaps you've seen professional players stay down on the shot for a very long time before pulling the trigger, and you wish to emulate this technique. We advise against that. These players might have particular vision demands that require this kind of lengthy focus; maybe it took years of practice and discipline to make it work for them.

Above all, if you notice that your eyes are beginning to tire, take a break from your practice session, or come back another day. Just like other muscles in your body, your eye muscles need time to train for specific tasks and to build up their strength to maximize efficiency. Overtraining can result in poor or lackluster performance caused by redness, burning, and even transient blurring in your vision as a result of cornea swelling. These are temporary conditions, but there's no point in continuing your practice session if your vision is blurred or if you're uncomfortable.

A sound program of vision exercises, relaxation techniques, and common sense allows your most valuable aiming tool, your eyes, to function at their best for as long as you play pool.

Cue Ball Control

If you've been taking your lessons in order, you've now developed solid physical fundamentals and have learned the principles behind aiming and understanding how your eyes work. You're well on your way to pocketing plenty of balls. For millions of players, that seems to be enough. But pocket billiards can be so much more. Simply pocketing ball after ball is like playing Monopoly without ever buying property or putting up houses and hotels.

The next logical step in your progress is to get control of your cue ball. Chances are you've been noticing, at least a little, where the cue ball goes after you make a shot. If not, you can now start paying attention. On each and every shot you have numerous options to send the cue ball in a direction that gives you an easier attempt on your next shot. You hear people say, "The pros make it look so easy." Indeed, it seems as if they never have to shoot a tough shot. That's no accident—that's position play. And you can't achieve it until you develop cue ball control.

The elements of cue ball control include speed control, mastering center ball, and the use of follow, draw, and english. The combinations of all these elements, and how each affects speed control, are endless. No matter how many years you play pool, you'll always be learning a new combination that works for a new position on a new shot. What few players realize is that, despite the desire we all have to take the easiest path from point A to point B, there are dozens of ways to get there on the pool table, and hundreds of places you can make your cue ball travel with every shot.

In the exercises provided for stroke development using various forms of english, we've included position drills using one rail and, where applicable, two and three rails. With these variations, you'll work not only on your english but also learn an important part of position play that many players never reach: using the rails for effective position. You'll also get the chance to invent a few shots of your own. Although we can't possibly illustrate all the results of using combinations of english on every shot, we can let you know what to expect as you begin to experiment.

BUT FIRST, CHALK UP!

Chalking the tip of your cue is a simple but vital part of the game that many players take for granted. You should chalk your tip before every shot, especially for any shot in which your cue tip is not addressing the cue ball at its center. Don't think

photo by Jerry Forsyth

Charlie Williams has been keen on cue ball control since he emerged on the pro scene as a junior champion.

of chalk as an optional accessory; you need to chalk to maintain friction between the cue tip and the cue ball to prevent the cue tip from sliding off, which is called a *miscue*. You've probably seen plenty of players miscue, and you might have also heard them mutter just afterward, "Chalk is free." It's a quip well worn by time, and you'd do well to heed it. It would be difficult to do any of the exercises in this chapter effectively without a little basic chalk knowledge, so we'll start here (and more experienced players will benefit from the review, especially if you've been stingy with your own use of chalk.)

To chalk the tip of your cue properly, place the chalk on the tip with a feathering motion, making sure the tip is completely covered. Avoid caking on the chalk too thick. If you do, chalk might transfer to the cue ball, which could cause problems if the chalk transfers to the same spot that the cue ball contacts the object ball. This causes a clinging effect, and your object ball will tend to skid or slide. Also be sure not to let tiny chalk chunks leave your cue tip and transfer to the bed of the table; they'll not only make a mess but might alter the path of the balls as they hit these accidental speed bumps.

The most common material used today for cue tips remains leather, whether in a single pressed piece or a laminated assembly of several layers. Either version suffers continual abuse from constantly hitting the cue ball. The leather becomes smoother and shinier with every shot, which doesn't help you a bit when it comes to holding chalk. To combat this, try one of the dozens of tip tappers and scuffers on the market to scuff, shape, and maintain your tip. Use these products with a light hand. You don't want to tear up your cue tip—just to scuff it a little so the chalk holds better.

Chalking up regularly helps prolong the life of your cue tip. Without regular chalk use, your tip will flatten out faster and need more care and scuffing, resulting in quicker wear and tear and requiring more frequent replacements. Develop a good habit in your game by putting chalk on your tip before every shot. Eventually you'll chalk up automatically without even thinking about it.

SPEED CONTROL

Once you've learned the basics, everything, and we mean *everything*, in pool comes down to speed control. Pool is called a game of inches, and for good reason. You can send your cue ball three rails and 15 feet around the table, be an inch off, and get *snookered* (hidden) behind another ball, losing control of the table. You can be a few inches on the right side of your shot and well poised for a simple run-out, but get a few inches on the wrong side and you'll spend the rest of the rack trying to get back in line. Good speed control in a well-played safety can guarantee you *ball in hand* on your next shot, whereas bad speed control can force you to give up the table for your opponent to run instead. Get the picture? Watch any tournament on television, on video, or in your local club, and you'll see the deciding factor in most matches is speed control. The cue ball went too far, or it didn't go quite far enough—you'll hear these tales of woe for as long as you wield a cue.

There will always be conditions affecting cue ball speed that you can't control (most notably equipment), but what you need to learn and study are all the fascinating ways in which you *can* control the speed and position of your cue ball. The possibilities of controlling the cue ball are virtually endless; you could spend the rest of your life working on various techniques for speed control. But knowing the basic elements you can control will speed you on your way.

Thin Versus Thick Hits

The angle at which the cue ball hits the object ball is the first and most obvious physical element that makes a tremendous difference in the resulting speed of the cue ball after contact. Did you pay attention in high school physics? Remember that whole bit about transfer of energy? A full hit on an object ball by the cue ball leaves little energy on the cue ball as energy transfers to the object ball. This means a full hit results in the cue ball traveling only a short distance after contact. Conversely, a thin hit (greater angle) leaves most of the energy on the cue ball. Even with the same force of hit, the cue ball will travel a much greater distance after contact with the object ball if it's only a glancing blow. Think of it this way: When you're running at a pretty good clip and someone bumps you going the other way, the contact barely slows you down. But if that same person stands squarely in front of you, and you hit him or her head on, he or she goes flying, and you slow down significantly.

In figure 3.1 we show a couple of shot scenarios that help illustrate the principle of energy transfer. In both shots the cue ball is the same distance from the object ball. The object ball is the same distance from the pocket. Shoot them both with a medium hit and with the cue tip addressing the cue ball at its center. Measure the result. The cue ball travels much

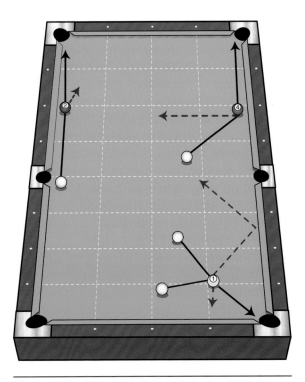

Figure 3.1 The cue ball travels farther in shots at a greater angle.

Equipment Affects Your Speed Control

When it comes to controlling speed on the table and controlling your cue ball for optimal position play, some variables come into play that you can't control. Types of equipment, wear and tear of the equipment you're using, and even weather conditions can affect speed control.

Speed of the billiard fabric covering the table is the most obvious factor. Your speed of stroke is largely influenced by how worn the cloth is. A new cloth will be quite quick. Balls have a tendency to skid more easily because the cloth has less chalk, dust, and dirt in its fibers to increase friction. Over time, the cloth becomes worn and will slow down. Nonworsted wools have a tendency to pill because fibers loosen from the strands, making the playing surface less consistent. Conversely, once the cloth becomes old and worn (note the dull shine on such tables), balls tend to speed up again because of reduced friction between the ball and the playing surface.

If you're playing in a billiard club that properly maintains its equipment, dirt and dust should be minor factors. If you do come across a dirty table that hasn't been vacuumed, recognize that it will play slower. If you have a home table, try to vacuum it weekly. Keep in mind that billiard fabrics come in directional versus nondirectional varieties. A directional cloth is in the direction of the nap and must be brushed or vacuumed with the nap (from head spot to foot spot) and never against it. Most clubs today are leaning toward the napless variety of fabric.

Another big variable you'll run into is humidity, which can wreak havoc on any player's game. Humidity has such a tremendous effect on playing conditions that manufacturers have invented tables with heated slates to keep tables warm and dry. These tables haven't really hit the mainstream yet, but they are popular in tournament play, especially in Europe. Humidity slows down the cloth but actually speeds up the rails. These effects become even more noticeable on older tables on which the rubber rails have aged and become more porous, thus allowing in more moisture. Humidity also affects the angle at which the cue ball rebounds off the rail, causing difficulties in position play.

The age of the rubber rails can also affect speed control. New rubber tends to cause farther rebounds off the cushion. Also, remember that the rubber cushions on your pool table are glued to the rails of the table. If someone has sat on the edge of the table, the glue seal might be broken, and you'll end up with a dead spot on the rail. You can recognize a dead spot by the unusual *thud* the ball makes on the cushion. The ball won't carom off the rail as far as it should or in the exact direction you might expect. Add to these factors the variables of different textures of rubber and different heights of rubber cushions. The higher the cushion, the less chance of the ball contacting the cushion at its center, resulting in the ball coming off the cushion at a lesser angle.

Of course the balls themselves affect speed control. Newer balls have more elasticity and will go farther. After years of being beaten on, older balls won't be completely round and won't roll quite as far. Dirty balls don't roll as far as clean balls. Balls that have been waxed will be slippery and tend to skid.

Remember this—when you're playing an opponent, he or she is playing under the same conditions. Direct your attention to pocketing balls and getting close to your next target ball. Getting within 18 to 24 inches (46 to 61 cm) will usually do the trick. Your shots will be much easier to execute, and the factors we've described won't be as difficult to overcome.

farther on the shot with the sharper angle. Now set up a few for yourself and note the differences. A half-ball hit results in about half the energy left on the cue ball. A quarter-ball hit results in three quarters of the energy remaining on the cue ball. An eighth-ball hit results in . . . well, you get the idea. If only physics had been so easy!

Cue Stick Speed

The force you put into driving your cue into the cue ball obviously influences speed control. Cue stick speed alone offers an unlimited amount of variations: the faster the cue's speed (i.e., the greater the force imparted), the farther the cue ball will roll. Slower speed means less distance. In fact, most of the game can be played with follow, draw, and center-ball shots with a proper stroke, and it's definitely to your advantage to master these techniques that allow you more control of your speed. It's much more difficult to control speed once you add the variables of spin.

Many beginning and intermediate players tend to hit balls too fast and too hard. They try to overpower everything. Pool is a sport that requires more finesse than power. You want a smooth and level swing that provides for the most action on the cue ball.

Using the Cushions

You can use the cushions on the pool table to control the speed of the cue ball. The softer the hit into the rail, the more speed is taken off the cue ball as it leaves the rail. The harder the hit, the less speed is taken off because the rubber cushion tends to spring the cue ball back out onto the table after impact. You can also use the cushions to take speed off a shot. Say you have a very thin cut on an object ball, but you don't want to lose control of the cue ball traveling up and down the table. Every cushion you contact takes more speed off the cue ball. You hear different theories on how much speed is taken off with each subsequent cushion, such as 60 percent diminished off the first rail, 30 percent off the second, and 10 percent off the third. But of course much depends on the speed at which the cue ball entered the cushion in the first place. You'll learn much more about speed control off the cushions in chapter 6 on pattern play.

Bridge and Grip Hands

Here's a little speed control gem. The closer the bridge hand is to the cue ball, the easier it is to take speed off the cue ball. The farther the bridge hand is from the cue ball, the easier it can be for the player to follow through farther for power shots. For example, there are the little *nip shots*—short bridge shots with an inch or less of follow-through—that benefit from keeping your bridge hand very close to the cue ball. You'll see pros kill (stun) the cue ball on these short shots despite extreme angles. They use a short bridge and more grip pressure to achieve the stun effect. By contrast, your length-of-the-table position shots will require more follow-through, and thus a longer bridge.

As we discussed earlier, grip pressure affects speed control, too. Grip pressure dictates the speed at which the cue ball leaves the cue stick. The lighter and looser the pressure, the more speed generated. Tighten the grip for a slower reaction. As just mentioned, when players want to kill the cue ball, they'll tighten up their grip to take the spin off the cue ball and produce a stun effect instead. You'll see that same player produce a beautiful long draw shot with a wrist that's loose as can be.

Using English

Finally, english is often used to control speed. For example, inside english (right sidespin if you're cutting a ball to the right, left if you're cutting to the left) can be used to stun the cue ball so it doesn't roll as far, though extreme angle shots require a great deal of experience and feel to accomplish this stun. The opposite takes place with outside english (often called *running english*). Outside english can lengthen the distance the cue ball travels; the cue ball will run (roll) a lot farther. With all else equal (same force, same stroke and grip), the speed of the cue ball will still change depending on your use of english.

CENTER BALL

Before you can begin learning and experimenting with different forms of english, you need a reference point. At this stage of development in your pool game, it's time to find the center of the cue ball. The easiest way is to use a simple drill.

Begin by facing the width of the table to keep the shot very short and easy to execute. This will help you gauge your initial progress. Place two balls about 3 inches (7.6 cm) apart (no more than that) and about 6 inches (15 cm) from the long rail, as shown in section A of figure 3.2. You'll be shooting the cue ball between the two balls, and, because standard pool balls are 2.25 inches (5.7 cm) in diameter, you'll have more than enough space for the cue ball to pass through. Place your cue ball 12 inches (30 cm) from the long rail directly opposite the middle of the two balls. Finally, to give yourself a reference point at which to aim, place a piece of chalk on the opposite long rail closest to the two balls and midway between them.

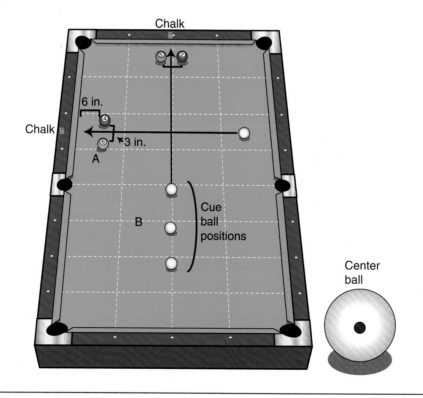

Figure 3.2 Use this simple drill to locate the center of the cue ball.

Using the piece of chalk as your target, step into your stance, aim the ball at the chalk, and shoot. Be careful to contact the cue ball directly at what you believe to be its center. If everything is lined up correctly, and you execute the shot with slow speed, a proper swing, and a smooth follow-through, the cue ball should hit the long rail and bounce back without disturbing the two balls. Ideally, the cue ball will pass between the two balls and directly back into the tip of your cue stick.

If this doesn't happen for you, make one of the following adjustments:

- If on the rebound off the long rail the cue ball hits the left ball, you're putting unwanted left english on the cue ball. Reposition the cue ball and shoot again, this time aiming a touch to the right of what you see as the center of the cue ball.

- If your cue ball hits the right ball on the rebound, you're putting a little unwanted right english on the cue ball, so compensate by aiming a touch to the left.

What looks like center ball to you might not result in a center-ball hit. Why? One of three explanations generally applies. You either have a slight natural crossover in your stroke; your head might have a slight tilt and not be directly in line over your cue stick; or your dominant eye (as discussed in chapter 2) might be giving you an illusion. If things don't *look* right, but you're achieving center-ball effect, trust what you're doing.

Practice this drill until you get the same results 10 times in a row. Once you've mastered the first part of the drill, set up the same shot, this time down the length of the table, as shown in section B of figure 3.2. Use short distances at first until you feel comfortable. Gradually increase the distance between the two balls and the cue ball until you can achieve a true center-ball hit over the length of the table.

Finally, perform the same exercise, but add an object ball, as shown in figure 3.3. Use the chalk on the rail as your target. Keep the cue ball 12 to 18 inches (30 to 46 cm) from the object ball. You want the cue ball to stop and the object ball to rebound off the cushion and directly back to hit the cue ball. This drill should give you a bit of feel for the speed of the object ball and the cue ball. Move the cue ball and the object ball farther apart, in increments of 6 inches (15 cm) at a time, to increase the difficulty of the drill.

Here's another helpful hint when you're trying to find center ball: Determine your dominant eye (see chapter 2, page 36), and then close your nondominant eye to see if you're really looking at center ball.

After you're sure that you've found center ball, you need to play a few racks using that center-ball hit on every shot. While you're doing this, focus on one thing and one thing only: how the cue ball reacts off the object ball. Which way does the cue ball travel after contacting the object ball?

The line on which the cue ball travels after contact with the object ball is called the *tangent line* (see blue dashed lines in figure 3.4 for examples). The tangent line is at a 90-degree angle to the target line. With a middle-ball hit, your cue ball will normally glance off a ball on the tangent line. Another way of looking at it is to add up the angles. For instance, with a 25-degree cut shot, the cue ball comes off the object ball from the approach line at about 65 degrees (25 + 65 = 90 degrees). Knowing the tangent line is the first critical step to knowing where your cue ball is headed. Only by knowing the reaction with center ball will you know what paths can result when altering that line with follow or draw or different stroke forces.

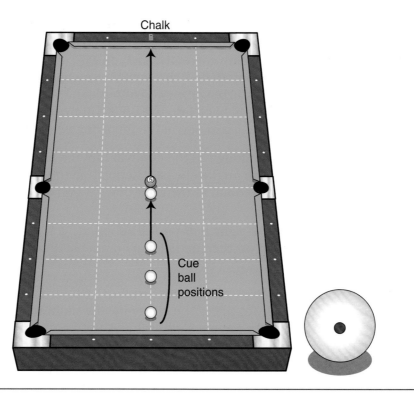

Figure 3.3 Adding an object ball to the mix.

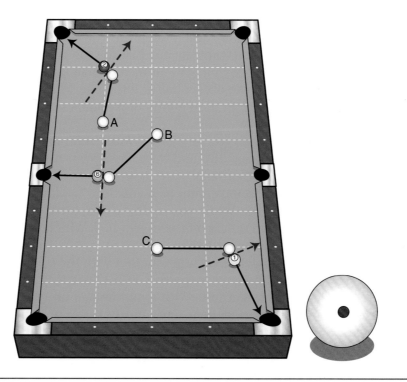

Figure 3.4 The line the cue ball follows on a medium-speed, center-ball hit is called the tangent line.

Another important thing to note is where the cue ball travels after contacting the object ball and then the rail. Ideally, the cue ball should roll from the cushion out onto the table at about the same angle it traveled into the cushion, as shown in figure 3.5. This is that old physics principle of angle in equals angle out, and of course, this too can be altered with speed, left or right english, or a combination of these.

Confused yet? Don't be. It gets more interesting from here!

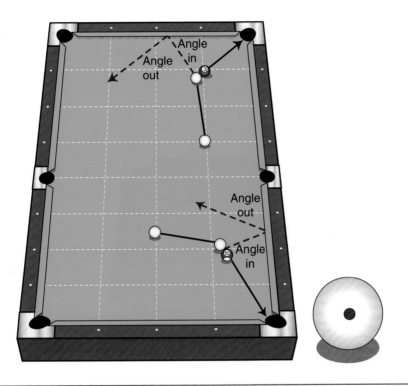
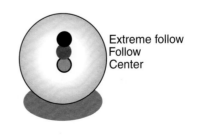

Figure 3.5   Angle in equals angle out, but remember that this line can be altered drastically with speed, english, or a combination of the two.

FOLLOW

Because it's easier to learn initially, we'll begin our study in cue ball path alterations with the follow stroke. As the name implies, your cue ball, when hit above center, will follow the object ball after contact. You're putting topspin on the cue ball, which causes it to continue rolling forward.

To execute a follow stroke, you will, in most cases, need to shoot a one-half to full cue tip above center, as shown in figure 3.6. For maximum results you should never need to be much more than a full cue tip above center. Shooting too high on the cue ball causes miscues and is really not necessary. The most important factors to remember while executing your follow stroke are to keep your cue stick level (simply elevate your bridge hand slightly to raise the cue tip) and to follow through completely.

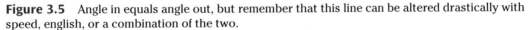

Extreme follow
Follow
Center

Figure 3.6   Cue tip position for a follow stroke on the cue ball.

If you're shooting a ball straight into a pocket, a follow stroke will send the cue ball directly into the pocket after it—which is rarely a desired result. But few of your shots will be straight in, so you need to understand the benefits of knowing how follow affects all other shots you'll attempt on the table. Follow can be effectively used to minimize the angle at which your cue ball travels after contacting the object ball, because follow in fact alters the tangent line—that is, the 90-degree line at which your cue ball will normally glance off a ball with a middle-ball hit, as shown earlier (figure 3.4, page 52).

The softer and smoother the hit, the more you can minimize your angle coming off the object ball. This skill becomes an important tool in your arsenal, especially when you want to avoid a scratch or avoid hitting other balls on your way around the table, as in our example in figure 3.7.

An excellent way to develop your follow stroke is to set up a simple follow shot (figure 3.8) and play position for the spots labeled A through D by arriving

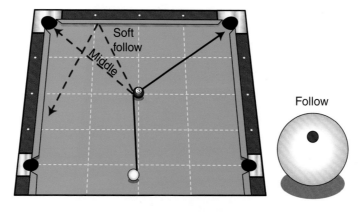

Figure 3.7   Use follow to minimize your angle after contact with an object ball.

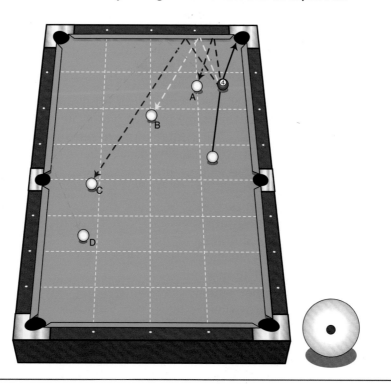

Figure 3.8   Set up this simple follow drill to improve your follow stroke.

at the corresponding labeled areas. As you'll note, to arrive at area D you'll need to hit your shot harder than you did for area A, which changes where the cue ball contacts the cushion. The greater the force of your hit, the more the cue ball will skid or slide sideways off the object ball before starting its forward roll.

While learning position play and cue ball control, it's simpler to picture your pool table divided into small quadrants and to visualize having your cue ball arrive in that desired quadrant when shooting. This is called "area" position. (As your stroke and speed-control skills develop, you'll play more and more for "pinpoint" position.) Once you can successfully position your cue ball in each of these areas, you'll have a good idea of the difference in the hit needed to get to position A or B as opposed to position C or D.

Now try the shot shown in figure 3.9. This shot is a thinner cut on the object ball. Note that to get to the position indicated by the illustration, you need only hit the ball as hard as you did in speed A of figure 3.8, but your cue ball will travel much farther. Remember that cue ball speed is dictated not only by follow-through of the cue stick but also by the angle at which the cue ball comes off the object ball. In shot A of figure 3.8 you had to hit the ball very full, transferring most of the energy to the object ball. But in this shot, a thin hit allows most of the energy to stay with the cue ball, causing the ball to travel much farther with less effort.

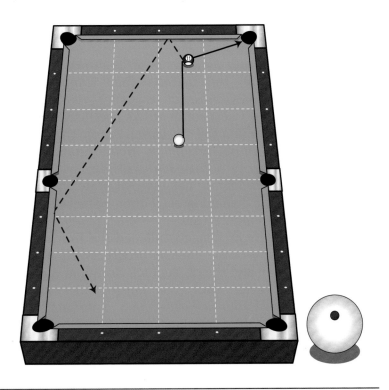

Figure 3.9 Expand your follow position skills with this drill, noting that the cue ball will travel farther with less force on the thinly cut shot.

THE DREADED DRAW

Quite a few amateurs think that if players can draw their ball, they must play good pool. This isn't a reliable indicator, however, because the draw stroke isn't as tough as some make it out to be. It's true that the stroke *looks* impressive. There's nothing that gives you quite the same feeling of power as a well-struck draw shot that commands the cue ball to come whizzing back toward you. If you remember a few simple rules of pool and physics, you too can experience that feeling and look like a champ (well, at least to the amateurs).

Figure 3.10 Cue-tip position for a draw stroke on the cue ball.

Rule 1: Keep your cue as level as possible. You'll be using a below-center hit, which, after contact with the object ball, allows the cue ball to hesitate, and then "magically" reverse its path. Figure 3.10 illustrates draw position of the cue tip on the cue ball.

Rule 2: Keep your grip loose. A loose grip keeps the wrist loose, and a loose wrist creates more draw. A death grip on the cue will kill your follow-through, and thus stun, or kill, the cue ball.

Rule 3: Don't jump out of the way of the shot. The cue ball will not roll back and hit your cue. Trying to get your cue out of the way too quickly, or pulling your cue stick back as if a string is attached to the cue ball and your cue, are the biggest mistakes new players make. Only follow-through brings the cue ball back toward you. The exercises we've described in this section allow you to follow through completely without fear of the cue ball hitting your cue; this will help you develop a feel for the draw shot and its timing for those short, straight-in shots in which you will need to get your cue out of the way a little more quickly.

Begin with a shorter shot, as shown in figure 3.11. The slight angle shown allows you to draw the cue ball without fear of bringing it straight back into the opposite pocket. As you execute this shot, visualize trying to move a heavy ball with your cue stick. Use a softer stroke and develop a feel for the shot.

The farther the object ball is from the cue ball, the more chance the cue ball has to run out of backspin as friction from the table slowly removes the draw effect. Because of this little law of physics, you'll need a very well-developed stroke and follow-through to get any real draw on a long shot. Shooting too hard won't produce the desired effect, either, because the force of the hit gives the cue ball more forward momentum.

Once you've accomplished the first shot a few times, gradually increase the difficulty of the shot by progressively adding 6 inches of distance between the cue ball and the object ball. Note that it might take slightly more force to get the same results each time, but focus less on force and more on follow-through to improve your accuracy. Also experiment with moving your cue stick lower, but only if you're keeping it level. Shoot too low without a level stroke and you'll be miscuing more often than shooting the ball. Remember that if your cue ball is too close to the rail, a draw is impossible because you can't keep your cue level. You'll merely dig your cue stick into the table (most likely irritating the owner of the establishment).

Once you feel comfortable with your draw stroke, try to imitate the results in figure 3.12. Note the path taken by a center-ball shot, and how that path is altered

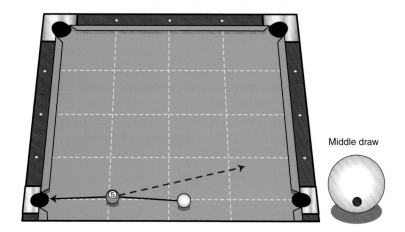

Middle draw

Figure 3.11　Begin your draw shot skill practice with this simple shot.

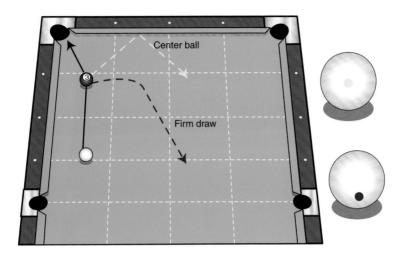

Figure 3.12 Note how the path of the cue ball is altered by a draw stroke.

with the use of a draw stroke. As you do these exercises, you'll begin to realize just how much difference the draw shot can make in position play.

COMPLICATING MATTERS WITH ENGLISH

Now you're ready to get fancy. But first a word of caution—fancy doesn't always equal great. If you haven't really developed a feel for cue ball control with center ball, draw, and follow, you're not ready to use english. If you have developed a feel of control over the cue ball, you've likely already been using a form of english. For example, if you're using center ball and cutting the object ball to the left, your cue ball picks up a bit of right spin, and vice versa. The amount of english picked up by the cue ball depends on the angle of contact (unless of course you're hitting a straight-in shot). The greater the angle, the less sidespin, if any, will be transferred to the cue ball. As you can see, english, as used in pool, can be a whole other language. Even the pros try to limit their use of english, or sidespin, to situations when it's absolutely necessary. There's sage wisdom in the old adage, "Keep it simple."

So, english refers to putting left or right spin on the cue ball to change the path of the cue ball after contacting a rail. Because you'll be approaching shot exercises using english from both sides of the table, it's convenient to use the terminology "inside" english (cueing inside the angle of the shot) and "outside" english (cueing outside the angle of the shot; outside english is also called "running" english). Figure 3.13 shows you two examples of inside english. Shot A uses left english; shot B uses right english. Both are inside english because you're cueing to the inside of the angle.

Now look at figure 3.14. In this case you're using outside english to lengthen the angle of the cue ball coming off the object ball. In shot A this is now right english. In shot B it's left english. This can be a bit confusing at first, so just remember to think inside and outside the angle of your shot.

Note in figure 3.14 that outside english alters the path of the cue ball by widening the angle it comes off the rail. Inside english shortens, or closes, the angle.

To execute a shot using english, you'll be applying the same technique you learned in follow and draw—use a level cue stick and a smooth follow-through. Begin by using no more than half to a full cue tip of english on either side, especially when you're still learning. Figure 3.15 illustrates left and right english tip positions on the

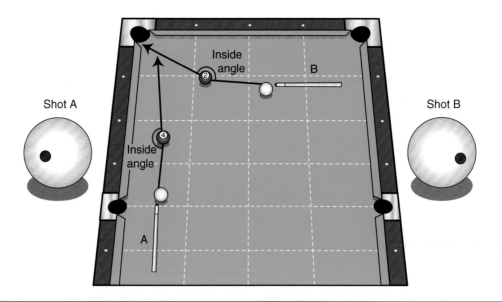

Figure 3.13 Examples of the effects of inside english.

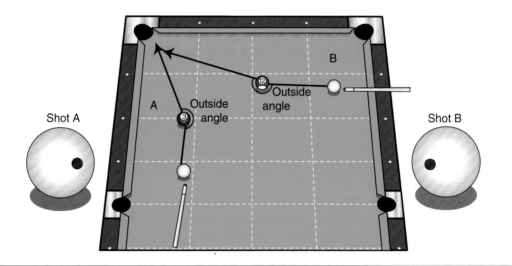

Figure 3.14 Examples of the effects of outside english (also called running english).

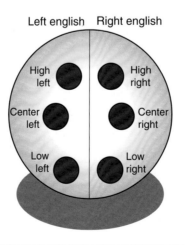

Figure 3.15 Cue-tip positions for left and right english on the cue ball.

cue ball. Avoid the tendency to steer the cue ball to one side or the other; begin in the proper position and follow through with a smooth, level stroke.

Now things get a little more complicated. You see, there's not just center ball, follow, draw, and left and right english. You have to contend with all the combinations that will make possible nearly any position on the table. In the next six diagrams (figures 3.16 to 3.21 pages 60-61), you'll see three examples of primary shot situations, representing a 15-degree cut, a 45-degree cut, and a 75-degree cut shot. In figure 3.16, you have shot results for the 15-degree cut using high-right, center-right, and low-right english. In figure 3.17, the same shot shows results using high-left, center-left, and low-left english. The same is then diagrammed for the 45-degree (figures 3.18 and 3.19) and 75-degree (figures 3.20 and 3.21) cut shots. The resulting path of the cue ball for each shot is shown using both inside and outside english, along with combining this english with high ball (follow) and low ball (draw). You'll see that all of the shots shown are cut shots to the left, with the cue ball coming off at an angle to the right. To get a real feel for the use of english, you should also set up each shot the other way to cut the ball to the right.

While trying each of the shots shown, keep these tips in mind:

- Execute the shots with medium speed, not too hard or too soft. A good way to gauge medium speed is to shoot the cue ball up and down the table once with a center-ball hit (as you would do in a lag). This is medium speed and will produce results similar to those in the diagrams.

- Look at the shots using inside english (in these illustrations, left english) versus the shots shown using outside (right english). With all things being equal, using a medium stroke as advised, the shots employing outside english will travel much farther. Inside english, as mentioned, can be used in your speed control to take speed off the cue ball, whereas outside english can lengthen the shot without requiring additional force.

- Now look at the difference in how far the cue ball travels between the fuller 15-degree cut and the thin 75-degree cut. Again, because less energy is transferred to the object ball in the thinner cut shots, the cue ball will travel farther.

So, which combination of elements will cause the cue ball to travel the least amount of distance? And how about the greatest amount of distance?

Now think of all the options you can exercise simply by changing the force of your shot. Set up the same three shots that we illustrated for you in the previous diagrams, beginning with the 15-degree cut shot. Experiment with different speeds of the cue ball for this shot. What happens to the cue ball when you shoot very softly? What happens when you shoot very hard? Play each shot not only with a range of area hits on the cue ball but also with a range of speeds.

Without getting too technical, we can tell you that the force of your hit can and will alter the path of the cue ball. The harder the hit, the more you can force the cue ball to slide. Force-follow and force-draw shots can be great assets in your game, but only if you've first mastered your swing. Too many players attempt to force everything, or, worse, develop a poor swing that results in too many force shots. You'll never learn the true reaction of the cue ball this way, and you'll be less able to predict your cue ball position after even the simplest of shots.

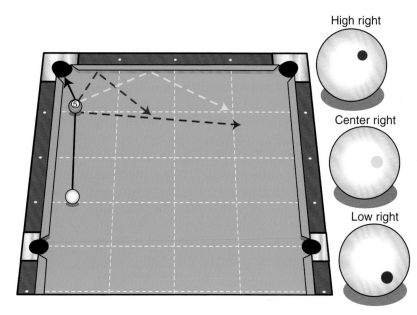

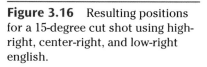

Figure 3.16 Resulting positions for a 15-degree cut shot using high-right, center-right, and low-right english.

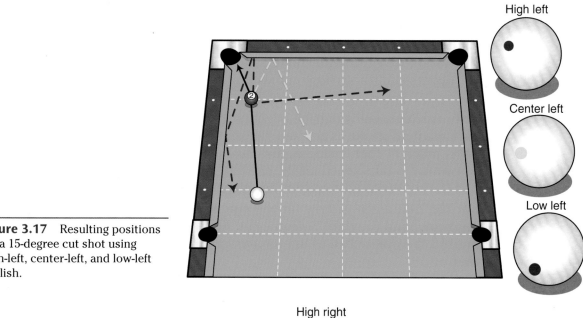

Figure 3.17 Resulting positions for a 15-degree cut shot using high-left, center-left, and low-left english.

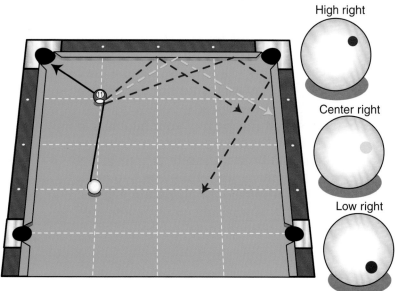

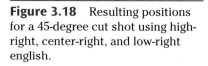

Figure 3.18 Resulting positions for a 45-degree cut shot using high-right, center-right, and low-right english.

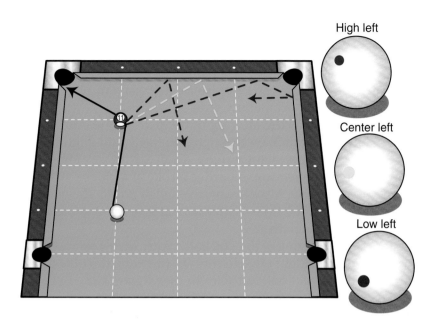

Figure 3.19 Resulting positions for a 45-degree cut shot using high-left, center-left, and low-left english.

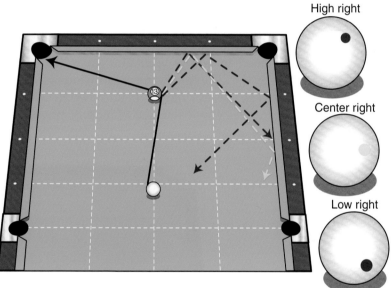

Figure 3.20 Resulting positions for a 75-degree cut shot using high-right, center-right, and low-right english.

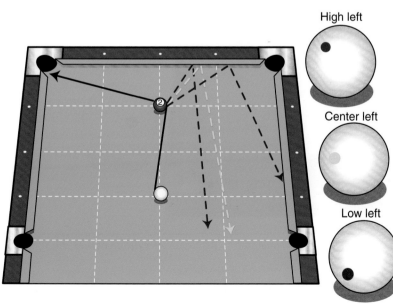

Figure 3.21 Resulting positions for a 75-degree cut shot using high-left, center-left, and low-left english.

DEFLECTION AND THROW

Deflection and *throw* are terms you're bound to come upon as you progress in your game, whether from other instructional materials or from other players. Let's define these terms, and then explain how they can affect your game.

Deflection, sometimes called *squirt*, is the altering of the path of the cue ball by using english. Simply put, a cue ball struck on the right side will shift slightly left, and a cue ball struck on the left will veer slightly right. A soft stroke at a short distance produces the least amount of deflection. A harder stroke at a longer distance produces the most amount of deflection. Also, the more english put on the cue ball (in other words, the farther away the cue tip is from the center of the cue ball), the greater the deflection of the cue ball's path.

Whereas deflection refers to the altering of the cue ball's path, throw refers to the altering of the path of the object ball. Right english throws, or veers, the object ball to the left; left english throws the object ball to the right (see figure 3.22). Because the cue ball hits less of the object ball on sharper cuts, the sharper the angle of the cut, the less throw will result. And, in the opposite of deflection, a softer shot actually produces more throw. Again, the more english used, the greater the result.

These are scientific facts of the game. Dozens of experts have rigorously tested these theories and have come up with expansive charts depicting how much you might need to adjust your aim for deflection and throw. As die-hard pool nuts, naturally we appreciate these laborious efforts to help better our game. In a sport such as ours, every nugget of knowledge is fascinating, and the more you learn, the more you *want* to learn. *Unfortunately*, however, studies like these, in the hands of

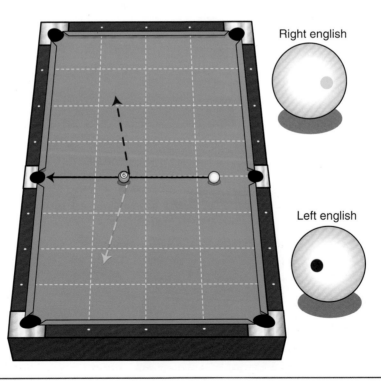

Right english

Left english

Figure 3.22   Using left or right english on the cue ball to produce deflection enables the shooter to throw the object ball to the left or to the right.

players already struggling to grasp nuances of the sport, can convince them that they must constantly question their aim when they plan to impart anything but center ball on the cue ball.

Why is it that the more you know, the more potentially frustrating it can be to get the proper shot off? Well, just try to apply your knowledge in a game situation. Say you're shooting at the 8-ball to get to the 9-ball. To aim correctly, you're going to need to predict the amount of throw you'll get, because you have a pretty good angle, which will minimize most of the throw, but you're going to hit the ball softer, which will give you more throw, but with the right english you want to put on the shot, your cue ball is going to head slightly to the left of where you want to hit it, though because you're not hitting it hard it shouldn't matter as much, but—*stop!* We've all seen this happen in the poolroom. Players study a shot so hard you can almost see the calculations moving across their brains behind their eyes. When they finally get the shot off, they have talked themselves out of making it.

If everyone thought about *all* the considerations on every shot, it would take a long, long time to finish a game, and the tremendous popularity of the cue sports would plummet. Ask pros how *they* compensate for squirt. Chances are good that their answers will range from "What?" to "I just do" to "Squirt and throw cancel each other out anyway."

Now, the third statement isn't true, but you get the idea; they're too busy making balls to think about all the ways they might miss. Every sport has interesting and unique physical properties. Just think of the football traveling through the air, spinning as it heads toward the receiver. Does the football player calculate the spin on its approach, combined with the day's wind velocity, to determine exactly where his hands should be to grasp the ball? Of course not. Students of football might study such things; players just play.

The lessons you should take away regarding deflection and throw are simple. First, the less english you use, the better off you'll be. This is another reason why only half to a full cue tip of english is recommended. Second, shooting too soft or too hard can be dangerous unless you have good reasons for doing so. The simpler you keep your game, the simpler the game will be.

Finally, although deflection and throw can't be disputed—they *do* occur—you don't need to take them into consideration on every shot. Try a few experiments of your own to observe the results with extreme english and extreme speeds so that you understand the possible effects on your shot. If studying more on this subject interests you, by all means find a book (Jack Koehler's *Science of Pocket Billiards* is a good one) that delves more deeply into this territory. Then move on—play pool. With observation and practice you'll learn to compensate for minor adjustments without having to consciously calculate them, and your body, if you've trained it for the sport of pool, will know what to do.

Once you have established the basics—learned center ball, tangent lines, and how balls react coming off the object ball and the cushions with the use of follow, draw, and english—the game of pool becomes one of feel and confidence. And, while each individual's ability varies, every student can create his or her own feel for the game and for each of its beautiful and mystifying shots, be it a length-of-a-table draw shot or a three-rail high-ball shot. Experiment with shots you're unfamiliar with, and allow yourself to try variations of shots as they occur. Some of you are just beginning a lifelong pursuit of the ultimate in cue ball control. Learn, and enjoy. Meanwhile, let's move on to another of pool's most interesting features—game breaks.

Game Breaks

When your ability at the table reaches a certain level of competence, the break shot becomes one of the most important shots, if not *the* most important shot in your arsenal. Games and matches are won and lost all the time on the break, especially in the professional arena. All too often, players treat the break like a pre-game shot, failing to give it the attention it deserves. In this chapter we help you absorb the full importance of a solid break.

There are two distinct methods of breaking: the power, or offensive, break, and the finesse, or defensive, break. The power break is used in games when it's to your advantage to scatter the balls on the table as much as possible, such as Eight Ball and Nine Ball. The lesser-known games requiring a power break are Six Ball, Seven Ball, Rotation, and Banks (if playing an offensive strategy). Games in which a finesse break is called for include Straight Pool, One Pocket, and Banks (if playing a defensive strategy).

Who breaks to begin a match is determined by either a coin toss or what's known as lagging for the break. In lagging, each player shoots a ball from behind the head-string up and down the table. Whichever player's ball lands closest to the rail behind the headstring then has the choice of whether to break or let the opponent break. In power-break games, it's to your advantage to break and keep control of the table. In games such as One Pocket, the finesse break is a strong advantage to the breaker, which is why the break shot is commonly alternated between players. Straight pool is a different beast because the player who breaks must drive at least two balls and the cue ball to a rail, making it likely to leave the opponent an incoming shot.

Before we get ahead of ourselves, we should stress that no matter which game is being played, the balls should be tightly racked. Older balls, imperfect racks, and worn or damaged foot spots and cloth are among the many variables that can cause gaps in the rack, but your goal should be to freeze as many balls to each other as possible. It's reasonable (and a professional courtesy) to expect a tight rack from your opponent and to give the same in return. Also make sure the rack is straight, with the center balls lining up down the center of the table, not twisted to either side.

And one more thing—whether working to develop your power break or your finesse break, pay attention to results that lead to a scratch or an illegal break. The penalty for either is losing control of the table to your opponent, and, in many cases, giving them cue ball in hand anywhere on the table. The break shot is all about control—keep control over the shot, and you won't lose control of the table.

The Right Way to Rack

Here we answer one of pool's most common questions: *What is the correct way to set up the break shot?* There is more than one correct arrangement for the balls in Eight Ball, Nine Ball, Straight Pool, and One Pocket racks; however, there is only one correct *way* to set up these arrangements. In other words, specific rules govern the way in which you rack the balls. Here's what you need to know for each game.

Eight Ball

All 15 balls are racked in a triangle with the 8-ball in the center of the triangle, the apex ball on the foot spot, a striped ball in one corner of the rack, and a solid ball in the other corner. The figure shows one example of a correct Eight Ball rack.

Nine Ball

The balls in this game are racked in a diamond shape with the 1-ball on the foot spot, the 9-ball in the center of the diamond, and the other balls placed randomly. Shown here is one correct 9-ball setup.

Straight Pool

Straight pool follows a triangular rack as in Eight Ball with the apex ball on the foot spot, the 1-ball on the racker's right corner, and the 5-ball on the left corner. The other balls are placed randomly, as shown.

One Pocket

In One Pocket you'll use a standard triangle rack with the balls placed entirely at random.

Rotation

Rotation also uses a standard triangle rack with the 1-ball on the foot spot, the 2-ball on the right rear corner, the 3-ball on the left rear corner, and the 15-ball in the center. All other balls are placed at random, as shown.

Banks

Banks, like One Pocket, uses a standard triangle rack with all balls placed randomly.

Six Ball

In Six Ball, the 1-ball is placed on the foot spot, and the 6-ball is placed in the center of the rear row. The other four balls are placed randomly, as shown.

We hope this information helps prevent any pregame battles on the correct way to rack the balls. To learn how to rack for other games, see the official rules of the Billiard Congress of America (go to www.bca-pool.com for contact information).

POWER BREAKS

In games in which balls must be pocketed in numerical order, the power break takes on added significance. The reason is obvious: Not only do you have to scatter the balls, but, to continue control of the table, at least one ball must be made and the cue ball should have an unobstructed path to the lowest numbered ball.

The two most popular games played today are Nine Ball and Eight Ball. They're also the games played in the majority of pro tournaments, because Nine Ball moves fast for the TV cameras, and Eight Ball is the game best known by audiences of millions of amateur players. In virtually all pro events, players compete in a race. Whoever wins the set number of games first (e.g., race to 11) wins the match. Formats vary between winner break, meaning that the winner of each game breaks the next rack, and alternate break, meaning players take turns breaking. In either case you must be able to control the table when it's handed to you. It's not at all uncommon to see a player, in a race to 11 in winner-break format, get control of the table to break and run out the last three, four, or five games to win the set, never letting his or her opponent back in the match. Likewise, it's hard to mount a comeback in an alternate-break format if you're not keeping the table when it's your turn to break.

In the professional arena, the Nine Ball break has become a contest of who can propel the cue ball into the rack with the most power. That said, it's more important to hit the 1-ball solidly than it is to hit it with great velocity.

Tests have been conducted with electronic devices to see just how fast the cue ball travels during the power break of some top pros. At your local poolroom, ask your fellow pool players to guess the speed of the cue ball. You'll probably get answers ranging from 50 to 200 miles per hour. In fact, the top speed reached by the cue ball in such tests has been only a little over 31 miles an hour. (An interesting note, though—more often than not the cue ball didn't contact the 1-ball solidly on the higher-speed tries, and the cue ball also tended to jump off the bed of the table.) If you could hit the 1-ball solidly at 31 miles an hour, the sound would echo through the room like a cannon shot. Impressive, maybe, but hitting the 1-ball with more accuracy at a lesser speed will result in a better outcome. Again, most aspects of pool are all about control.

Your body's foundation is critical for a power break, and your fundamentals used on most other shots on the pool table will need to shift slightly to accommodate your power break. To achieve more power and spring in your upper body, you need to spread your legs a little farther apart than you would on your normal swing. Place at least 60 percent of your body weight on your front leg. In doing so, you can rock your body forward on the break to increase cue-stick speed. Also stand up a little higher on the shot, which keeps your body from getting in the way of your arm and improves your follow-through.

Your grip will need adjustment, too. A good place to hold the cue stick is roughly 3 to 6 inches (7.5 to 15 cm) behind where you grip the cue for normal shots. This allows a greater follow-through toward the rack when you break the balls.

Finally, you might need to change your bridge. Top players debate over the use of an open bridge or a closed bridge in the power break. The advantage of the open bridge is that it provides no obstruction as you drive your cue stick toward the rack. With a closed bridge, you'll discover that you need to open up your bridge hand anyway to follow through toward the back rail within a second after impact. Begin with what feels comfortable and keeps you in control, but work up to the open bridge.

As we mentioned in chapter 1, when you're breaking the balls, you'll probably find that looking at the cue ball last—rather than at the object ball, as in all other shots—produces better results initially. The reason for this is that when you look at the cue ball last you'll create more of a stunning stroke. Looking at the 1-ball tells your brain to follow-through, which can create too much spin. When you create too much spin in your power break, you'll have a harder time controlling your cue ball.

But, that said, once you have worked for a time on your break and developed a feel for the power stroke necessary to execute the break, you'll probably want to return to looking at the object ball. In Nine Ball, it's often helpful to look at the base of the 1-ball when you break—the spot where the 1-ball and the table are in contact. This can help keep you grounded on the shot and give you a more definite target on your break shot. Many players having problems with their break have had great success with this visual reference.

Setting Up the Power Break

In each of your power break games, placement of the cue ball on the table is important. That placement depends a lot on your own preference. Most players find it's easier when starting out to break the balls with the cue ball at or near the center of the table behind the headstring. As you'll soon see, however, there are many variables in the games and in your own swing and personal preference, all of which can alter your choice of cue ball placement.

Nine Ball Break

Let's talk first about the break in Nine Ball (figure 4.1). If you're right-handed, the best place to set the cue ball is on the right side of the table. If you're left-handed, the best place is probably on the left side. But that's just a starting point.

Cue ball placement is also influenced by your stroke—whether you more often put left english or right english on the cue ball. Without getting too complicated, if you're a right-handed person who tends to put left english on the ball as the cue stick swings through and crosses over, especially when the ball is hit hard, you're better off putting the cue ball on the left side of the table or moving it in toward the center. Anywhere in this area at all and left english automatically comes into play on the 1-ball. This results in a better stunning effect to kill, or stop, the cue ball after it hits the rail. If, on the other hand, you tend to put right english on the ball, you're best off breaking from the right side of the table, again anywhere from the side rail to the middle of the table.

Players used to break from the center of the table until they discovered it's easier to make the corner ball from the rail. Various schools of thought remain on this. Some players still prefer breaking from closer to the center of the table to achieve what they feel is the fullest hit on the 1-ball. Remember that the most important part of the Nine Ball break is a solid—and we do mean *solid*—hit on the 1-ball. Shooting the ball from either side means you're hitting the 1-ball from an angle instead of head-on. You might thus glance off the 1-ball more than you would with a head-on hit from the center of the table. With the cue ball on the foot spot it's much easier to get a solid hit on the 1-ball because you're shooting at the whole ball, as with a straight-in shot. If you move the cue ball to either rail, it becomes more difficult to get a solid hit on the 1-ball.

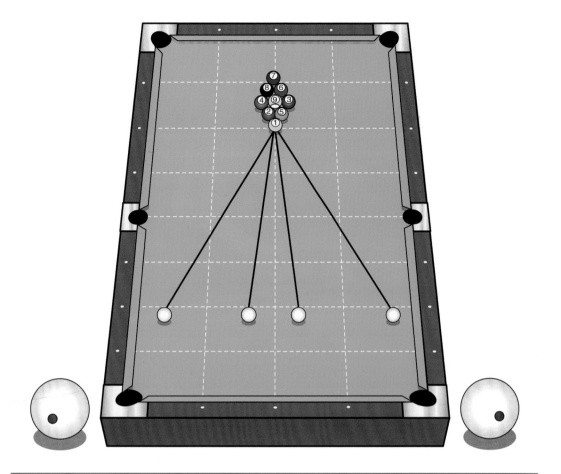

Figure 4.1   Various cue ball positions for the 9-Ball Break.

A good way to practice getting a solid hit is to visualize your cue ball driving right through the 1-ball into the rows of balls behind it. This should also help you focus on your follow-through as you execute your break shot.

Let's get back to those tendencies in your normal stroke. Suppose you naturally put right english on the cue ball, whether by accident or design. (Very few players in fact hit absolutely dead center on the cue ball because of variances in crossing over in their stroke, having a dominant eye, and so on.) In this case you would use just a bit of low-left english for your break shot. This is because your natural tendency is to cross over the cue ball with your cue stick. Without the compensating english, your timing would have to be perfect to hit dead center on the cue ball in order to attain a stunning effect (to hit the 1-ball solidly, with virtually no spin). In other words, you're trying to prevent spin on the cue ball; you want the cue ball completely dead, with no sidespin whatsoever. This allows the greatest transfer of power and the most control.

Years ago you could see top players dig the cue stick into the bed of the cloth after they broke. This is not recommended. Figures 4.2 and 4.3 illustrate the differences. The player shown in figure 4.2 employs the method of digging the cue stick into the table. We believe this actually slows the cue stick down rather than speeding it up. You also risk breaking the spine of your cue shaft, making it susceptible to warping. A better move is to raise the cue stick, bringing it up on your follow-through, as

Figure 4.2 World champion Jasmin Ouschan presses her cue into the table on her break shot.

Figure 4.3 2007 BCA champ Dennis Orcollo breaks without pressing his cue into the table, with impressive results (and less stress and strain to his cue).

employed by contemporary players like Dennis Orcollo and Johnny Archer. What you then accomplish is to put just a touch of forward spin on the cue ball. You want to hit that 1-ball as solidly as possible, and when the cue ball grabs, making contact with the cloth and the 1-ball, it will more or less just die in the center of the table, which is the optimal place to have the cue ball after the Nine Ball break. It stands to reason that if the cue ball is in the center of the table, your chances of having a shot at the lowest numbered ball are much greater.

Most top pros today break from the side rail, with the goal of pocketing the corner ball (shown in figure 4.4) so that they may continue shooting. You'll hear some commentators say that professional players intend to try to make the 1-ball in the side. That's ludicrous. What they're trying to do is control the 1-ball, keeping it near the cue ball for their first shot after the break. They don't necessarily want to make the 1-ball, because they have no control over the 2-ball! The 2-ball could be anywhere in the rack except in front where the 1-ball is or the center where the 9-ball is. So it makes sense that if you make the 1-ball, there's no guarantee of a shot at the 2-ball.

Can you predict where the balls will land on the break? Not all of them. But let's say that you hit below center on the cue ball. What happens most often is that the 1-ball will go above the head spot, and the cue ball will go to the bottom of the table, as shown in figure 4.5. Now let's say you use follow instead. The high ball will have the effect of sending the cue ball forward and the 1-ball to the bottom of the table.

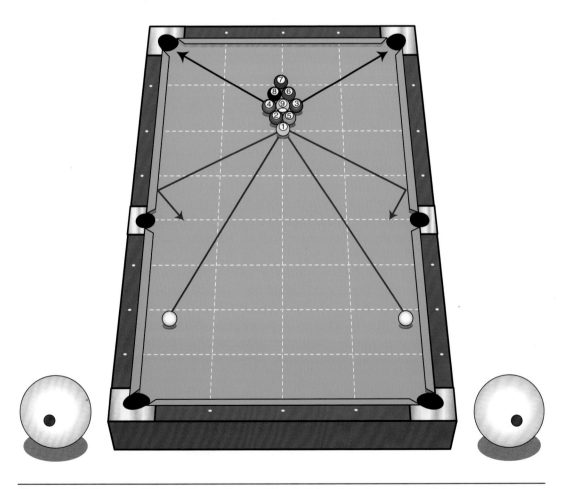

Figure 4.4 The most likely ball to go in on a Nine Ball break is the corner ball in the rack—it heads directly to the corner pocket.

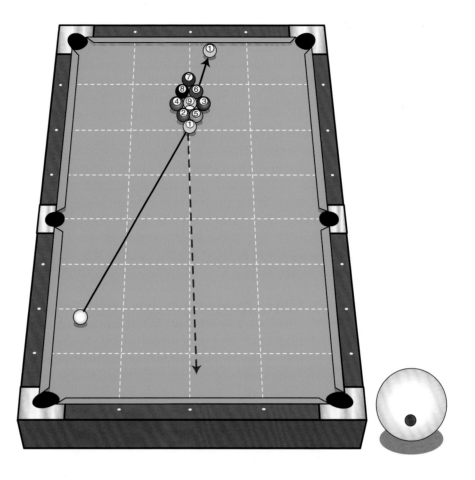

Figure 4.5 Predicting the typical outcome of a Nine Ball break using a below-center hit.

Neither option produces an optimal shot on the 1-ball. What you want to do is to hit the cue ball as close to the center as possible into the 1-ball. You'll be attempting to send the 1-ball either to the right or left rail, close to the side pocket. (Old-time players would call this trying to trap the 1-ball near the side pocket.)

You'll discover that although weaker players don't hit the balls as hard on the break, the balls still seem to gravitate toward a pocket. Yet you might see a very powerful player hit the balls 30 miles an hour and the balls seem to stun themselves. Think of it this way: If you hit the balls too hard, the balls will explode, then implode, then explode again. The energy gets trapped within the rack, rather like exploding a firework inside a can. There's plenty of noise but not much action. Thus, players with powerful swings never want to hit the balls with 100 percent of their strength. Accuracy is the key. The more solidly you hit the 1-ball, the better your chances of making a ball.

Eight Ball Break

Today's most popular game in amateur tournament and league competition is Eight Ball, and we're seeing more professional events try this format as well to appeal to spectators already familiar with the rules. Having the break in Eight Ball offers a few advantages. First, as in Nine Ball, with a well-scattered rack better players can run the table. Second, if a run-out opportunity isn't there, pocketing any ball on the break still gives the player the first option of which group of balls to shoot. This leaves the opponent with the less desirable group, where balls might be tied up or clustered on the rail.

The Eight Ball break, while also a power break, is totally different from the Nine Ball break. You don't try to hit the head ball in the rack but instead aim for a hit on the second ball. Because you don't need to hit the lowest numbered ball in Eight Ball, hitting the 1-ball or head ball on the break isn't required. Second, hitting the second ball gives you a much better spread of the 15 balls, as opposed to the 9 balls you're busting up in a Nine Ball rack.

For the Eight Ball break, move the cue ball toward one rail or the other, as close to the cushion as possible. Aim to hit the ball behind the head ball as solid as possible, with below-center spin (see figure 4.6). If you contact the cue ball with center or high ball, chances are good you'll scratch in the corner pocket. Hitting that second ball very solid and below center gives you a much better spread of the balls on the table. This is especially crucial in bar-league play because the tables are smaller (typically 3.5 by 7 feet [1.0 by 2.1 m] rather than 4.5 by 9 feet [1.4 by 2.7 m]), which promotes ball-clustering; a solid hit to the second ball will help break up the clusters.

On a table measuring 4.5 by 9 feet, things are a little different. Some players go for the second ball, or row, and some aim for the third row to promote a better spread of balls on the bigger table. For now, we don't think it makes any difference whether you hit the second or third row; the crucial thing is to hit the ball solid and below center to avoid scratching. The bonus of the below-center hit is that it tends to bring the cue ball back to the long rail just on the side of the rack and then closer to the center of the table. And, as we discussed for the Nine Ball break, you're more likely to have a good shot with your cue ball in the center of the table.

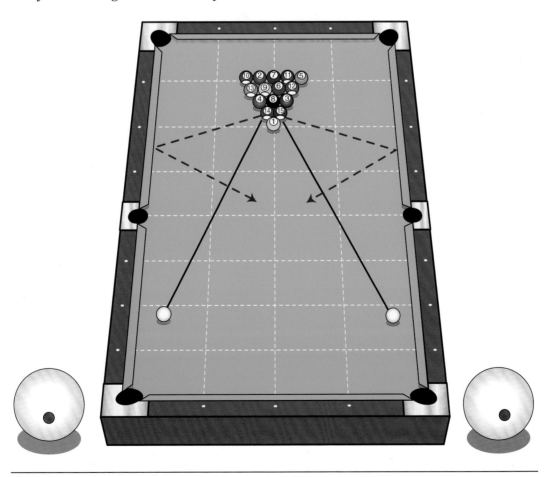

Figure 4.6 In an Eight Ball break, aim to hit the second ball.

Alternative Game Breaks

The break in Rotation is similar to the Nine Ball break. Once again, the 1-ball sits at the head of the rack, the 2-ball is in one corner of the rack, and the 3-ball is in the other corner of the rack, as shown in figure 4.7. You want to spread the balls as much as possible, make a ball, and also get a shot at the 1-ball. For the shot to be considered a legal break, you must hit the 1-ball first.

Breaking in the game of Banks straddles the line between offensive and defensive breaks. If you have a very tough opponent, and your games are quite similar, you'll likely want to opt for a safety break or a Straight Pool break. If you intend to play an offensive game of Banks, then you'd opt for a power break, similar to the Eight Ball break. Again, you want to spread the balls as much as possible and pocket a ball. Chances are then very good, if you keep your cue ball near the center of the table, that you'll have a makeable bank shot on your first shot after the break, especially considering you can shoot at any ball on the table.

For a Six Ball break you'll need a little different break technique because of the configuration of the balls. Here, break from one side of the table or the other with the intention of having your cue ball land near one of the long rails. Why? Because if you get a solid hit on the 1-ball from one side or the other, you'll tend to make one of the back two corner balls four rails in the corner. To execute this break, you hit on the cue ball well below center with the intention of drawing back from the rack of balls. If your cue ball stops in the center of the table, it could interfere with the four-rail shot outcome, as shown in figure 4.8.

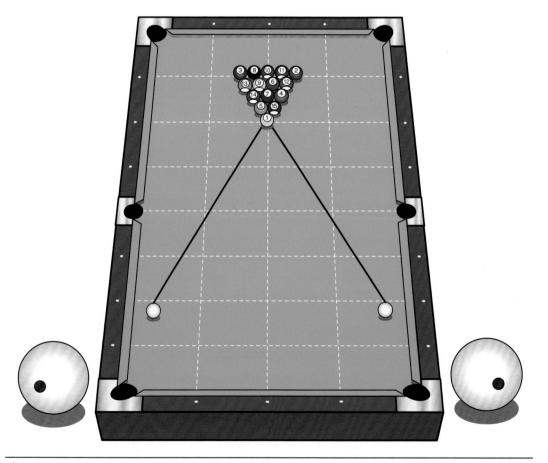

Figure 4.7   Set your cue ball for rotation break to the left if you have a tendency for right english and to the right if you have a tendency for left english.

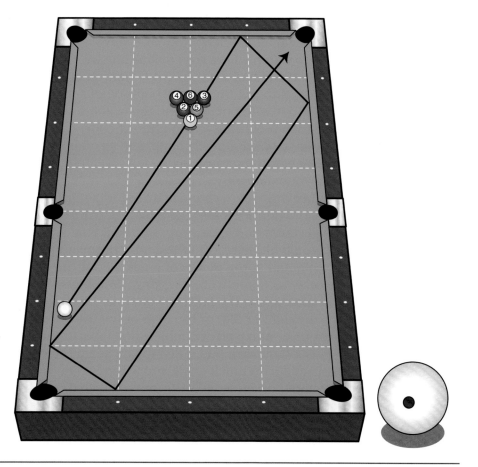

Figure 4.8 Keep your cue ball away from the table center in a Six Ball break.

All of these games are great for developing your power break while enjoying play. Even if you lean toward one game or another, take a bit of time to learn the other games and their related breaks. This is a great way to break the monotony of a tired practice routine.

Practicing Your Power Break

Developing a solid power break takes time, work, and effort. But doesn't everything? An important lesson to learn while practicing your power break is that you don't need to accomplish everything at once. Nobody hits a perfect break shot the first time. You have to slowly build up your speed with the cue stick. This might seem like a tedious process, but it's well worth the time. Getting a solid hit on the target ball is first and foremost. Building speed comes next.

Begin developing your break by exerting just 20 percent of your hit strength, similar to a slow or medium hit on the cue ball. Your objectives are simply to control the cue ball, control your speed, and get a solid hit on the target ball.

Gradually increase the speed of your stroke. Once you hit five to six solid breaks in a row, step up to 40 percent of your hit strength, then to 60 percent, and then to 80 percent. If you still have total control of the cue ball at this point and you're able to hit 100 percent of your stroke, go for it—but don't be surprised if you miss. Few players can exert 100 percent of their force and still get a solid hit on the target. You'll probably need to settle for 70 to 80 percent, which is just fine.

There are a couple of ways to determine how you're progressing on your break shot, or if you have physical adjustments to make. Have a partner stand either in front of you by the rack to watch where the cue ball hits the pack, or behind you to see where you contact the cue ball with the tip of your cue. This helps show you the kind of english you tend to put on the cue ball—dead center, a touch left, or a touch right. If you can shoot video of yourself, this will tell you even more. Many instructors now offer video recording as a matter of course, and the information you can glean about your stroke, follow-through, and so on is invaluable for a shot like the break, in which everything happens so fast; watching video play back in slow motion can teach you volumes.

Another method of checking where your cue tip is contacting the ball is to use the 8-ball in a single-ball test. Without racking the balls, put the 8-ball on the head spot with the number 8 dead center and facing you, so that if you're shooting exactly in the center of the ball, you'll hit directly in the center of the number. Scuff your tip to rough it up quite a bit, and apply plenty of chalk. Shoot the ball straight down table with plenty of force, as if you were breaking; then have your partner catch the 8-ball immediately after it hits the bottom rail. Now, check the chalk mark. Is it in the center? If it's to the right or left, or too high or too low, you'll need to adjust. You can also do this exercise with a bit of double-sided tape, or the tape that golfers use on clubfaces to check their own hits. The tape picks up the chalk mark left by your cue without the need for so much chalk and without requiring a partner. One company has even invented practice balls on which the chalk sticks to the ball.

On the power break (and many harder-hit shots in your regular game), the cue ball travels above the table surface, sometimes skipping along the way. The skip should be anywhere from one to three feet in front of the rack, so that the cue ball is back on terra firma before hitting the rack. A ball that is still in mid-air as it makes contact is more likely to fly off the table, causing injury to nearby spectators and glass objects. The skip is easier to detect on a table covered with new fabric. To determine where your cue ball skips, try this simple exercise. Lay out a line of dimes along your path from the cue ball to the object ball. If your cue ball hits the dimes right away, you're not getting enough power on your break. If it's landing on dimes close to the rack, you should be able to tell at about which point the ball has contacted the table during its skip. Most players are amazed at how far the cue ball travels without touching the table.

After your amazement, though, keep in mind that the point of the exercise is to create consistency. When you know that your cue ball is going to skip over the cloth, you then want to gauge with what power you have to hit the cue ball and to what point on the table the ball skips, given that power. You're literally hitting the 1-ball on a bounce. This is good to know because you really would like to hit the 1-ball on the fly, so that the cue ball comes down and into the 1-ball. This is a rare shot indeed, but you can strive for it by adjusting your power until you can perfectly time the landing of your cue ball. You can also learn to avoid the speed at which your cue ball jumps off the table, resulting in a foul. Keep your stroke as level as possible; too much of a downward hit at the increased velocity will send the cue ball airborne.

THE FINESSE BREAK

Games in which a finesse, or defensive, break come into play include Straight Pool, One Pocket, very defensive games of Banks, and some international rules of Eight Ball (where a single game can take hours). The finesse break requires a soft to medium

Selecting a Break Cue

The game has changed over the past few decades with the introduction of specialty cues in the billiard marketplace. Specialty cues include models designed for power breaking, jumping over impeding balls, and the hybrid break–jump cue combinations that allow removal of part of the butt of the cue to jump balls when not using the cue to break. Newer models of break–jump cues feature quick-release screws to turn your break cue into a jump cue in record time. Best of all, newer models of cases accommodate increasing numbers of cues, in addition to space for extra shafts and accessories, making the inclusion of a break cue in your arsenal more practical than ever.

The break cue has become increasingly important in the power break. Because you hit the balls so hard, this particular shot has a tendency to flatten out the tip of your normal cue. As many professional players will tell you, the break cue (although it takes some getting used to) has resulted in better break performance, along with increasing the longevity of their regular playing cue. Power breaks put stress on your normal cue shaft and require changing your tip more frequently.

What you'll want in a break cue is a flatter and relatively thinner tip, along with some form of phenolic (plastic) ferrule (preferably a slip-on as opposed to screw-in type of ferrule). Many players also swear by the newer layered tips (many layers of leather glued together to increase strength and better retain shape).

For shaft size, a good rule of thumb is to purchase a break cue anywhere from a quarter-millimeter to a half-millimeter larger than the cue stick you normally play with. The reason for this is twofold. First, you get a sense of security, because the cue feels a little more stable in your bridge hand, you have a little more control over the cue tip, and even your miscues will be a little closer to center. Second, the larger the millimeter of the tip, the more surface area of the tip will contact the cue ball, offering more control. A thicker shaft might also prove more durable over the long haul.

As for break cue weights, some professionals believe that the heavier stick creates more force, but most subscribe to the theory that the lighter stick allows more speed and thus more velocity. Professional players are leaning more and more toward the lighter break cues, which they claim provide more whip, translating to more action out of the cue.

We agree with the latter theory—the best cues are the lighter ones that allow more velocity. Think of a golf swing, in which greater club head speed generates more distance; the same principle applies to your pool swing.

Still other players rely on a cue that's as similar to their playing cue as possible, often even the same weight, tip size, and so on. The theory here is that they don't have to adjust, knowing they're playing with virtually the same cue, and that they have their break cue as a fallback in case of a malfunction in their regular playing cue. There's something to be said for this line of reasoning because even with an extra shaft in your case for a lost tip or broken ferrule, a cue can still lose a butt screw or have a joint loosen after repeated power breaks.

Also gaining in popularity are the graphite and other composite material cues. Even professionals who lean toward the traditional in their regular playing cue have made the move to graphite in their break cues, explaining that these models can offer more action and power in the break shot. We advise speaking to a reputable dealer or owner of a billiard club pro shop before making your selection. Also pay attention to what works for players or instructors whose opinions you respect.

hit. You're breaking the balls just hard enough to drive the required number of balls to the rail for a legal break, or, as in One Pocket, to drive balls toward your pocket. In both cases, you want to leave your opponent with no shot, or at least a difficult shot. Although not offensive in its execution, a solid defensive break is necessary for winning strategy in these games. Your opponent is left with a tough shot, and this can translate into one of pool's greatest strategies—forcing your opponent to take the tough shot and capitalizing on what's left to you.

Setting Up the Finesse Break

Finesse breaks, like power breaks, will benefit from various setups and points of aim, depending on the game you play and what you need to accomplish. The following sections discuss a bit of the technique necessary for your finesse break.

Straight Pool Break

When playing Straight Pool, it's to your disadvantage to break the balls (so the loser of the lag or coin toss is the one who has to break). In the rules of Straight Pool, you must drive two balls and the cue ball to a rail. The best place to put the cue ball on the break shot is 3 to 6 inches (7.5 by 15 cm) from the side rail. You'll aim to hit one quarter to one third of the corner ball in the back row with outside english (see figure 4.9). In other words, if you're on the right side of the table, you're going

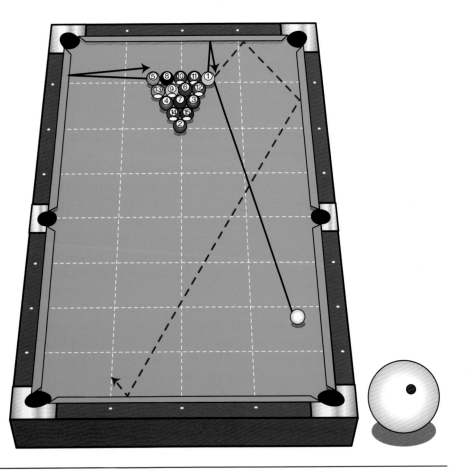

Figure 4.9   A typical opening break in Straight Pool.

to hit the right back ball with a touch of high-right english. The desired result is to drive the ball you've contacted to the bottom rail. The object ball on the other side of that row of five balls moves toward the long rail and, one hopes, back into the stack of balls. The cue ball bounces off the short rail, back into the long rail, and then travels toward the lower-left corner pocket.

A couple of fancy breaks used in Straight Pool attempt to pocket a ball off the break, but these aren't breaks we'd suggest in competition because of the conditions they require. Nevertheless, they can be fun, and impressive to witness. In the first of these breaks (figure 4.10), line up the cue ball between the head spot and the side rail and shoot it with about 80 percent of your power into the short rail, banking it back to hit the last ball in the back stack very solid. This sends the front ball two rails into the side. It's a fun shot when it goes, but a lot depends on the rack—that is, if all the balls are frozen, if the rack is straight or twisted, and so on. The conditions have to be perfect.

Another fancy break in Straight Pool is to make the side ball in the row of five at the back of the rack, as shown in figure 4.11. This is a straight high-ball shot with no left or right english to bank the object ball back. The side ball picks up right spin off the hit from the cue ball. Then, as it caroms off the ball next to it, the spin sends the ball straight back into the corner. This shot was played in competition by European champion Oliver Ortmann (Germany) during his win at the 1989 US Open in Chicago. Risky? Oh, yes. Impressive? You bet.

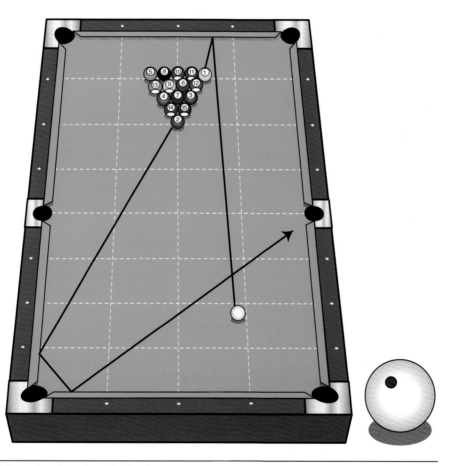

Figure 4.10   A fancy break in Straight Pool.

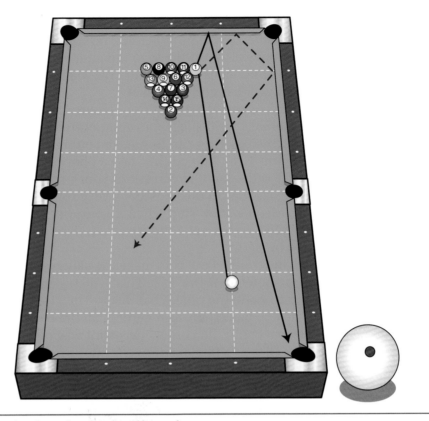

Figure 4.11   Another fancy break in straight pool.

One Pocket Break

The One Pocket break offers different types of breaks, from the ultraconservative to the more aggressive to every variation between. We've included a few of the favorites, beginning with a more aggressive break. Suppose that you have the upper-right corner as your pocket. You place the cue ball near or along the long left-side rail, and try to split the front two balls with your cue ball. In other words, you shoot the cue ball between the head ball and the row of two balls behind it, as shown in figure 4.12. Use high inside english (in this case, right english) with a nice, smooth stroke. You want to send as many balls as possible to your side of the table. Even if the left corner ball pops up by accident, the cue ball will tend to send that ball toward your side of the table. This is a very good break when executed correctly. Ideally, you want your cue ball to end up 3 to 6 inches (7.5 to 15 cm) above the side pocket, frozen on the side rail. When playing One Pocket, the best places to leave the cue ball for defensive purposes are frozen on the rail or frozen on an object ball.

Another One Pocket break is accomplished by kicking rail first into the balls. To execute this break, you take the cue ball to the right side of the table and shoot toward the first diamond past the side pocket on the left side of the table, using a below-center stroke, as shown in figure 4.13. The cue ball then travels with a high-ball effect after it contacts the rail. When it hits the rack, it will stick, pushing balls toward your pocket. You're trying to freeze the cue ball on the stack while sending balls toward your side of the table.

For a more defensive break, line up the cue ball with the row of balls going toward your pocket and in line to hit the front ball solid. What you're attempting here is to freeze the cue ball to the head ball and move just one ball toward your pocket

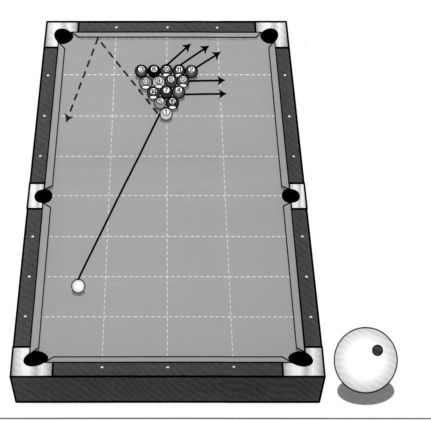

Figure 4.12 An aggressive One Pocket break.

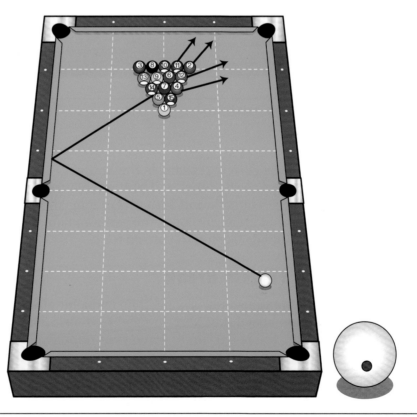

Figure 4.13 Kicking rail first in a One Pocket break.

(figure 4.14). This is a weaker, defensive brand of break, and remember that in One Pocket one ball must hit a rail for the break to be legal.

We've also seen people playing One Pocket who use a Straight Pool break, but this is a very weak shot unless all you want to do is bunt balls around the table for the next three hours. This shot is too defensive for most players' tastes and accomplishes nothing to either player's benefit.

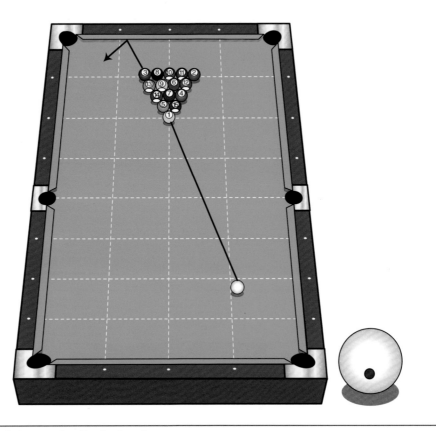

Figure 4.14   A defensive One Pocket break.

Banks Break

The safety break in Banks closely resembles the Straight Pool break; the object is to send the cue ball down to the other end of the table and leave your opponent with the rack pretty much intact—and with a very long shot. This break, like the very defensive One Pocket break, prolongs the game and immediately sends it into a safety battle. If this sounds like fun to you, go for it.

Practicing Your Finesse Break

Developing a finesse break also takes some time and a bit of work. You don't have to work on building up speed, but you do need to develop a proper feel for the shot. Hit too hard, and you're certain to leave your opponent a shot. Hit too soft, and you risk not making a legal break, giving your opponent control of the table. You won't need to change your stance or bridge for these shots as you would in the power break; execute them as you would a normal shot. This eliminates part of the work, but only if you've invested the time to feel the shot and know what you need to accomplish.

Set up the various breaks we've shown in this chapter and practice them with special attention to the amount of force you're giving to the shot. If you have the opportunity to play on various sizes of pool tables, you'll notice that it takes less force to perform the same shot on a small table than it does on the bigger table. As you learned in chapter 3, speed of the equipment also comes into play. If you're preparing for a match involving a defensive break strategy, take a couple of practice break shots before you play to gauge the speed of the cloth and the cushions.

In the finesse break, it's especially important to achieve a smooth swing and follow-through. Anticipating the hit on this break can lead you to hesitate and undershoot the shot, or you might force your arm through it, resulting in a choppy stroke that won't allow control over your resulting cue ball position. Visualize a gentle, relaxed, and controlled swing through each shot.

Finally, in the finesse break, knowledge is power. Have an exact idea of where you want your object balls and cue ball to arrive. Decide on this before you get down in your stance. Once you've made your decision, step into your stance, let your body take over, and perform the break shot as you would any other shot.

No matter your choice of game in the cue sports, it pays to practice the breaks for each of the games we've discussed. Different breaks, whether power or finesse, allow you the opportunity to witness different focus points on the rack and different reactions of the cue ball off the rack. Once you've honed your breaking abilities, you're ready to tackle some critical shots—shots, like the break, that can make or break your game.

CHAPTER 5

Critical Shots

Critical shots are those shots seldom fully discussed or taught, namely, the stop shot, stun shot, and drag shot, along with rail shots, banks, combinations, caroms, massé shots, and jump shots. Some of these shots are underestimated (the stop, stun, and drag shots), whereas others are considered shots only the pros can pull off (combinations, caroms, and massé shots). But you can and should learn each of these skills to the best of your ability. Mastering them can mean the difference between winning and losing. In discussing each of the critical shots, we present information on the technique used for the shot and suggested applications in game situations. Understand that some critical shots, while impressive when performed perfectly, can be low-percentage shots. When possible, you might want to opt for a safer alternative. But when no alternative exists, a well-played critical shot can win you the game.

THE STOP SHOT

Many assume the stop shot is the easiest shot to master. Perhaps. But until you master it, sliding or rolling your cue ball beyond contact with the object ball will cost you position play and, consequently, games. Stop shots, by design, decrease the distance the cue ball travels after contact with the object ball. What's the advantage of less distance traveled? Simply put, predictability. You may have heard a player comment on a game or match, "Ah, well, the guy had nothing but stop-outs." This means the player didn't have to move the cue ball around the table as much, resulting in less margin for error in subsequent cue ball positions. When appropriate, a stop shot is a great position play because you know exactly where your cue ball will be for the following shot. The stop shot is a vital skill that you must master to play your best game.

Keep in mind that when you execute a stop shot, the cue ball does not replace the space of the object ball, as many players mistakenly believe. This common misconception can result in bad position plays, especially when executing pattern plays that demand pinpoint position, such as being able to see the next ball from where your cue ball lands. Just remember that because the cue ball stops on contact, it comes to occupy the space 2.25 inches (5.7 cm) *behind* where the object ball was prior to contact.

Here's how to perfect your skill in performing a stop shot. Take one of the striped balls from your rack and place it on the table (around the head spot) with the stripe horizontal, or parallel to the bed of the table. Now hit the ball toward the other end of the table with a below-center stroke and observe the stripe on the ball. Watch how the ball, while moving forward, will reverse for a period of time, then slide, then begin rolling.

Once you've seen this initial physical reaction, you can experiment with different types of strokes and different aiming points, as shown in figure 5.1. Attempt the shot in three different positions, with a just-below-center hit (one-half cue tip), a full cue tip below-center hit, and even farther below center (maintaining as level a stroke as possible). Use the same force on your stroke in each of the different positions. You'll quickly recognize that the farther below center you go, the farther the cue ball will skid forward before it actually grabs and starts rolling forward. This action, when the ball begins the forward rolling motion, is sometimes referred to as a *perfect roll*. A perfect roll describes the cue ball rolling forward with absolutely no sidespin or english on the cue ball.

Figure 5.1 Practicing the stop shot with different strokes and hits.

Now you're ready to transfer this knowledge to proper execution of the stop shot. What you're trying to achieve with the stop shot is to have the cue ball hit the object ball at the point when there's still a touch of backward spin on the cue ball, just before the cue ball ends its slide and starts its perfect roll. First, before using any object balls, practice the simple shots shown in figure 5.1 to see how the cue ball reacts with the different strokes. This will give you a good idea of the distance the cue ball is traveling before it grabs in each of your cue tip positions. Once you get the technique down, you're ready to move on to the next exercise.

The other exercise we've set up for you (in figure 5.2) will do two things for quick development of your stop-shot skills. First, you'll learn to quickly recognize a stop-out pattern when you see one. As you'll note in the diagram, no balls are tied up or clustered together, and nothing is too close to a rail. Without these conditions, a stop-out will be nearly impossible. The point of the exercise is to run the balls in rotation, as indicated, executing a stop shot with each shot. It's easy to set up variations of this exercise on your own, keeping in mind that no balls should be too close together or too close to a rail.

Second, you'll practice stop shots at short and long distances. While in normal play it might be more practical to draw the cue ball back for better position, this exercise is designed to let you develop a feel for executing the stop shot from varying distances. You'll discover that lower cue ball position (slight draw), combined with a slightly harder hit, will be necessary to stop the cue ball on the longer shots. Again, this is because in a stop shot the cue ball will slide to the object ball, ideally

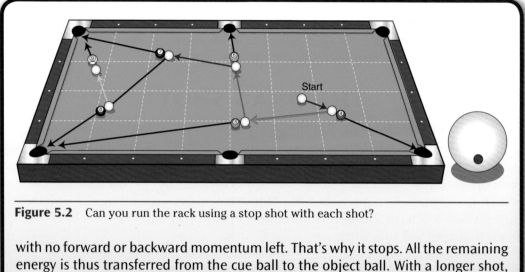

Figure 5.2   Can you run the rack using a stop shot with each shot?

with no forward or backward momentum left. That's why it stops. All the remaining energy is thus transferred from the cue ball to the object ball. With a longer shot, the cue ball will need extra force and a lower hit to maintain the slide before the natural forward roll takes place and causes the cue ball to drift after contacting the object ball.

THE STUN SHOT

How do you adjust a stop shot if the shot isn't exactly straight in? Let's add some shots with a slight angle and see what occurs. Note the shots in figure 5.3 and the resulting cue ball positions. As you can see, knowing how to perform the stun shot can help you minimize drift of the cue ball and allow you to play pinpoint position, as well as avoid impeding balls.

The stun shot is a variation of a stop shot that's used when you're not quite straight in on the object ball. As you've learned already, your cue ball will come off at a 90-degree angle from the angle to the pocket (the tangent line). If you have a 10-degree-angle shot, executing the stun shot is just like a stop shot, only the cue ball will react sideways off the object ball rather than forward or backward. The stun shot then becomes an equally good way to control the cue ball off the object ball without sending the cue ball very far, or having to go back and forth across the

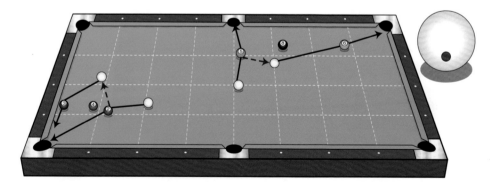

Figure 5.3   Slight angle stop shots or stun shots can minimize cue ball movement.

table for position. Set up several off-angle shots to develop your stun-shot skills, noting in each how the cue ball reacts and how little distance you can make it travel. Obviously, the greater the angle, the more energy is left on the cue ball and the harder it is to control how far it travels after contact.

THE DRAG SHOT

The drag shot, like the stun shot, is useful when you want to move the cue ball a short distance. The drag allows you to roll the cue ball forward just a little, anywhere between 3 and 12 inches (7.6 and 30 cm). Skill development in this shot requires a bit more feel. You'll continue to use a below-center hit, but in this shot the cue ball will stop sliding before it reaches the object ball. After contacting the object ball, the cue ball will have forward spin remaining, and you must be able to recognize when that spin will take over.

In the drag shot, most of the energy you put on the cue ball is gone. Take a look at the shots in figure 5.4. In both cases, you want the cue ball to drift forward a bit for ideal position on the next shot, but you also want to maintain control of the cue ball. A follow stroke will allow the cue ball to travel too far; a stop shot will bring you up short. A soft, slightly below-center hit will get you where you need to be. Experiment with several drag shots to develop a feel for allowing the cue ball to drift forward.

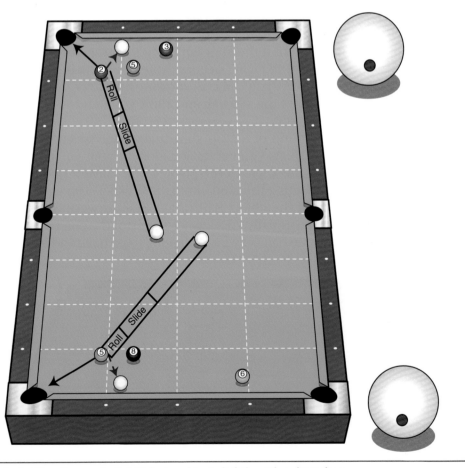

Figure 5.4   Letting the cue ball drift forward just slightly with a drag shot.

FROZEN SHOTS

Very often you'll be left with shots in which the object ball is frozen on (touching) the cushion. These shots are easy to make, but they fall into the category of critical shots because so many players fail to develop their skills in this area. There are three options on how to pocket a ball frozen on the cushion. You can contact the object ball and cushion at the same time, you can hit the cushion first, or you can hit the object ball first. The force of the shot and to which point your cue ball needs to travel should dictate which option you choose. If you need to hit the shot hard to achieve position on the next shot, hit the object ball first. If you hit the object ball first, you are also able to keep more english on the cue ball, whereas if you hit the rail first, the hit will take the english or any spin off the cue ball.

See figure 5.5 for an example of an object ball frozen on the long rail; three rail positions are indicated for the cue ball after execution of the shot. Using inside english (in this case, right english), if you hit the object ball first, or the ball and cushion simultaneously, your cue ball will *grab*, meaning it will pick up the necessary english, enabling you to go around the table three rails. If you hit the rail first in this shot, you'll almost always come off sideways, no matter what spin you've put on the cue ball. In other words, your cue ball will never get to the short rail to go three rails (figure 5.5). Instead the cue ball will shoot straight across the table to the other long rail, no matter what sidespin you have on the ball, even with draw.

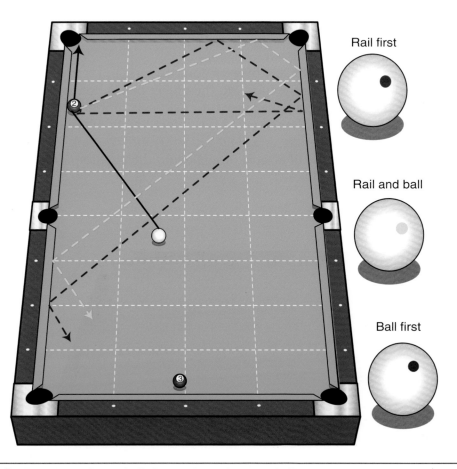

Figure 5.5 Executing a frozen ball shot, with resulting cue ball positions.

When executing the frozen ball shot, don't get caught up in so-called optical illusions, of seeing too much of the rail and losing focus on the ball. Aim as you would for any other shot, and shoot the ball. Again, this shot is easier than some people think—actually easier than a ball just off the rail, which can be over- or undercut. Fear of the shot translates into a poor follow-through, which often reinforces the miss. Here is a little secret, then: When practicing frozen-to-the-cushion shots, attempt to execute them with an exaggerated follow-through. This forces you to stay down on the shot and allows you the best opportunity for full, firm contact with the object ball. With a little practice, you'll have plenty of confidence in making any ball that's frozen to the cushion.

BANKS

The bank shot might be the most misunderstood shot in the cue sports. There's been so much written about the bank shot, and there are so many variables to take into account to pull off a bank shot, that players get just plain confused. Here, then, are the basics of the bank shot, and a couple of different systems for banking.

Speed

The main variable to concern yourself with in bank shots is speed—how fast (or how hard) you hit the object ball. Figure 5.6 shows a graphic illustration of this. Each shot has been hit with center ball, but the red shot has been hit too hard, the yellow shot too soft, and the black shot just right. As you see, the harder you hit the ball, the shorter the angle coming off the cushion. The angle into the cushion won't equal the angle coming out.

Simple so far, right? What many players don't understand is why this is so. There are two reasons. First, with the hard hit, the object ball is not rolling but skidding off the rubber cushion. Second, because the cushion is rubber, a ball hit into it with force will compress the rubber, causing the object ball to bounce back off the rail at a shorter or shallower angle. A ball hit too softly into the rail, then, will roll long in comparison to the angle of attack, or angle into the cushion. This is why speed is the most crucial part of banks.

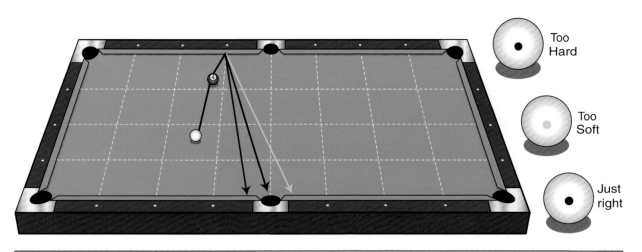

Figure 5.6   Using speed to increase or decrease the bank shot angle.

Figure 5.7 shows you how this knowledge can translate into a game-winning opportunity. You are presented with a bank shot on the 8-ball that, if hit with medium speed, will send the cue ball to poor resulting position for the 9-ball. But, with a harder hit, you can open up the angle coming off the 8-ball because you have to cut the 8-ball more to pocket the ball. This allows you to send the cue ball down table for the 9-ball, using a middle-ball hit (no english required). This is just one example of how speed affects the angle at which you aim to make a bank and get position at the same time.

So far, so good. Let's add another variable. In figure 5.8 we show you the same shot, hit with medium speed, but we've changed how we hit the cue ball. The red shot has been hit with follow. The yellow shot has been hit with draw. And, again, the black shot, hit with middle ball, is just right. High ball on shot A will transfer low ball to the object ball. As the object ball picks up the draw off the cue ball, it will spring off the cushion with low-ball effect, thus cutting down the angle at which it bounces off the rail. If, on the other hand, you put draw on the cue ball, you will be putting follow on the object ball, and the high-ball effect will result in the object ball coming off a little longer, depending on your angle of attack into the cushion.

The best way, then, to initially practice your bank shots and to get a feel for each individual bank is to begin with a medium hit using center ball on the cue ball.

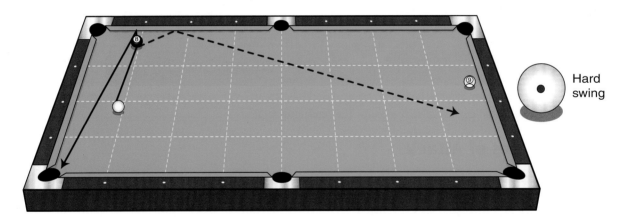

Figure 5.7 Your knowledge of bank speed will benefit your position play.

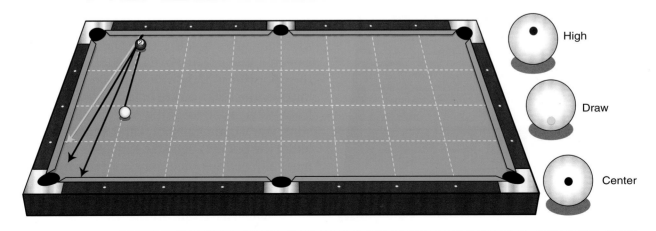

Figure 5.8 Using follow and draw to change the bank shot angle.

English

The next variable that affects your bank shot execution is the use of english. As occurs with follow and draw, the resulting spin on the object ball will be the opposite of that imparted to the cue ball. That is, left english on the cue ball transfers to right english on the object ball, and right english on the cue ball puts left english on the object ball. Again, results will differ depending on the angle of attack. And if you wish to impart english, you can transfer more spin to the object ball with the use of low ball—that is, low right or low left as opposed to high right or high left. The speed of the swing also determines how much spin is transferred to the object ball. The slower the swing speed, the more spin transferred. Figure 5.9 illustrates the altered paths using right english and left english versus center ball.

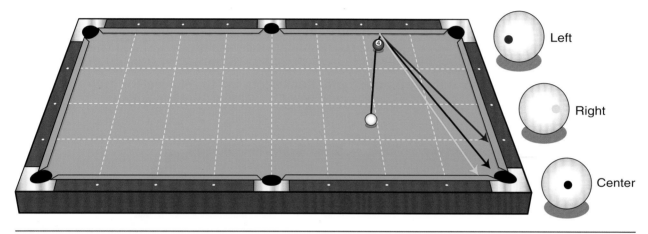

Figure 5.9   Using left and right english to change the bank shot angle.

Angles of Attack

The final variables that influence bank shots are the angles of attack. These include the angle from the cue ball to the object ball and from the object ball to the cushion. Let's first discuss the angle from the cue ball to object ball. Figure 5.10 shows a crossover bank, so named because you cross over the angle of the bank shot with your cue ball. A glancing blow on the left side of the object ball puts left spin on the object ball, even with a center-ball hit. This will cause the ball to go long (sending it to the right of the corner pocket—see red arrow). Also remember that the fuller the hit, the more sidespin that's transferred. Figure 5.11 shows the opposite situation. Here, you're not crossing over the ball; you are in fact shooting away from the bank angle of the object ball. On this shot, you'll come up short on the bank (to the left of the pocket) because english is put automatically on the object ball from the glancing blow away from the angle of attack. In other words, the angle will change from the natural angle (which we've already learned is about the same angle out from the cushion as the angle at which it approached the cushion).

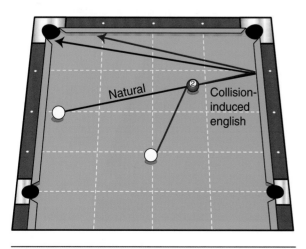

Figure 5.10   Crossing over the angle on a bank shot.

Which brings us to the angle from the object ball to the cushion. Angles between 20 and 60 degrees pick up the most collision-induced sidespin. After about 60 degrees, the more severe the angle, the less sidespin is picked up on the object ball. A cross-side bank with very little angle (5 to 10 degrees) won't pick up much sidespin coming off the cushion. With a center-ball hit, then, the only variable that affects the shallow angle bank is the speed at which you hit the ball. The more shallow the angle coming into the cushion off the bank, the less distortion you're going to get off the cushion.

A steep angle coming into the cushion allows the object ball to pick up a great deal of sidespin, or running english. Figure 5.12 illustrates a steep-angled, two-rail bank shot and its resulting altered path from the cushion. *Angle in* does not equal *angle out* in this case; you'll pick up sidespin, which will force the object ball to go longer. This will occur on the first rail of a bank shot, and also on the second rail in shots using multiple rails. By the third rail, the spin will be gone. This will also hold true for kick shots. Take this factor into account when hitting multirail banks; aim that shot shorter than you actually would on the shallow-angle shot.

Banking Systems

Chances are what we've told you so far has either made you take up tennis or really whetted your appetite to try a few banks on your own. We hope the latter is true. If you've experimented at all, and studied the figures provided, you'll have noticed that everything starts with angle in equals angle out and then adjusts based on the aforementioned variables. Now it's time to take your knowledge one step further with a few fun systems built just for banks.

Creating a Mirror Image

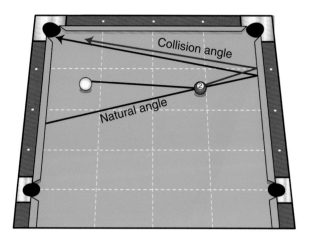

Figure 5.11   Shooting away from the angle on a bank shot.

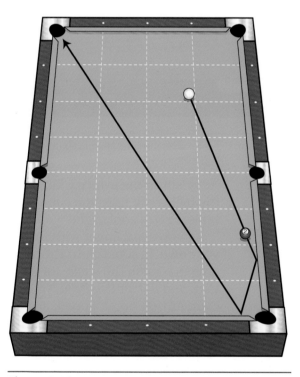

Figure 5.12   A steep-angle bank shot causes the cue ball to pick up sidespin.

The first system involves aiming the bank shot with the use of a mirror-image table. The theory can be explained and illustrated in a few different ways. If you practice with a partner and have access to a mirror large enough for that person to hold up directly next to the table, this could be the best visual you'll ever get of a bank. If you don't have this luxury, you can recreate the mirror image using your imagination. In figure 5.13, a simple cross-side bank shot is illustrated on the primary table.

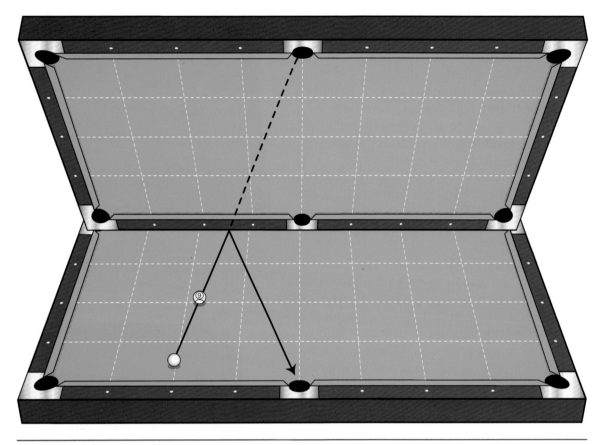

Figure 5.13   The mirror-image system for aiming a bank shot.

Adjacent to the primary table is your imaginary table—your mirror image. To bank the ball cross side, you simply aim to make it in the side pocket of the mirror image table. Pretty cool, right?

As you experiment with this system, you'll probably come up with variations of your own. In some clubs the tables have everything mapped out. There are actually tape marks on the walls, furniture, other tables, and so on. Some people swear by that, and if it amuses you, you can decorate your home rec room with tape of your own. At that point, speed, english, and angle of attack are the remaining variables that dictate how you execute the bank.

Spinning the Bank

Here's a method for pocketing bank shots that we've seldom seen taught: using english to spin the bank into the pocket. After you have ascertained the angle of the bank itself, continue the imaginary line through the object ball from the rail so that you can visualize the point at which you need to make contact with the object ball. Line up the cue ball and the object ball head on, and then adjust the cue tip to that contact point. This imparts english on the object ball that will send the ball straight to the rail and then throw it back to the pocket.

Now we'll add an illustration to simplify this explanation. In figure 5.14, we have an object ball on the foot spot, and the cue ball is dead in the middle of the table. We want to bank this ball straight back to the right. The angle at which the object ball must hit the bottom short rail in order to bank it back (the angle of attack) is shown. But rather than shooting straight center ball into that angle, you line up for a fuller hit on the object ball. Then, looking at where you have to hit the object ball

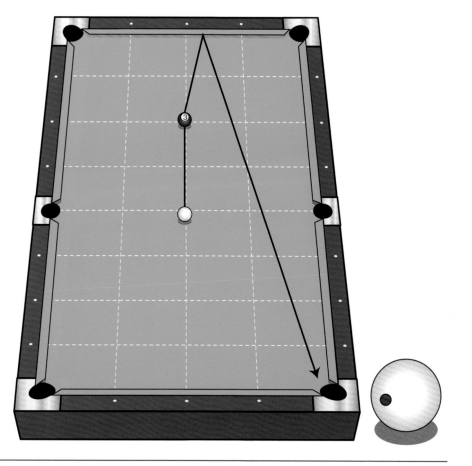

Figure 5.14 Spinning a bank shot into the pocket using left english.

at that angle, you instead put that much english on the cue ball. In other words, you know that you will have to hit the object ball to the right, so you put left english on the cue ball to throw that bank into the short rail in order to bring it back into the pocket.

This becomes a very easy banking system once you've learned where the object ball must contact the cushion. You'll hear this method called *throwing the bank*, *englishing the bank*, or *spinning the bank*. And it works with inside or outside english, depending on where you want the cue ball to go after the bank. In figure 5.15 we've illustrated the same bank, back to the right, only now we want to use right english. Line up the cue tip with right english, and observe that you have to cross over just about the entire cue ball to make the bank. Try a couple of these to expand your banking versatility, and at the same time learn the myriad of options you have to place your cue ball after a bank shot.

Now let's take the theory of spinning the banks one step further. Some of the best bank players who ever lived would rather bank the balls with inside english. Why? They execute banks this way to transfer the english to the object ball; thus the bank bounces off the rail at a shallower angle, increasing the size of the pocket. Look at figure 5.16. A center-ball hit is shown for a simple bank, along with a hit using inside english (in this case, left english) to pocket the ball. Notice how the inside english allows a more shallow angle, which increases the size of the target pocket. This method also takes the spin off the object ball that you would naturally get from hitting it at an angle. That is, if you're cutting a ball to the left or right, you've already learned that you will naturally put sidespin on the object ball. So, in

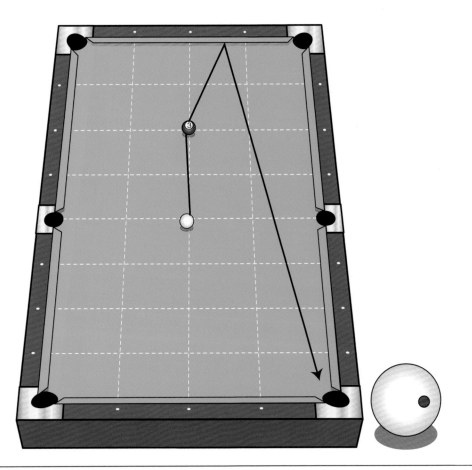

Figure 5.15 The same bank shot using right english.

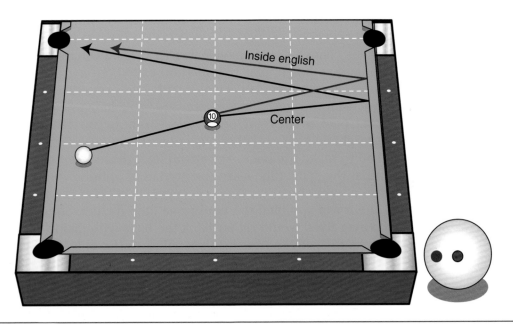

Figure 5.16 Note how inside english allows a more shallow angle, thus increasing the size of the pocket area you can shoot it into.

this example, if you put left english on the cue ball, you'll offset the natural sidespin on the object ball. Taking this sidespin off the object ball gives you a truer roll and allows you greater margin for error.

When spinning in a bank, keep in mind that the amount of english transferred to the object ball depends on how much english you put on the cue ball. Once the object ball hits the cushion, much depends on your equipment. How tightly stretched the cloth is dictates how much english is kept on the object ball. Loose cloth decreases the spin; worn cloth, which allows more contact with the rubber than thicker new cloth, increases spin. New cushion rubber holds more spin, but if the rubber is detached from the rail, it will be virtually impossible to hold the spin coming off the cushion.

With all the variables that you now know can affect your banking, you should also realize it's better to observe where the object ball must be hit in simple banks and apply this knowledge to learn more banks. As we've pointed out in other parts of this book, simple keys to shots and situations lead to more keys and more knowledge. You'll progress farther and faster by experimenting on your own.

Most pros will tell you that they've learned much of the game of pool, and particularly critical shots such as banks and kicks, strictly by rote and memory. Once they've tried so many of these shots during practice and experimentation, their subconscious takes over and knows what to do. Sure, it takes some time for the subconscious to adapt to different conditions on different tables, but once this occurs, banking becomes automatic. You'll find that it's not so difficult to memorize different angles and then let your subconscious adjust to game and table conditions. This allows you to make subtle changes necessary to continue pocketing balls.

KICK SHOTS

Kicking at balls, which means having the cue ball first contact a cushion and then come back into an object ball, is really just a form of banking without the object ball. Instead of figuring placement of the object ball to the pocket, you're trying to figure placement of the cue ball to the object ball. The object ball could be one diamond from the side pocket or one diamond from the corner pocket, and all you do is adjust your banking to kick at the ball.

The mirror-image system of banking can be used in kicking balls anywhere on the table. "Angle in equals angle out" works on a one-rail kick shot the same way it does on the bank shot, provided you're working with medium speed and a center-ball hit. You'll need to experiment here, too, learning exactly how the cue ball reacts as it bounces off the cushion.

Practicing the Kick Shot

To begin practicing kick shots, eliminate the object ball. Just try shooting the cue ball into the rail, with the intention of making it cross-side and cross-corner until you get a little bit of feel for the shot. Once you can regularly scratch (pocket the cue ball) using just the cue ball, place a ball in front of the pocket. Try the two shots shown in figure 5.17. These use angles under 45 degrees, which lets you practice the "angle in equals angle out" theory. Once the angle becomes wider than 45 degrees, the cue ball will pick up sidespin (just like the effect on the object ball in banking). Your cue ball will seldom scratch on this shot, unless it's hit in exactly the right spot to follow the object ball into the pocket. The chances of scratching increase the closer the object ball is to the pocket.

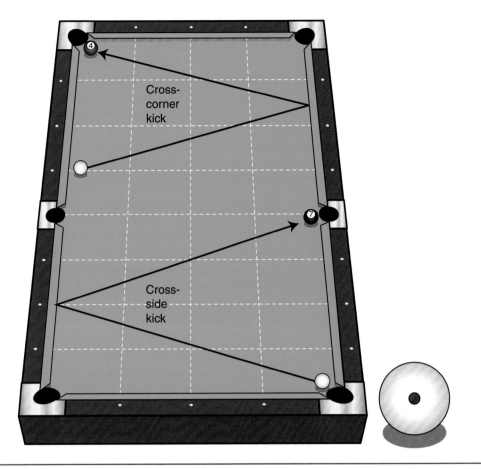

Figure 5.17   Try these two simple kick shots to get a feel for this critical shot.

As you become proficient at the first exercise, start moving your cue tip off center, in increments of a quarter cue tip, to see how the reaction of the cue ball changes coming off the rail. Note how much you have to adjust your aim on the cue ball to the cushion to still bounce off and pocket the object ball. English used to one side or the other will change the angle of the cue ball on the first rail but won't affect the angle coming off the second rail. If you paid attention to your lessons in banking balls, you'll quickly develop a feel for the kick shot using all the variables that can occur in banks, and you won't have the object ball to confuse you.

Two-Rail Kicks

When you can't achieve a hit on your designated object ball using just one rail, a two-rail kick is usually available to you. We have a great system that will have you making impressive two-rail kicks in no time. Refer to figure 5.18. Note that this is a Nine Ball rack, and you must hit the 2-ball to make a legal shot, but you have no one-rail kick available to you because of impeding object balls. Find the point on the table that's midway between the 2-ball and the cue ball, and aim an imaginary line from that point to the corner pocket (as indicated by the yellow dashed line in the diagram). That angle represents a line parallel to the line at which you must shoot the cue ball into the first rail. As you see, the cue ball will naturally bounce off the first rail, into the second rail, and out again at the line parallel to the angle of attack to contact the object ball.

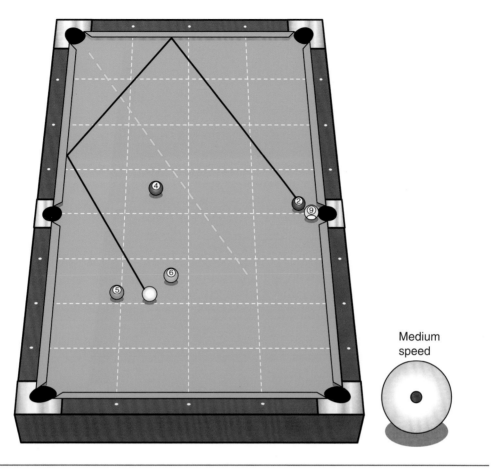

Figure 5.18   Finding the aiming point on the cushion for a two-rail kick.

Three-Rail Kicks

Think you're ready for the challenge of three-rail kicks? Frankly, we think you'll be surprised to learn how easy these shots can be. To line up a three-rail kick, begin by placing the cue ball near one of the corner pockets, as shown in figure 5.19, with the intention of sending it three rails around the table and resulting in a scratch in the other corner. You've heard about using the diamonds to calculate shots—here's your chance. To aim at your first rail, you'll shoot roughly five and a half diamonds up from the corner in which you are trying to pocket the cue ball. Simply count the diamonds up from the corner, using the side pocket as the fourth diamond. Again, you must extend your visual field out beyond the table to a point on an imaginary table or the wall beyond your shot. Now go ahead and execute the shot, using your center-ball hit and medium swing.

How did the cue ball react? Did it come up long (hitting the short rail adjacent to your intended pocket), or did it come up short and hit the long rail first? Depending on where it landed, make an adjustment to the point you are aiming at beyond the pool table and try the shot again. Once you've found your spot, you know where the track is for this table at this time. What this tells you is that anywhere on the table, so long as you can see the point past the long rail that you shoot into first, you can make that three-rail kick shot. When executing a three-rail kick, first make sure your cue ball can be shot toward that starting point. If it can, you can make it.

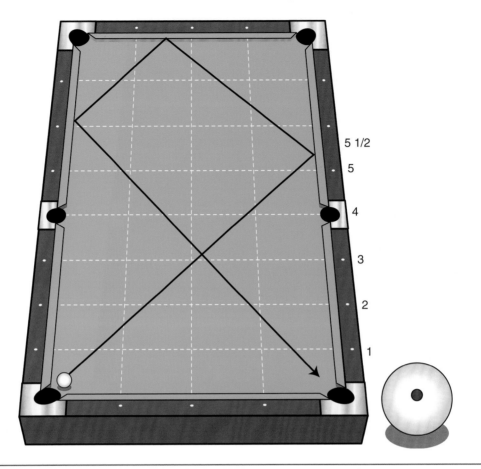

Figure 5.19   Learning to line up the three-rail kick shot.

This exercise works as a good starting point to practice your three-rail kicks. With a little practice and careful observing, you can become proficient in no time, noticing how the ball stays on that track to go three rails. By learning this, you'll also understand that if you're trying to go three rails but can't see your starting point off the first long rail, you can't make the three-rail kick with a medium-speed, center-ball hit. You might try a little massé or extreme english to make the shot, but it's not highly advisable except in the most dire circumstances. Do your best in this case to look for another option.

The Offensive Kick Shot

The offensive kick shot is a critical shot that's often overlooked. Players seldom recognize opportunities that await them with these game-winning shot selections. In figure 5.20, you cannot see the 1-ball to make it directly. But a well-placed offensive kick shot will allow you to pocket the 1-ball and end up in perfect shape for the 2-ball. Best of all, there's a clever system for measuring this shot. Using your cue stick as a measuring device (eventually you'll be able to visualize and will need no such aid), run a perpendicular line with the cue stick from the spot you wish to hit on the object ball to the rail. Say this distance is about 4 inches (10 cm). Extend the line 4 inches out past the edge of the cushion. That point off the bed of the table is your aiming point for the cue ball. Use middle-ball hit or a touch of follow with a smooth stroke. Your cue ball should kick into the cushion, contact the 1-ball to

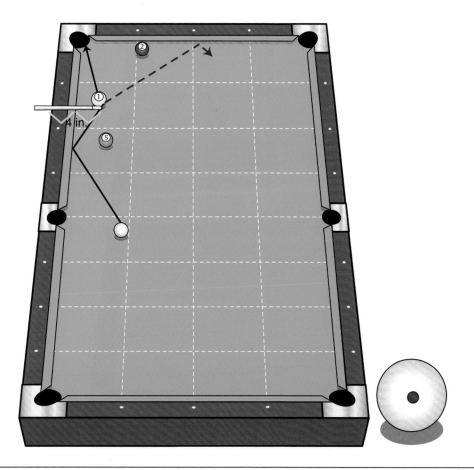

Figure 5.20   Recognizing an offensive kick shot opportunity can keep you at the table.

pocket it in the corner, and deflect at roughly a 90-degree angle (the tangent line), arriving in perfect position to make the 2-ball in the corner pocket. You can use this aiming method anywhere on the table simply by remembering that you figure the distance from the object ball to the cushion, and then match that distance from the cushion out beyond the table surface to find your aiming point.

Figure 5.21 shows another offensive kick, this time using a billiard off the 2-ball. Again, once you decide where to hit the 2-ball, measure that distance to the cushion and extend it for your aiming point on the cue ball. This is a soft shot requiring a light touch. You'll come into the cushion, glance gently off the 2-ball, and pocket the 9-ball. Because the 9-ball is close to the pocket, you have some margin for error here. The cue ball can go straight into the 9-ball, or if you contact the low side of the 2-ball, your cue ball will contact the long rail adjacent to the 9-ball first, which will still pocket the 9-ball. Nevertheless, players often assume this is too fancy a shot and opt for a safety when the win is well within their grasp.

If you've seen professional players in action, whether live or on TV, you know that they have the ability to kick extremely well, especially in the game of Nine Ball. Ninety-nine percent of the time, if you hit the correct side of the ball when you're kicking at the object ball, your opponent won't have a decent shot, which is discussed further in chapter 8 on safety play. The point we want to make here is that once you have some ability to kick at balls, experiment even further by trying to contact one side of the object ball or the other. Don't just aim to hit the object ball; aim to send your cue ball to an advantageous position for you. The biggest

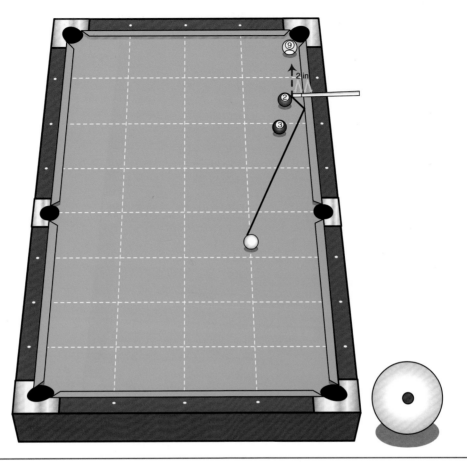

Figure 5.21   An offensive kick shot using a billiard off the 2-ball.

secret to kicking on the correct side of the object ball is not to try too hard. Don't begin calculating new aiming systems, and so on. Rather, let your subconscious do the work by visualizing the cue ball coming off the object ball on one side or the other. You'll be surprised how your body will make the minor adjustments for you if you let it.

COMBINATIONS AND CAROMS

Combinations and caroms are critical shots that use object balls to make other object balls. Combination shots require shooting one object ball into another to pocket the ball, whereas in a carom shot, you'll shoot your intended object ball off a helper ball, allowing it to carom off that ball and into the pocket. You'll also learn how to make a successful billiard shot, caroming the cue ball off a helper object ball to pocket your intended object ball. Knowledge of how to make these shots can prolong a run that otherwise looks dismal, allow an excellent safety opportunity, or shorten the game with a crowd-pleasing winning shot. The bottom line is practicing the proper execution of these shots will win you many games.

Types of Combination Shots

We'll talk about combinations first because they seem to be easier for most players to understand. Let's begin with the execution of the frozen ball combination.

In figure 5.22, you have two balls frozen together, and they don't line up exactly to the pocket. The black arrow shows that if hit full, the shot will play to the right of the pocket. This is one of those situations that reminds you that pool is often a game of opposites. Most people would assume that you'd want to cut the 2-ball to the left to make the second object ball go to the left. Wrong. Instead, you contact the 2-ball on the right side to throw the second ball to the left, as shown with the yellow arrow. The farther the shot is from the pocket, the

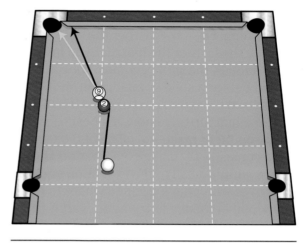

Figure 5.22 Throwing the object ball in a frozen ball combination.

more you can alter the final destination of the object ball. In figure 5.23, you have such a shot. From a shorter distance, this shot wouldn't get thrown enough before reaching the pocket. But at this distance you have plenty of room for the path of the object ball to be altered enough before it reaches the pocket. The more you cut the shot to the right, the more throw is induced.

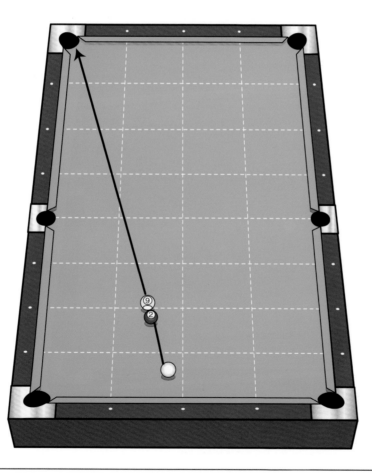

Figure 5.23 The greater the distance to the pocket, the more room to alter the frozen ball combination shot that isn't in line for the pocket.

In combinations in which the balls aren't frozen, two rules of thumb are worth mentioning. First, the farther the object balls are apart, the more difficult the shot. Second, the farther the ball that you intend to pocket is away from that pocket, the more difficult the shot becomes. Look at the two shots shown in figure 5.24. Shot A is a good bet for a solid combination shot. Shot B is a lower-percentage shot because the balls are farther apart and the 9-ball is a bit of a distance from the pocket. And, as you might already know, it's best to stick with the high-percentage shots and let your opponent make the mistakes.

To consistently make combination shots, you have to keep your focus because you're adding a ball to the execution equation. If you're not ready to make the shot, your eyes won't have decided where to focus, and you'll be in trouble. The mistake many players make is trying to watch the entire shot at the same time. This can throw you off. If you take your eye off the first object ball to anticipate the hit on the second object ball, you're cheating yourself out of the possibility of making the combination. Remain focused on the first ball for much better results. One trick players find helpful is to aim at parts of the rail. Once you line up toward the hit on the object ball, aim right through the ball to the point beyond it on the cushion. This will help you to stay down on the shot and visualize the whole shot without trying to look at each ball during your execution.

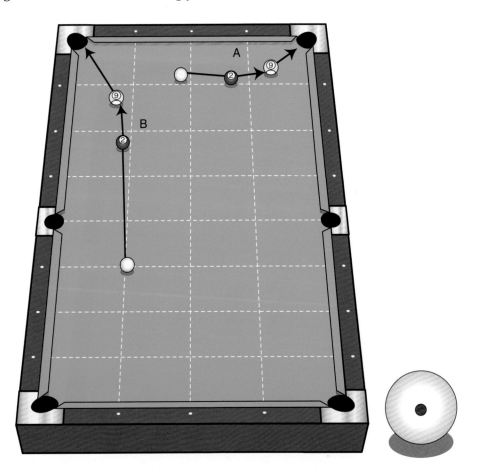

Figure 5.24   A high-percentage versus a low-percentage combination shot.

Figure 5.25 shows a simple combination shot. The target 9-ball is 6 inches (15 cm) from the pocket (a reasonable distance at which to try the shot under normal game conditions), and the 2-ball is 12 inches (30 cm) from your target ball, not allowing too much room for error. Ignore the cue ball for a minute. Instead, line up the 2-ball as your cue ball to make the 9-ball. When you have chosen the spot where you would hit the 2-ball to pocket the 9-ball, then go back to the cue ball and line up to contact the 2-ball.

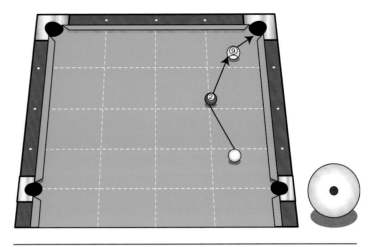

Figure 5.25 Lining up the combination shot.

Now, here's a hint. If you're cutting the first ball to the right to make the combination, you will naturally put left english on your first object ball. This has to be put into your equation. But, if you hit the ball firmer, the shot will incur less spin, and you're more apt to make it. Thus, when shooting a combination shot, you're always better off trying to keep the hit on your cue ball as close to center as possible. The use of english magnifies the variables. There are players and teachers who believe you should use outside english to straighten out, or take the spin off your first object ball. There's a lot to be said for this, but less experienced players tend to overdo it. If you'd like to experiment, we strongly advise that you use no more than a one-quarter to one-half tip of english. (With the english, you'll have to hit the combination a bit fuller than with a center-ball hit.) Your goal is to take the sidespin off the first object ball before it hits the second object ball. Abundant use of english won't accomplish that goal.

Players often find themselves in trouble on combinations if they don't properly plan where the first object ball and the cue ball will travel after pocketing the second object ball. They end up hooking themselves on the combination and are forced to kick at the ball they could see just fine on the last shot. Be sure to have a destination for the cue ball and the first object ball. Sometimes, if your second object ball is hanging in the pocket you might want to make both balls (the ball in the pocket and the ball you're shooting into it). This works quite well when you know you can pocket both of these balls and that your cue ball, after contact, will be in perfect position for the next ball in your run. The only way to force your first object ball to consistently follow the hanging ball into the pocket is to use draw on the cue ball. This allows the first object ball to pick up follow spin.

Caroms and Billiards

Like the combination shot, a carom shot also involves more than one object ball, but the ball you intend to pocket will glance off the helper object ball rather than being driven into the pocket by it. Caroms can be simple. The biggest problem is that few players know how to line up a carom shot correctly. We can solve this mystery for you.

First look at figure 5.26, which shows a simple carom shot. As you can see, the object ball must be shot into the helper ball. As you learned earlier, the object ball you intend to pocket will glance off the ball on the tangent line. If you want to find what spot on the helper ball you must contact with your intended object ball, just line up the outside of the pocket with the edge of the helper ball. This is the point at which you must aim your object ball because the outside of the pocket compensates for aim versus the actual contact point. Now go back to the cue ball and simply line up middle ball to shoot your intended object ball at that point on the helper ball. Visualize shooting straight through the helper ball. This will help your stroke and targeting. Use center ball with a medium hit in your swing.

Depending on what force you use and where you put the cue tip on the cue ball (high, low, or center), you can slowly increase and decrease the speed and learn to carom off object balls at many different angles. The speed of the object ball determines the angle coming off the carom ball. Experiment by using different speeds and cue tip placements on the cue ball to learn at which angles the object ball will glance off the helper ball.

To avoid complicating matters with spin, let's first look at speed only. If the object ball is sliding (it will from a hard hit), the angle coming off the helper ball is shorter than if the ball were rolling, as with a slower speed of the object ball. So use a fuller hit for a slow-speed shot, and a thinner hit for a faster-speed shot.

Using high ball (follow) will send the cue ball forward off the tangent line, whereas draw will bring it back. You'll want to experiment a bit with this because the force and swing used on your hit will affect the resulting path and the position of your cue ball, as mentioned earlier.

Now look at figure 5.27. If the balls end up like either of the examples here, consider yourself fortunate. With a medium, center-ball hit, these are considered to be dead caroms, and the 2-ball in both examples can travel to the pocket as if pulled by a string. Now set up either of the same shots and use draw. As you'll see, the shot is no longer dead. On the other hand, a frozen carom that isn't quite dead can be altered in your favor with the use of draw or follow, as shown in figure 5.28. Draw or low ball on the cue ball will actually push the 5-ball forward and make it in the corner. High ball or follow on the other ball will bring it back off the carom line to make the 2-ball in the corner pocket. Set up these shots a few times and see how far you can move them off the carom line.

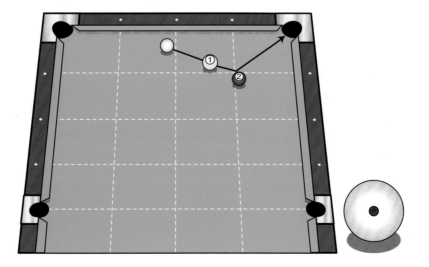

Figure 5.26   The object ball must be shot into the helper ball in the carom shot.

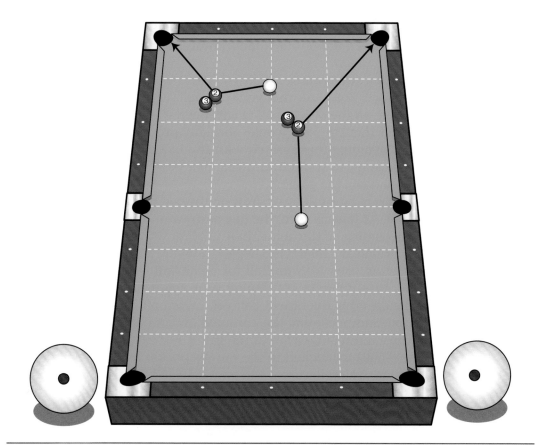

Figure 5.27 Examples of dead caroms with a center-ball hit.

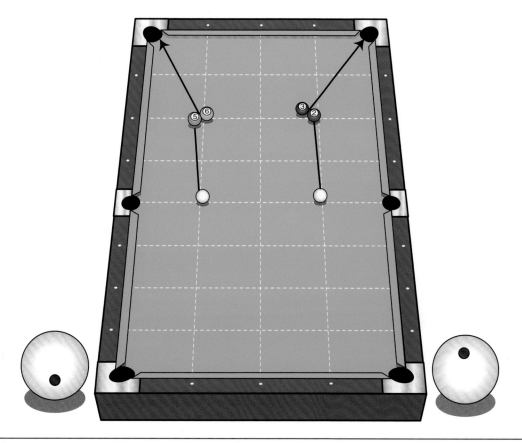

Figure 5.28 Altering a frozen carom with the use of follow and draw.

Now say you want to pocket an object ball using the cue ball to carom off the helper ball. This is called a *billiard*, but it incorporates the carom theory. Take a look at figure 5.29.

You're presented with a situation in which you can carom your cue ball off the 1-ball and pocket the 9-ball. You know that your cue ball (with medium speed and a center-ball hit) will come off the object ball at a 90-degree angle (the tangent line). And you also know that this cut shot would normally produce a scratch. You've probably experienced avoiding this scratch with the use of follow. But now you can use this knowledge to try to scratch, knowing that your cue ball will knock the 9-ball into the pocket and win the game.

Let's look in figure 5.30 at how follow or draw on the cue ball will alter its natural path off the object ball. As you can see, the use of draw or follow will change the tangent line of the ball coming off the helper ball. In other words, the cue ball won't not come off the helper ball at a 90-degree angle.

Billiards are most often used in Nine Ball for game-ball (pocketing the 9-ball) situations. This is because if you're continuing your run it becomes much more difficult to control the speed of the object ball you carom off when you're already controlling the cue ball and pocketing the caromed object ball. In rare instances, however, it can produce a run-out earlier in the game. For example, in figure 5.31, your object ball (the 6-ball) is blocked to the corner pocket by the 7-ball but lies near the 8-ball in the side. A simple carom will pocket the 8-ball, and you know that

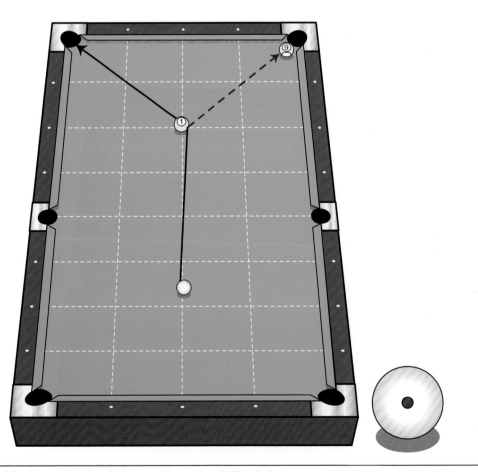

Figure 5.29   Incorporating the carom theory in a billiard shot.

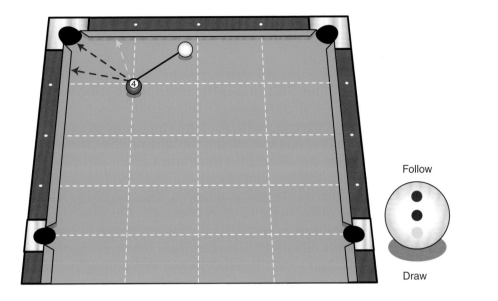

Figure 5.30 Draw or follow will change the tangent line in the billiard shot.

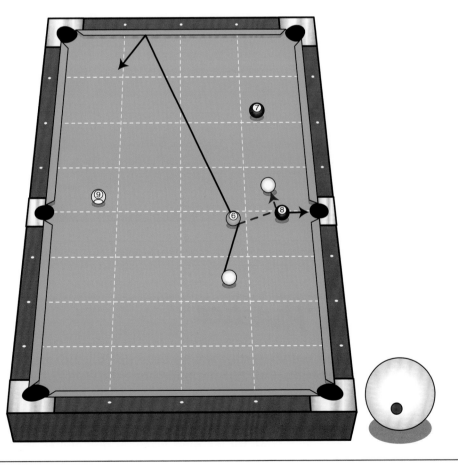

Figure 5.31 Using the critical billiard shot to win the game.

the 6-ball (hit with soft to medium speed) will travel down toward the short rail and back out. Your cue ball will travel very little, offering you a shot on the 6-ball with position on the 7-ball.

Now let's explore how the use of english can alter the path of a carom shot and expand your options. In figure 5.32, you can't pocket the 6-ball–9-ball combination because you can't hit the 6-ball thin enough to contact the 9-ball at the proper spot. Instead, line up the carom. On this particular shot you'll want to use inside, or right, english to throw the 9-ball to the left, taking the spin off the carom with your cue ball and literally throwing the 9-ball into the corner. Little variations of this shot come up quite frequently, and few players are aware of the possibilities.

Remember that caroms can be game winners, like the Nine Ball shots we've illustrated, but they can also extend your run earlier in the game. In Nine Ball, the difficulty will be in making sure you control the lowest numbered ball on the table that you've used to carom off and into another ball. It won't help to carom off the 2-ball, pocket the 5-ball, and send the 2-ball sailing into a disadvantaged point on the table.

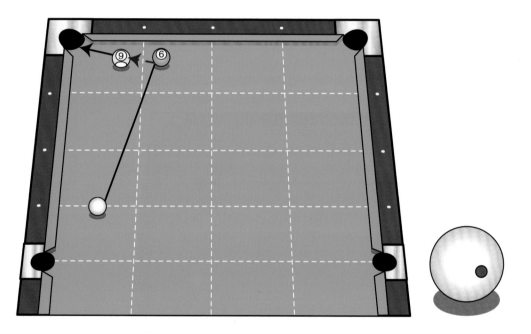

Figure 5.32   Expanding your carom options with the use of english.

Put It in Practice

If you're seeking a fun and interesting way to bone up on your carom skills, try the game of Philadelphia. Rack all 15 balls, but replace the front ball with the cue ball. Break the balls with the object ball you removed from the rack and attempt to pocket balls by caroming each of them off the cue ball. (Helpful hint: continuing a run in this game is much easier if you keep the cue ball close to a pocket.) Philadelphia is an excellent game for learning reactions and angles off balls and to control the speed of the object ball.

JUMP SHOTS

With today's rules of one foul, ball in hand (where the incoming player gets the cue ball in hand anywhere on the table if the opponent doesn't hit the intended object ball), the jump shot, like kicking, has become a vital part of the player's game. Years ago, before the advent of the jump cue, only a few players could jump a full ball with any kind of accuracy, and did so with their regular playing cue. Today there are all sorts of jump cues available. If you're interested in adding a jump cue to your arsenal, first check your local league or tournament rules for regulations dictating their use. Though most models are effective, not all are legal in competitive play; they are often restricted based on composition or size.

A legal jump shot is executed by sending the cue ball into the bed of the table, causing it to bounce from the table bed and over an impeding ball to contact the object ball. You may not use the cue stick to dig under the cue ball and lift it from the table. Not only is this particular shot illegal, but also you will be the likely candidate who incurs the cost of irreparable damage to the table fabric.

The jump shot requires a different type of physical approach, inasmuch as you must move your body sideways to elevate the cue to the proper height. Figure 5.33 shows a typical stance used to jump the ball, but it will take some experimentation on your part to develop a stance that's both effective and comfortable for your body

Figure 5.33 The stance used for a jump shot allows you to elevate the butt end of your cue stick.

type. The mistake most people make is to elevate the cue too high. If you do this, chances are you'll end up approaching the cue ball too high and trap it between the bed of the table and your cue tip. It's much better to come in at a 30-degree angle than a 45-degree angle (depending on the distance of the shot and the force with which it must be hit). A little experimentation will show you that you simply don't need to elevate your cue too high.

Now, for a tried-and-true method to quickly develop your jumping skills. Begin by placing a piece of chalk about 12 inches from the cue ball. Keep the cue ball at least a few inches from the rail but not so far that you need to stretch for the shot. It won't take much effort to jump the piece of chalk, and this will give you an immediate feel for the jump shot. The swing required of a jump shot is more of a throwing action rather than your normal smooth follow-through. The shot is difficult to describe, but you're really sort of whipping the cue down at the ball. At the same time, you don't want to force the cue down; you still need to keep your back hand loose. The first time you successfully jump the piece of chalk, you'll feel the stroke that allowed you to make the jump, and successive attempts will become easier.

Once you've jumped that piece of chalk a couple of times successfully, move the chalk up and down the table, toward and away from your cue ball. This will help you see at what distance the cue ball reaches its highest point during its airborne flight down the table.

Assuming you've accomplished these exercises without damaging any equipment or fellow players, you're ready to replace the chalk with an object ball. You'll find that it's more difficult to jump impeding object balls that are very close to the cue ball. Typically, unless you have a great jump cue, are adept at jumping with just the shaft of your own cue, or simply have a rare talent for this shot, you'll need 6 to 10 inches (15 to 25 cm) before the cue ball can reach the height required to clear an object ball. The ideal distance to have between your cue ball and the impeding ball is 12 to 18 inches (30 to 46 cm), depending on the force of shot. In a match situation, if the impeding ball is too close, you'll most likely be looking at a kick shot. If it's too far, you'll need more force to keep the cue ball higher in the air for a longer time.

When you're practicing your jump shots over impeding balls, aim your cue ball at one of the corner pockets. This gives you a target to shoot at so that you learn to jump balls and still maintain a degree of accuracy in contacting your object ball. It won't help to clear the obstruction and miss your shot! This also helps you get comfortable in manipulating your body into its jump stance for maximum effect. One secret to aiming your jump shot is to look at that target and *not* at the ball you intend to jump over. If you look at the impeding ball, your body will naturally aim toward it rather than over it.

Time to add a little variation to your exercise. Set up the object ball so that it isn't directly in line with the path of the cue ball to the pocket, as shown in figure 5.34. You should immediately recognize that this is an easier shot, but you'd be surprised how many players don't realize that you can jump over edges of the impeding ball and not have to hit the ball anywhere near as high.

Where you aim on the cue ball dictates how high the cue ball will jump. Picture the face of a clock imposed on the face of the ball as you're looking down on it (see figure 5.35); you'll be aiming at roughly 6 o'clock to get over the ball. Many players tend to look at the center of that clock face. This is the forbidden zone, where the cue ball will get trapped between the bed of the table and your cue stick. Shooting at 6 o'clock will allow your cue to go "through" the cue ball, or through the shot, with the least amount of resistance. The lower you can get (below 6 o'clock) with-

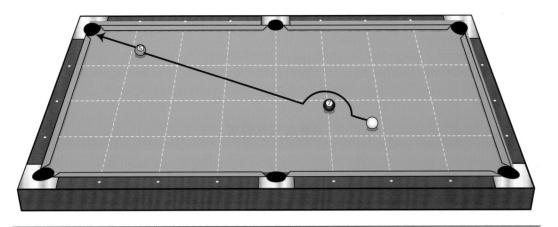

Figure 5.34 Jumping over edges of impeding balls requires less lift of the cue ball.

out digging under the ball, the better. If you hit a pure enough jump shot, you'll actually achieve draw on the cue ball.

This brings us to your aim on the object ball. You might have already noticed in your preliminary jump shot practice that you're having a harder time hitting your target (the corner pocket) with consistency. No need to despair. This is a common predicament, and it might help you to understand why you're having a difficult time, when you can pocket other shots pretty consistently. Because the jump shot doesn't use a normal stroke, you're likely to get a bit of an optical illusion. You won't be approaching your line of aim, as you normally do, from behind the shot. Rather, your approach is most often from the side. This illusion will vary from player to player and will typically correspond to

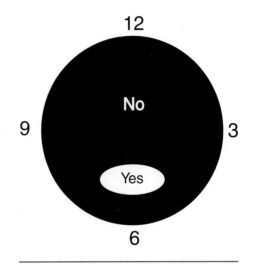

Figure 5.35 Using the face of a clock to determine your cue-tip position for the jump shot.

your size and body type. The taller you are, the closer you'll be able to get in line behind the shot because it's easier for you to elevate the cue with minimal stance distortion. But taller players, or players with longer wing spans (which dictates where you hold the back of your cue), might have a difficult time with the shorter jump cues on the market. If this is you, first give your own cue a try. You might have more success jumping with a full-size model and simply choking up (moving your grip hand closer to the center of the cue).

Besides having to deal with the optical illusion involved in your aim, you might also overcut many of your shots because you hit the object ball on the fly. This is one of the reasons it's important to learn just how far the cue ball travels in the air before rolling on the bed of the table again.

Finally, while we're on the subject of hitting the object ball on the fly, here's a tip that even many pros don't recognize—or refuse to believe, as we see them try these shots anyway. Don't attempt a jump shot when the object ball you want to hit is too close to the rail and you're shooting directly at the ball into the rail, especially if your cue ball is within 2 feet (.6 m) of the object ball. With the force you already know is necessary to get your cue ball over an obstruction, you also know that the cue ball will arrive at the object ball on the fly. This means it's likely also going to hit the adjacent rail on the fly and leave the table, resulting in a foul. Frankly, the whole reason you're jumping over a ball in the first place is to avoid a foul, so what's the point of risking another one? Opt instead for a well-played kick.

MASSÉS

For many shots that look otherwise dismal, you won't need to kick or go airborne, even with obstructing balls littering your path to a successful hit. Curve shots and massés are critical shots that allow you to magically veer, curve, and twist the path of your cue ball. They are extremely fun shots to execute, and sometimes they're easier to learn than the jump shot.

Again, let's work with our visualization of the clock face, beginning with a simple curve shot. In figure 5.36, two shots are shown that require just a slight curve to get around the 2-ball and successfully pocket the 1-ball. The same shot is shown on either side of the table. With just a slight elevation on the butt of your cue, visual-

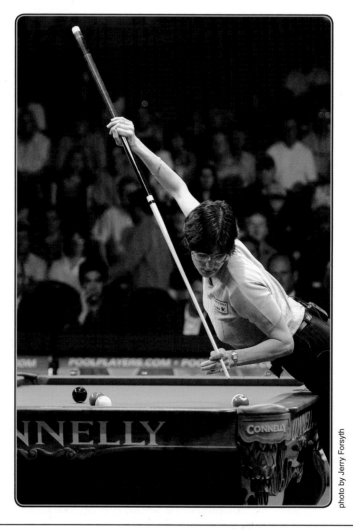

photo by Jerry Forsyth

Karen Corr, winner of dozens of international titles, considers each shot, especially if it requires a difficult curve or massé.

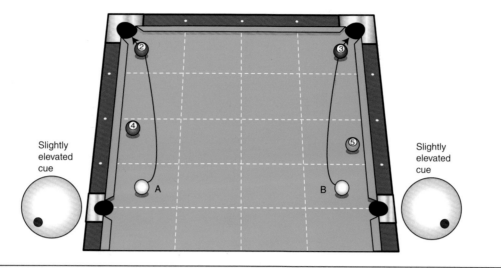

Figure 5.36 Visualize a clock face on the cue ball to help you line up a massé shot.

ize the cue ball having the face of a clock, and, as you elevate, the clock face will elevate also. In shot A you want to curve the ball just to your left, so you'll use left english at 7 o'clock on the cue ball. In shot B you'll need to curve the ball to your right, which means using right english, aiming at about 5 o'clock.

Time to get a little tougher. Figure 5.37 shows two shots requiring more curve. Again, as you elevate the butt of the cue, you get more turning action on the cue ball. The face of the clock moves with the elevation, and now you'll be aiming at about 8 o'clock for shot A and about 4 o'clock for shot B. Experiment with several more shots on your own to find just how much curve you can get on a ball comfortably, continuing to increase the elevation of the back end of your cue until you get up to a 90-degree angle straight down, as in the massé shot.

Figure 5.38 shows a massé stance. As you can see, the cue stick is now perpendicular to the bed of the table. A massé shot allows you to send the cue ball forward, whereupon it will grab the cloth and come straight back to you. Before we go any further in this discussion, a quick warning is in order on behalf of billiard club pro-

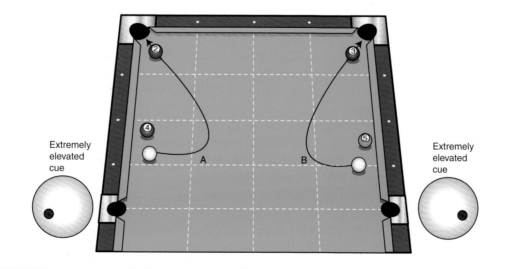

Figure 5.37 Shots using the curve technique.

Figure 5.38   A massé stance with the cue perpendicular to the table.

prietors everywhere. When you're first learning massé shots, be very careful of the cloth because you don't know yet how the cue tip will react off the ball, and you have no feel for the shot. It's easier than you might imagine to drive the tip straight down through the cloth and rip it. Try to obtain a small piece of billiard fabric (many poolroom owners keep scraps for break and massé practice themselves) or obtain a sample from your local dealer and place this on top of the cloth you're playing on to protect it until you get familiar with this shot.

Shot A of figure 5.39 shows a path typical of a massé shot. Your clock face has elevated so that you're now looking straight down at the clock, and you need a 6 o'clock hit on the cue ball.

Let's say you want to completely curve the cue ball around the object ball, and the cue ball is just to the left of the object ball. You would hit it at about 5 o'clock, shooting straight down at the imaginary clock face on the cue ball to massé it to the right. To massé to the left, you would shoot down at about 7 o'clock. Examples of massé shots to the right and left are shown in shot B of figure 5.39, along with their corresponding aiming points for the cue ball.

Curve and massé shots are critical shots that are often misunderstood; players try to overpower them. You really don't have to hit them too hard to get a reaction on the cue ball, and a 45-degree turn around the object ball won't take much force at all. Your biggest hurdle, as in the jump shot, will be to get comfortable with your

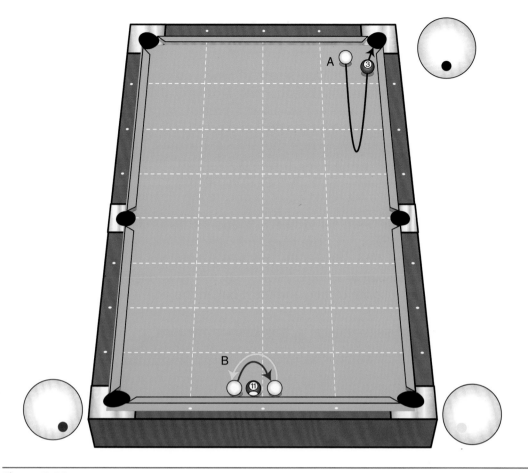

Figure 5.39 The path typical of a massé shot (shot A) and examples of massé shots to the right and left (shot B).

own body and your cue to properly aim and execute these shots. But, once mastered, they are shots that can be used effectively. Many players overlook them, so skills in this area will give you an edge.

From stop shots to jump shots, the critical shots we've discussed can significantly improve your chances of game and match wins. Nevertheless, even the best shot makers can't rely solely on their expertise with crowd-pleasing critical shots to win games. Up until now, we've focused on developing your skills to make a single shot. But perfect pool is really about continuing to shoot, ball after ball, while keeping your opponent in a chair. Master your single-shot skills and you're ready to turn these single-shot successes into multiple-ball runs.

Crowd Pleasers

If you've been around pool for any length of time, you've seen fellow players, or pros in exhibitions, perform a trick shot or two. Most trick shots are set up, meaning they take little skill if the balls are placed in a predetermined position. There are shots, however, that do take a bit of talent and practice to pull off, and these can be great for practicing certain critical shot skills at the same time. We've offered a little of both. If you enjoy trick shots, there are books on the market devoted solely to shots that will make spectators' mouths drop open.

The following shots must be set up according to the diagrams. Good luck!

Which Ball Goes First?: Set up the 1, 2, and 3 balls as shown in figure 5.40. To perform the shot, your cue must hit exactly in the center of the 2-ball at a medium speed. (Too soft and the shot will dribble; too hard and you'll tend to slide off one ball or another.) The 1-ball will go in one corner pocket, the 2-ball in the opposite corner, and the 3-ball in the side.

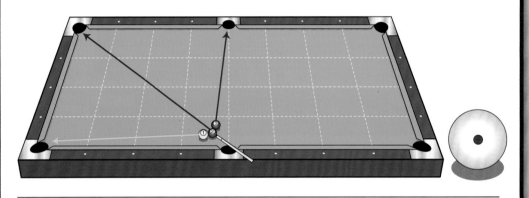

Figure 5.40   Which ball goes first?

The Slam Dunk: A firm, steady stroke and a direct hit are all you need to make this shot, but you'll really wow the crowds as the 8-ball pops up from the other three balls and falls into the corner. See figure 5.41. Depending on the table you're playing on, test this shot first. It's easy to fly the ball right off the table if you shoot too hard.

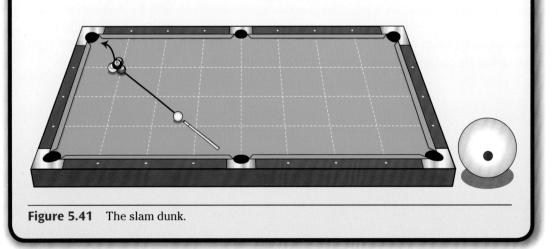

Figure 5.41   The slam dunk.

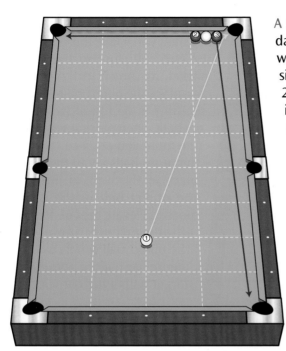

Figure 5.42 A simple proposition shot.

A Simple Proposition Shot: In the old days, gamblers made money off what were called proposition shots. Here's a simple but impressive one. Line up the 2-ball, cue ball, and 3-ball as shown in figure 5.42. The proposition was (before you set up the shot) that you could pocket the 1, 2, and 3 balls in different pockets, in order, and the cue ball would end up in the exact same place it started. The trick? Shooting the shot with the 1-ball instead of the cue ball! This shot requires a medium-hard hit, with a touch of high-right english. (Hint: if the 3-ball contacts the long rail before the pocket, move the entire row of balls slightly farther from the pocket.)

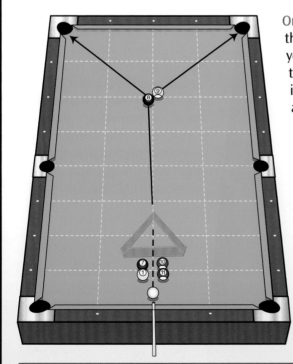

Figure 5.43 On the fly.

On the Fly: This shot demonstrates both the frozen ball carom technique and your jumping skills. Set up the 9-ball on the foot spot and the 8-ball frozen to it and aiming into the corner pocket, as shown in figure 5.43. Place the cue ball on the other end of the table, and put the interfering rack and balls as shown near the head spot. Using your newfound jump skills, you'll jump over the interfering balls, through the upright rack, and pocket the 8-ball in the left corner pocket and the 9-ball in the right corner. Now that's impressive!

(continued)

(continued)

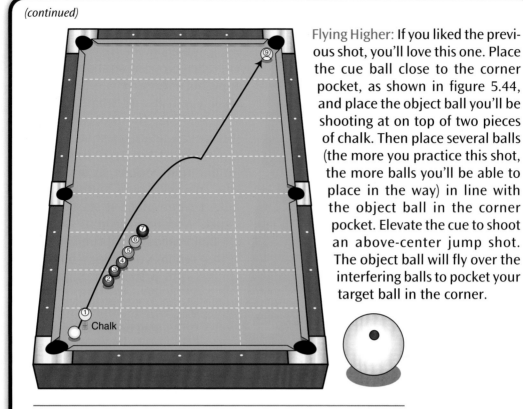

Figure 5.44 Flying higher.

Flying Higher: If you liked the previous shot, you'll love this one. Place the cue ball close to the corner pocket, as shown in figure 5.44, and place the object ball you'll be shooting at on top of two pieces of chalk. Then place several balls (the more you practice this shot, the more balls you'll be able to place in the way) in line with the object ball in the corner pocket. Elevate the cue to shoot an above-center jump shot. The object ball will fly over the interfering balls to pocket your target ball in the corner.

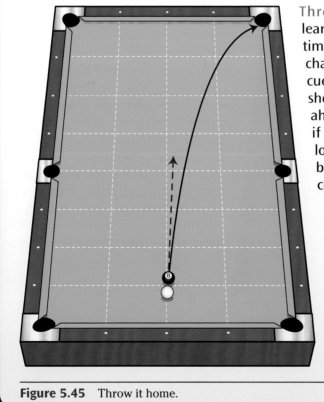

Figure 5.45 Throw it home.

Throw It Home: Think you've learned the throw reaction? Well, time to show it off. (Hint: a little chalk on the contact point of the cue ball and the 8-ball makes this shot much easier.) Aim straight ahead (or toward the right corner if you're having trouble) with low-left english and watch the 8-ball head straight into the right corner pocket. See figure 5.45.

Out of the Pack and Over the Rack: Tell people you actually had to shoot this shot in a tournament once when someone thought they could interfere with you by throwing the rack up on the table. Freeze the four balls together as shown in figure 5.46 and set the rack upright on the opposite corner, with a target ball (we've used the 9-ball) near the pocket. With a center-ball hit, shoot firmly into the 1-ball. Too hard can jump the 3-ball over the intended object ball and into the pocket (which also makes a nice shot if you announce it ahead of time). Too soft, and the 2-ball won't clear the rack. You might have to move this shot up or down the rail a few inches to hit your target, depending on your equipment.

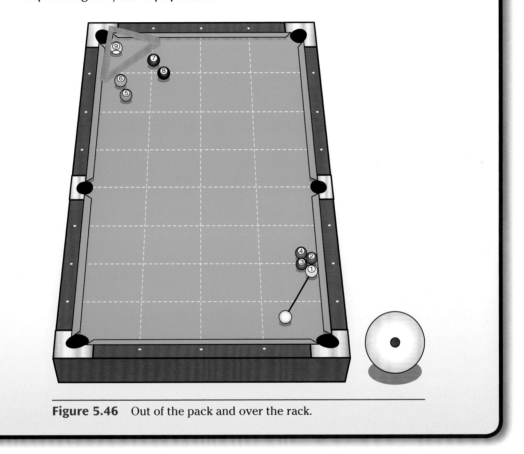

Figure 5.46   Out of the pack and over the rack.

CHAPTER 6

Position Play

Now that you can move your cue ball around the table and have learned all the critical shots that can make or break your game, it's time to find out what all the fuss is about! You're ready to use all that knowledge to play position and run racks—which requires learning the basic rules of pattern play.

Playing patterns, simply put, involves making your first shot with the intention of placing the cue ball in an advantageous position for your next shot, with an angle to get to the shot after that, and so on. To be able to do this consistently, you need to learn basic patterns that are the linked steps that move you through each rack. Pattern play is where the power of your game kicks in; you want to control your execution of the rack and leave opponents sitting in their chairs.

THE FIVE COMMANDMENTS

Our five commandments of position play apply to all the cue sport games and will help you recognize patterns and position play opportunities no matter which game you prefer. Keep these simple rules in mind, and your pattern and position play will develop quickly. Let's look at each of the five commandments—look ahead, be on the correct side, don't cross the line, let the table be your guide, and think backward—in some detail.

1. Look Ahead

In the various games of pool you get plenty of chances to be a chess player, fortune teller, and weather forecaster all wrapped into one. With proper forethought and planning, your predictions will most often come true. If you plan poorly, your opponent will be the one predicting the outcome and pocketing the win.

No matter what your game of choice, you should always be looking at least two or three balls ahead. Let's take Nine Ball as an example. If you're shooting at the 1-ball to get on the 2-ball, you should already be looking to get to the 3-ball; you should also know what angle you need from the 3-ball to the 4-ball. As you move the cue ball from point A to point B, you're constantly working on making your next shot as easy as, or easier than, your current shot. Eventually, you'll recognize right after the break how the entire rack should be played. You'll be able to predict where each ball should be pocketed and know what angles you'll need to get in position for each of these balls. If balls are tied up, you'll know whether there's an opportunity to break up clusters with early shots in the rack or whether to play it safe.

You might find this part of the game difficult at first, but don't let yourself get lazy about it. Whether you think you can run the rack or not, keep developing good habits in your planning. In time you'll be able to break the balls and with a glance recognize which pocket you'll put each ball in for the entire rack. True, you'll find players, even a few top players, who claim to look only one ball ahead in their games. Is this possible? To an extent, it can be, but only if your cue ball control is so phenomenal that your resulting position on each shot doesn't matter. To the rest of us, planning and pattern play are imperative for a solid game.

See figure 6.1 for a sample five-ball run-out in Nine Ball. The player broke the balls and ran up to the 5-ball with the resulting position. Test yourself—plan this run in your head. Take some paper and a pencil and mark how you would play this rack. Then take a look at the series of shots labeled A through D in figures 6.2*a* and 6.2*b*, which show the proper method to the run-out. How did you do? Were you able to quickly analyze the rack and decide how to make all your subsequent shots simple ones?

Here's the reasoning behind the run—in figure 6.2*a*, shot A, we're shooting the 5-ball into the left corner pocket. We have well over a foot of breathing room in which the cue ball can land to get an angle on the 6-ball, giving us the best chance to get back down table for the 7-ball. If you play the 5-ball too weakly and end up in the shaded area, you'll have a more difficult shot on the 6-ball to get back to the 7-ball.

Shot B, then, represents the ideal area (shaded) to be on the 7-ball. Because the 7-ball is off the rail, it's even OK to wind up straight in on this ball, but an angle will make it easier and more natural to execute. This allows you an angle to make the 7-ball and bounce off the rail toward the 8-ball.

The ideal area for your position on the 8-ball is shown in figure 6.2*b*, shot C. This position, close to the center of the table, allows you to use the right long rail to

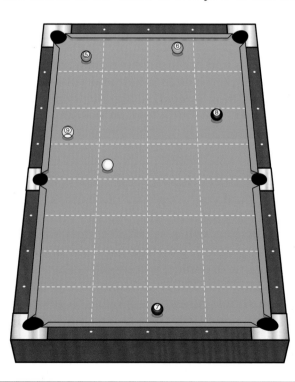

Figure 6.1   A sample five-ball run-out.

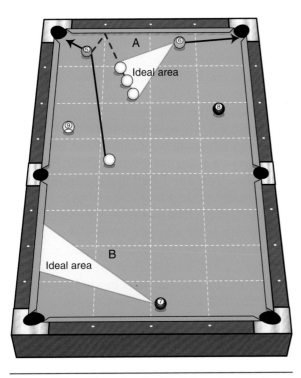

Figure 6.2a Shooting the 5-ball in order to get an angle on the 6-ball, which will open up a chance for the 7-ball.

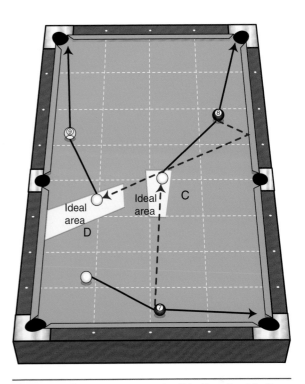

Figure 6.2b Getting from the 7-ball to the 8-ball to arrive in an ideal area to make the game ball.

bounce back across the table toward the 9-ball. By now you should begin to see how much easier it can be to run a table if you look ahead and plan proper angles in advance.

Finally, in shot D, note where your cue ball—after pocketing the 8-ball—can cross over the table into the shaded ideal area for an easy shot on the 9-ball. Shoot the 8-ball in the corner with a bit of low right spin. Though you're crossing over the table, this is a safe shot as long as you don't scratch in the side pocket. Plan to have your cue ball arrive below the side pocket because your margin for error is much greater in this area.

If you didn't do so well on this first exercise, take heart and read on. There's more than one rule to make your task simpler.

2. Be on the Correct Side

Suppose you're shooting at the 1-ball to get on the 2-ball and then the 3-ball. You make the 1-ball, and you have a shot on the 2-ball, but you ended up on the opposite side of where you planned to be on the 2-ball. Ugh. Now there's no way to get to the 3-ball without doing something difficult or unusual.

You're bound to hear players talk about having gotten on the wrong side of a ball. If you get on the wrong side of any ball early in the rack, it can easily throw off your position play for the remainder of the game. There's always a right side and a wrong side to be on when you're playing position, except in those rare instances when you can play all your remaining balls straight in with stop shots. By not thinking out the rack ahead of time, too many otherwise good players run the 1-ball through the 6-ball but have the wrong angle when they get to the 7-, 8-, or 9-ball. They've gotten

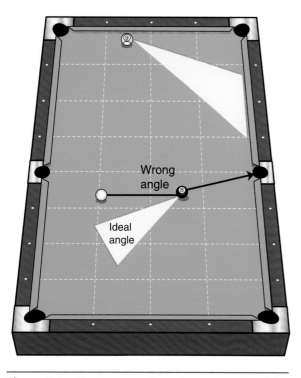

Figure 6.3 Don't get stuck on the wrong side of the ball.

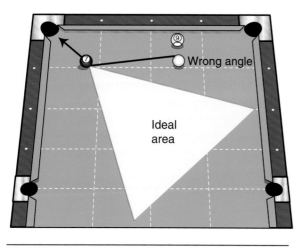

Figure 6.4 Another wrong angle shot resulting in a tough trip to the 9-ball.

on the wrong side of the ball and now have to do something drastic to obtain position and get back in line for the rest of the rack. This most often results in missing the ball or getting out of position and giving up the last two or three balls to the opponent.

In figure 6.3, we've illustrated a typical situation in which some poor player has ended up on the wrong side of the 8-ball. Poor position was played from the 7-ball to the 8-ball; what's left is a nasty angle going away from the 9-ball. With the balls in this position, you really have to come up with a super stroke shot to get the cue ball to go around the table to get in position for any kind of shot on the 9-ball. By contrast, if the cue ball had landed anywhere in the shaded area, representing the correct side, this player could simply float the cue ball down to the other shaded area for a relatively easy shot on the 9-ball.

Just in case you're still not a believer in this commandment, figure 6.4 shows another case of ending up with the wrong angle. You're shooting the 7-ball, trying to get position on the 9-ball. Because of your poor resulting cue ball position, you'll have to go three rails to get position on that 9-ball. Even worse, you now have a greater chance of scratching because you're turning the cue ball loose and running it around the table another 20 feet (6.1 m). (Note that the farther you have to make your cue ball travel, the more control you lose and the greater chance you have of making an error.) That's really a shame in this case because the shaded area represents the best (and vast) area where you could have planned to arrive on the 7-ball for an easy position play to the 9-ball. Make it a habit to note the zone you need to reach to stay on the right side of every shot.

3. Don't Cross the Line

The line we're referring to is the line from the pocket through the object ball and extended out across the table, as shown in figure 6.5. As you'll note in this shot, even after the cue ball crosses the line of the 9-ball to the pocket (but not until after contacting the rail), you have a makeable shot at the 9-ball, with a much greater margin of position than if you were to try and go back and forth across the table. When the cue ball must cross over this line too soon in order for you to get position on the shot, it means you're undoubtedly sending the cue ball back and forth

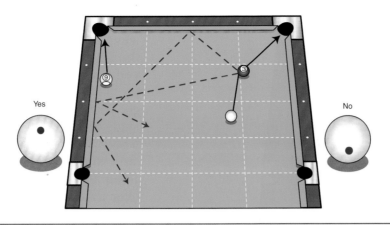

Figure 6.5 Don't cross the line from the pocket through the object ball and extended out across the table.

across the table to get there. Your speed control on the cue ball must be excellent for you to be able to control that shot. If you think you have no choice but to cross the line, look for another option first. In figure 6.6, the obvious shot on the 3-ball results in crossing the line to get on the 4-ball, as shown by line A. Instead, use the natural two-rail shot option to go *away from* the line of the 4-ball, as illustrated by line B.

As you plan the path to your next object ball, you'll always be looking for a path *to* the angle you want on that object ball or *away from* the angle you want on that object ball. When you head away or toward the line, your margin for error can be measured in feet. Conversely, crossing the line can cause a margin of error measured in inches as it becomes easier to break the second commandment and land on the wrong side.

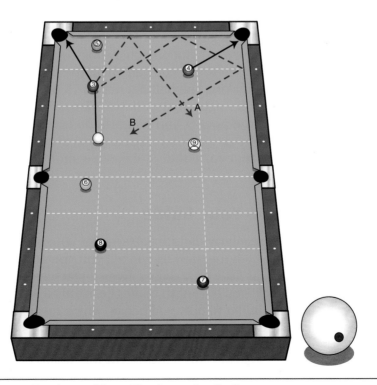

Figure 6.6 The better option for position without crossing the line.

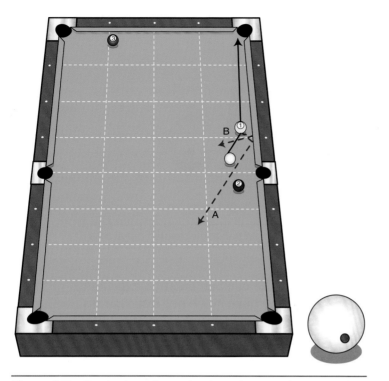

Figure 6.7   Coming into the angle of attack to avoid crossing the line.

Figure 6.7 shows two possible ways to get on the 2-ball from the 1-ball. But, knowing the angle you want on the 2-ball to get to the 3-ball, shot A is the way to go; you're again coming into the angle of the shot you want on the 2-ball. Your margin for error is indicated by the entire line to the 1-ball. In shot B, you're crossing over that angle, with your error zone indicated by the red dashed arrow. Notice how much smaller your position zone is when you cross the line.

Heading into or away from the angle obviously gives you the best chance to be in line for your next shot. Even if your speed control is off a little one day, your position play won't suffer as much. Ideally, on each shot, you want to be no closer than 1 foot (30 cm) away from your next object ball, and no farther than 2 feet (60 cm) away. And it's easier to control speed for position play on the next shot if you always have a 45-degree angle or less on your current shot. If you can achieve this, you're playing perfect pool.

Sometimes, particularly on your first shot on the table, the lay doesn't allow you the angle you want. When you get straight in on a ball, your options will be fewer. You can move the cue ball forward, but obviously not too far without scratching. You also can move backward. Sometimes you can cheat the pocket or spin the ball. But if you do, your chance of making the ball decreases 75 percent or more—because any form of sidespin on a straight-in shot is transferred to the object ball, which tends to bounce around the pocket and hang there. In the case of the straight-in shot, you need to know the range of forward and backward motion and what can bring you into the best range for either a makeable shot or a safety maneuver on your next object ball.

4. Let the Table Be Your Guide

The lay of the table will regularly dictate patterns for you, especially if the balls are wide open. The way in which the balls lie will tell you how to plan your attack. Your goal is to move the balls as little as possible. Even if you have a cluster that you can break up early in the rack, you'll want to move these only a little. In this way, the lay of the table will remain similar to how you began, which means less revision of your plans in the middle of the rack. If the rack presents several shots that you must travel back and forth down the table for, this tells you that your cue ball will be traveling a lot. In this case, immediately look for patterns up and down the table, using the rails to control your speed. The longer the distance from shot to shot, the easier it is to control your speed using the rails. Look to go one rail instead of none, or two rails instead of one, so long as you can still head into or away from the angle of your next shot.

Conversely, if most of your balls are grouped together at one end of the table, your plan will automatically adjust to stop shots, with very little movement of the cue ball or use of the rails. Staying on the correct side of subsequent balls becomes critical. Being on the wrong side could force you to send your cue ball all the way around the table to get back to your next shot. If several balls in the rack are clustered, with very little chance of a breakout, the lay of this table indicates a safety, in which case you'll look to the table for when and where a safety opportunity best presents itself.

In other words, don't fight what the table is trying to tell you. In figure 6.8, you can see that you are straight in on the 4-ball. You could try to cheat the pocket, heading into the short rail, then the long rail, and come down to try breaking up the 5–6 cluster. Let's face it, though—that's tough enough to explain, let alone shoot, even for a pro. The table offers you another option. The most prudent play stops the cue ball after contact with the 4-ball. Then you can simply shoot the 5-ball as

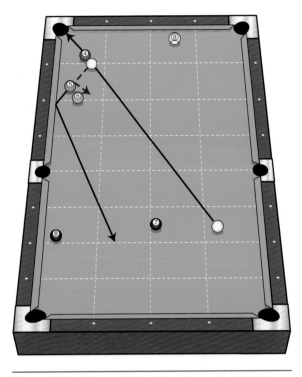

Figure 6.8 Every table tells a story; don't fight what the table is telling you.

a stop shot or roll up slightly to allow your cue ball to freeze to the 6-ball, letting your opponent kick at the 5-ball. If you ignore what each table situation tells you and go for the crazy breakout, or take flyers at shots because you didn't plan closer position, you've lost the advantage of the table being your ally. Your opponent will be the one who listens to the table and wins.

The size of the table affects the lay of the balls and thus dictates alternate patterns and strategies. With smaller bar tables of 3.5 by 7 feet (1.0 by 2.1 m), less surface area means less room to work. You're better off playing pinpoint position, and you must have a definite destination in mind before you execute a shot. Bigger tables and fewer balls allow the use of more area position play. Complicating the size of the bar table is the game of choice typically played on this table: Eight Ball, which involves using all 15 balls. This means more clusters and more shots that are difficult to get at, which calls for not only pinpoint position play but also stealth and planning in your execution.

5. Think Backward

This commandment works especially well in the games of Eight Ball, Nine Ball, and Straight Pool. In Eight Ball and Nine Ball, you begin with the game-winning ball (the 8 or 9). In Straight Pool, you begin with the shot you want left on the table as your break shot for the next rack to continue your run. Thinking backward doesn't work for One Pocket because you might never know which ball will be your game ball. (The most manageable way to play your patterns in One Pocket is to think three balls ahead.)

Thinking backward is rather like working a crossword puzzle. You complete the words you know first, using them as clues to the next words. In the same fashion, by beginning with the last ball you intend to pocket, you pick the pocket it will go in, and proceed from there.

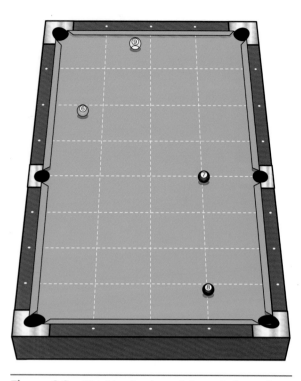

Figure 6.9 Thinking backward through the rack, beginning with the 9-ball.

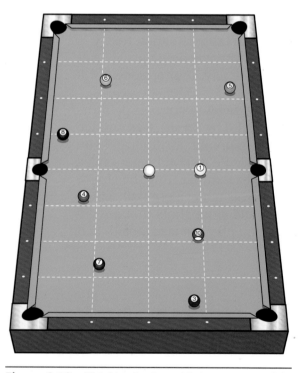

Figure 6.10 Thinking backward is important in the game of Eight Ball.

Nine Ball is the simplest game in which to think backward because you know every ball you need to make and in what order. You'll never need to decide which ball to play first, only how to play the ball to get to the next ball, right up to the 9-ball. But at the same time, thinking backward is critical because you don't have the luxury of changing your mind about which ball to shoot first, as you might in Eight Ball or Straight Pool.

In figure 6.9 your opponent has been kind enough to miss and leave you a possible run-out. Of course, it becomes a probable run-out if you first establish where you want to pocket the 9-ball. Looking at the lay of the table, you decide to pocket the 9-ball in the left corner pocket. So, how will you get from the 8-ball to the 9-ball? Then, how will you get from the 7-ball to the 8-ball? Finally, where must you go from the 6-ball to be on the 7-ball? As you look at these balls, you should realize that you must begin by shooting the 6-ball in the upper-left corner. Draw the cue ball off the long rail, attempting to get straight in on the 7-ball in the side. Shoot the 7-ball as a stop shot; then shoot the 8-ball in the corner and allow the cue ball to go three (or four) rails. The biggest mistake players make in a run-out like this is not getting on the 8-ball correctly to have the easiest and most natural path back to the 9-ball. It's critical in Nine Ball to play the correct patterns as they come up in game situations.

Thinking backward in the game of Eight Ball requires you to pick the pocket for the 8-ball, and then decide how you'll manage the trouble balls on the table; then pick a key ball (the ball before the 8-ball) and work backward from there. This might often present a slightly more difficult first shot, but it will be to your advantage to take the tougher shot first in order to run the rack the right way. See figure 6.10. Your opponent has missed her last ball before the 8-ball (the 10-ball). She did you a big favor in the process by removing all the clutter of her own group of balls. As you can see, the 8-ball is in a relatively difficult position near the left side rail. Now you need to make a pattern-play decision. You have a few key balls to choose from—the 7, 3, or 4 ball. We'd opt for the 4-ball in the side because this will allow you to work from one end of the table to the other and give you the easiest route for a resulting easy shot on the 8-ball. Begin with a stop shot on the 1-ball, which will leave you fine for the 5-ball.

You'll want to come off the rail for the 6-ball, and when shooting the 6-ball, bring it out for the 7-ball. You shoot the 7-ball, and then the 3-ball, bringing the cue ball up the table for a straight-in or slight-angle shot on the 4-ball. A simple shot on the 4-ball results in another simple shot on the game ball.

The run was made easy by first looking at the 8-ball, then determining your best key ball to the 8-ball (the 4-ball), and then finding the least difficult way to click off the other balls, slowly working your way to the bottom end of the table.

Figure 6.11 illustrates how you might manage a Straight Pool run, again by thinking backward. There are six balls remaining on the table. Unlike Eight Ball or Nine Ball, in which

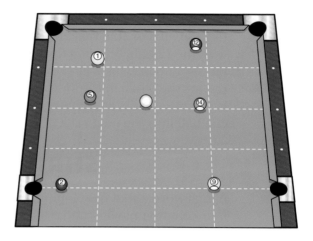

Figure 6.11 Thinking backward in a straight pool run-out.

you always know the 8-ball or 9-ball will be your game ball, in Straight Pool you must choose which ball will allow you the best break into the next rack. We've shown two balls that would make good break shots here—the 5 and the 14. Either will work fine, but if you have this luxury, know that this is where being right- or left-handed can come into play. If you're left-handed, the best ball for your break shot would be the 14. Right-handed players will be more comfortable shooting the 5-ball. If you're left-handed, you'll use the 9-ball as your key ball for the 14 break ball. If right-handed, you'll use the 2-ball as your key ball to the 5-ball.

Put It in Practice

A fun exercise to learn these principles of position play doesn't even require a pool table. Just watch TV. That's right, find a match on ESPN or ESPN2 (there's at least one every week; www.poolmag.com/calendar. cfm lists TV schedules daily), and see how many of our five commandments you can identify. It's trickier than you think, so pay close attention. There's no better way to learn than observing how the pros get it done, rack after rack. Also note just how often they play safe when an opportunity doesn't exist. You'll soon be predicting their every move faster than the color commentators.

photo by Jerry Forsyth

Top pro Johnny Archer has won numerous titles, including pool's most prestigious: The US Open 9-Ball Championship. Catch him on TV to see how he uses the five commandments of position play to run the rack.

Continuing to work backward from here, you would shoot either the 1-ball or the 12-ball. For this rack, let's assume you're right-handed. In this case you begin with the 12-ball, bringing the cue ball back to the center of the table for a stop shot on the 14-ball. This will allow a shot on the 1-ball, playing the cue ball off the long rail for the 9-ball in the side. Again, a stop shot for another stop shot on the 2-ball in the other side, and you're left with a perfect angle to pocket the 5-ball. Send the cue ball into the next rack of 14 balls and continue the run.

SHRINK YOUR TABLE

A final word about developing your position-play skills and then we'll delve further into common playing patterns. As you're examining our five commandments, you can make your plans easier if you reduce the surface of the table you're playing on by a foot. No magic here—just think about placing your cue ball 6 inches (15 cm) in from each of the cushions on whatever size table you practice on. Take a look at figure 6.12 and visualize the table surface ending at the shaded area. If you think about playing position inside this area, you'll always have the full complement of cue ball control options at your disposal because your cue ball will never be on or close to the rail. Playing position to one cushion or another will drastically limit your options, as you'll be forced to shoot high on the cue ball. Center ball, stop shots, and draw shots are virtually impossible with the cue ball adjacent to the cushion. Your opponent, if clever, will leave you on the rail enough without you doing it to yourself.

If when attempting to keep the cue ball off the rail you find that you're landing there quite a bit, you'll know immediately that your speed control needs a bit of work. This could be leaving you in increasingly difficult positions throughout each rack. It could also mean that you're using one rail when you should be using two, or two rails when you should be using three. When using the rails, plan to come into a rail and out again, not just get to the rail. This will increase your chances of landing at least 6 inches (15 cm) away.

You're now equipped with the knowledge to execute pattern plays for better position. Our five commandments are key to developing your sense of the game. The more you play, the more you'll recognize basic patterns and observe what works for the games you play most frequently. Be open to learning as much as you can, but always keep in mind the keys you've learned here to avoid developing poor pattern habits in the future. As you play and practice, continue careful observation in your pattern play to recognize when a good pattern doesn't exist. Once you can recognize that a run-out isn't possible, you'll be ready to execute a clever safety and still turn most games to your favor.

Figure 6.12   Shrink your table size with this visualization to keep your cue ball off the rail.

When in Doubt, Head for the Center of the Table

No matter how well developed your pattern play game becomes, there will be occasions when you're just not sure where to head next, or where what you perceive as ideal position now might present danger a few shots down the road. When in doubt, head for the center of the table.

As the games of Nine Ball and Eight Ball have evolved over the years, it has become crucial that you hit the correct ball on the table first, or else suffer the consequences of the one-foul rules and give your opponent ball in hand. In Nine Ball you must always hit the lowest numbered ball, driving it to a rail, or hit the ball and drive the cue ball to a rail. In Eight Ball, you must always hit a ball from your group of balls (stripes or solids), there again making a legal shot, safety, or pocketing a ball by hitting your ball first and then pocketing one of your opponent's balls.

Whenever you're in trouble, think you're in trouble, or just plain don't know what to do next, the best place to have your cue ball arrive is at or near the center of the table. From the center you will always have more avenues and paths available from the cue ball to other object balls and better access to a wider array of shots on the table.

From the center of the table you'll naturally have a shorter shot. What you're basically doing is cutting the table in half. For example, say you're playing on a table measuring 4.5 by 9 feet (1.4 by 2.7 m). With the cue ball in the center of the table, your next shot will never be more than 4.5 feet away, making it much easier to see and hit your next object ball. If you end up with a straight-in shot, you're close enough to the ball to have a better chance at cheating the pocket and creating an angle for your next shot. This means you won't have to worry as much about using the rake or stretching for a shot. Being closer to the ball means you'll probably be able to assume your normal stance and use your normal bridge. Keeping the cue ball in the center of the table also automatically avoids the difficulty of being frozen on any rails, which allows you to retain control of the full range of draw, follow, and english options.

But the list of benefits doesn't stop there. Shooting from the table center also gives you an unlimited number of options to hit the ball if you're playing safe. Again, you're able to use any english in your repertoire, it's easier to see the actual shot and the hit, and it's much easier to control the cue ball. If you're stuck with a bank or a kick, your options are still greater from this position.

Best of all, learning to maneuver your cue ball to the table center is an easy and fun way to practice. Begin by placing the cue ball in the center of table. Throw the remaining balls in the rack (nine if you're practicing Nine Ball, 15 if you're honing your Eight Ball or Rotation skills) and shoot every shot with the intention of having your cue ball arrive back in the middle of the table. This exercise lets you work on your use of english and speed control and gives you a feeling of real power and control.

Now try breaking a rack of balls. After the break, place the cue ball in the center of the table. After your first shot, place the cue ball in the center of the table again. See how many times you can do this and have a clear shot. Obviously there will be times when another ball can obstruct your view, so heading to the center of the table won't always be the answer. But it does tend to save the day when you're undecided about which way to go.

(continued)

(continued)

This is also a good exercise for working on your kicks and banks because these critical shots are much easier to develop and practice from shorter distances. Beginning the same way, attempt first to bank every ball in from the table center—again, trying to get your cue ball back to center. This helps you to focus not only on your banking skills but also on your cue ball control. (The same goes for kicking at balls, though you won't be able to bring the cue ball back to center as often, especially with softer kicks.) By shortening the table, you'll find that banks and kicks you previously thought mysterious and intangible become well within your reach.

CHAPTER 7

Pattern Play

At a certain point in your game, pocketing balls becomes second nature. This is when your position play will flourish. When you don't have to concentrate as much on cinching the ball, you can focus on where your cue ball is headed. This is when patterns, position play, and speed of the cue ball begin to really come into play. Once you learn the rules of pattern play, it's time to dial into some common patterns.

As your pool game develops, you'll notice different tracks for one- and two-rail positioning—for example, the cue ball coming off the object ball, into the short rail, then into the long rail and back into the middle of the table. This is what pattern play is all about—the joining of position play elements into cohesive patterns that allow you to thread your way through a rack with the precision of a surgeon. As you take note of these tracks and patterns, you'll use them more and more as time goes on. Your use of patterns and position play will depend, to some extent, on whether you're right- or left-handed. For instance, a cue ball on the upper-right side of the table presents a better shot for the left-handed player. Right-handed players like the left side of the table, so they'll play different patterns from those left-handed players use.

Be aware of a couple of pitfalls that could mar your progress. First, many players begin playing poor patterns early, but they win a game or two and mistakenly continue to believe they executed the rack correctly. This will hurt you down the road. You'll remember that the incorrect pattern worked and think it's going to happen again and again. When it doesn't, you won't know why. If a pattern you seem to play again and again flies in the face of the rules you've already learned, take a step back and look for an option that gives you a more reliable future.

The second pitfall arises if you become inflexible in your pattern play. You have to be willing, when necessary, to change your mind. Say you're playing Nine Ball, and you have a good shot on the 1-ball. No balls are tied up. You plan your run-out, run to the 4-ball, and discover that you're out of line. At this point, you have to be ready to change your pattern plan because you can't get to where you want to be on the 5-ball. Take advantage of the fact that you're the player still at the table, and make a new plan. Start over. There's no point in doing all the work and then giving the win to your opponent because you were caught in a particular pattern and weren't willing to regroup.

In this chapter we'll give you insight on how to develop your knowledge and pattern-play skills in four of the most popular games: Nine Ball, Eight Ball, One Pocket, and Straight Pool. Equally important, you'll begin to learn when a good pattern doesn't exist so you can plan your strategy for a well-played safety.

NINE BALL

In Nine Ball, because you're required to hit or pocket the balls in connect-the-dot order, all your decisions on which ball to make next are made for you. Once you break the balls, you'll always plan your entire rack at the moment the balls have stopped rolling. True, balls might be tied up, in which case you'll plan a safety, or you might get out of line at some point and have to rethink your strategy. Regardless, you'll always start with a plan that will take you as far through the rack as you're able to go.

Put It in Practice

In figure 7.1, you're left with the remainder of a Nine Ball rack. You're presented with a straight-in shot on the 4-ball. Using your five commandments, what would be the best and most common way to play this rack? Begin by asking yourself how to get from the 8-ball to the 9-ball. Play the rack yourself to see what you come up with, then try this. Shoot the 4-ball with draw, attempting to get straight in on the 5-ball in the side pocket. Shoot the 5-ball, and roll the cue ball up just a bit to get straight in on the 6-ball. Play the 6-ball with draw on the cue ball, back into the long rail on the left side of the table. This gives you a natural angle on the 8-ball (the 7-ball was pocketed earlier in the game) to come around the length of the table with a nice, easy stroke, leaving you a makeable shot on the 9-ball in the lower-right corner pocket. If you had gotten straight in on the 8-ball, you'd be in a tougher position to make the 9-ball. You could end up on the other side of the 8-ball and draw the ball down table, but this is a tougher shot, and you want easier shots toward the end of your rack.

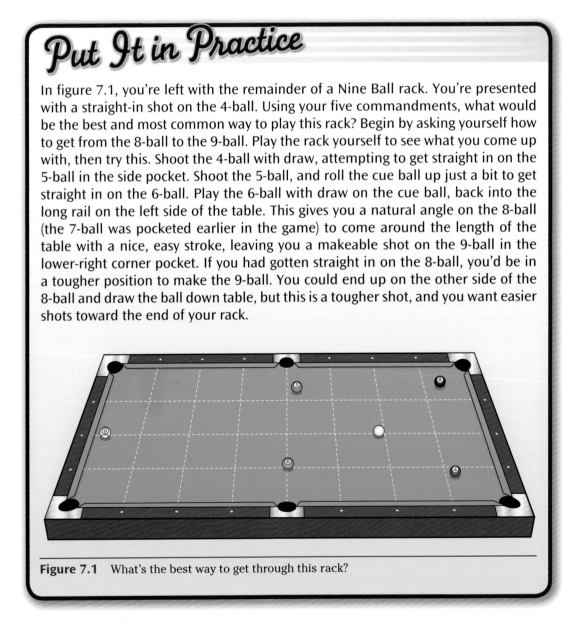

Figure 7.1 What's the best way to get through this rack?

Although patterns are endless in every game, your Nine Ball game, because you get used to the order of pocketing the balls, will present typical patterns that connect over and over again. If you have a good memory for situations that have come up in the past, your pattern play will pick up speed in leaps and bounds. It won't be long before you realize that a particular situation has come up before and your mind already knows what to do. The more you pay attention to Nine Ball patterns, the more automatic your response will be to the table layout in front of you.

You might be able to get away with straight-in or relatively straight-in shots early in the rack of a Nine Ball game, but having angles at the end of the rack is crucial to running out consistently. Nearly always this is where less-experienced players will fall down in Nine Ball. They have no problem with the first five or six balls on the table, but they're suddenly out of line for the remainder of the rack. Even at the pro level, we see players over and over again get straight in on the 8-ball and have to execute a very difficult shot to wrangle position on the 9. Never take a run-out for granted, even when there's only a ball or two left on the table.

Another significant element to Nine Ball pattern play is recognizing key balls in the rack. See figure 7.2 for a simple example. Your opponent has broken the balls without pocketing a ball and has left you a great run-out opportunity. In fact, this pattern is so simple that the cue ball doesn't even have to hit a rail. But let's play it right. Begin with a stop shot on the 1-ball. Pocket the 2-ball and allow the cue ball to swing off the long rail on the right side for a straight-in shot on the 3-ball. This allows you to roll up slightly for another straight-in shot on the 4-ball in the opposite side. Stop the cue ball, and shoot the 5-ball in the corner. Stop again, and shoot the 6-ball in the side. Stop again, and shoot the 7-ball in the corner. Depending on exactly where your cue ball has landed after you pocketed the 7-ball, you have two options on the 8-ball to get position on the 9-ball. You can either allow the cue ball to contact the long rail on the right side and come back for the 9-ball in the same corner pocket in which you just made the 8-ball (the right corner), or roll up for the 9-ball in the left corner pocket.

Did you recognize the key shot in the rack? Probably the toughest part of this rack is to watch for being on the correct side of the 3-ball. If you get on the wrong side of the 3-ball, you might need to change your plan because it will be impossible to just roll up for a stop shot on the 4-ball, and consequently the 5, 6, and 7 balls. It pays to keep your attention on this type of pattern, as you can see just how easy a

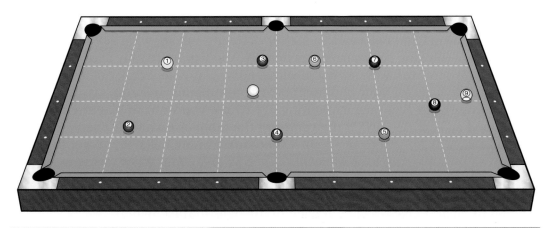

Figure 7.2   Identify the key ball in this rack.

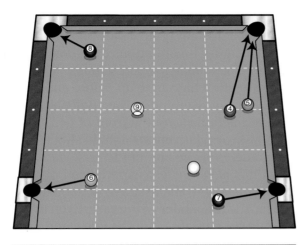

Figure 7.3   In this rack there are two key shots to get you on the right side of each ball.

rack can be with the proper angle on the key ball and how difficult it will be without the proper angle.

In figure 7.3, you actually have two key shots. You'll need the correct angle on the 6-ball to get to the 7-ball, and then the correct angle on the 7-ball to get to the 8-ball. Think ahead. When shooting at the 4-ball, make sure to get on the 5-ball with a proper angle on the 6-ball. This way you can roll up for a shot on the 7-ball, and then roll up again for a shot on the 8-ball. From here, it's conceivable that the 9-ball can be made in any of the six pockets, but make sure you pick one *before* you pocket the 8-ball. Never make the mistake of not having a destination for the cue ball. Always allow yourself correct position on the key balls in each rack because they'll be crucial to your successful execution of run-out patterns.

The best way to begin seeing more common patterns in Nine Ball is to practice first with just the 8 and 9 balls. Throw them out on the table, and make the 8-ball to get in shape on the 9-ball. Then add the 7-ball. Shoot the 7-ball to get an angle on the 8-ball to get to the 9-ball. Then add the 6, 5, 4, and so on. This kind of practice forces you to develop a keener insight into what angles are necessary and useful, what key shots will make or break a rack, and how to plan your pattern from the beginning.

EIGHT BALL

Figuring out your pattern in a game of Eight Ball presents a few more challenges than in Nine Ball, in which you know which ball you must shoot to hit. On the other hand, in Eight Ball you'll have options for shots that you won't have in Nine Ball, giving you a bit more latitude in your pattern selection. As a result, a great deal more strategy is involved in Eight Ball. You might have a choice of six or seven balls of your group (stripes or solids) to shoot at, but there's always the one right shot that will lead to the most productive run-out, breakout, or eventual safety attempt.

Pattern play in Eight Ball is also a matter of timing—of knowing when to run out. This is where thinking backward plays heavily. You'll more readily know when you have a pattern to work with, or if you will need to play safe, break out a cluster, or create trouble balls for your opponent before continuing your run.

Begin your Eight Ball rack by figuring out where you want to play the 8-ball. Is it in a good spot or tied up? In the center of the table or on a rail? Then pick your key ball that will get you to this ball. If there are trouble balls, try to get to those as soon as possible, but exercise caution in this area. You're not trying to hit the clustered balls too hard. If you head into them with too much force, you'll likely end up creating a cluster somewhere else on the table. Instead, your plan will be to open them up to have a shot at each of the balls in the cluster.

Smart Eight Ball players will also attempt to have a safety ball positioned near a pocket or hung in the pocket. Even with a great breakout plan, sometimes the unexpected can happen. Balls can freeze up against each other, or the cue ball might get stuck between them. With a safety ball, once you send the cue ball into the cluster, you'll have something to shoot at if you didn't end up with a good shot after breaking up the cluster.

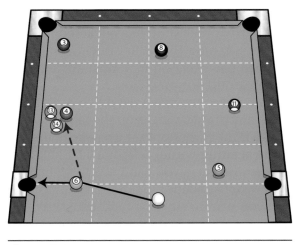

Figure 7.4 Running an Eight Ball break with the use of safety balls.

Let's take a look at a couple of Eight Ball racks that demonstrate these skills. In figure 7.4, you have solids. The 4-ball is tied up with the 13 and 14 balls in your opponent's group of balls, but you're still in a fine position for the run-out. Don't shoot the 3-ball or the 5-ball first, even though they're attractive shots at first glance. Instead you'll want to shoot the 6-ball in the side pocket. With this shot you have a natural angle on the 6-ball to go into the cluster. Don't head into the cluster with too much force because this could create other clusters and compound your problem. The real advantage of this table layout is that you have two safety balls: the 3-ball and 5-ball. Should you get stuck somewhere in the cluster, you'll still have a shot at one of these balls. The remainder of your run-out will then depend on the resulting position of your 4-ball. Give this rack a try and see what works for you.

Eight-Ball wizard Dave Matlock is known for playing clever patterns that keep him at the table.

In figure 7.5 you have an Eight Ball table layout in which your opponent, despite a powerful break shot, has pocketed nothing, leaving you with an open table. This means you have the luxury of choosing whether to play the solids or stripes. The cue ball has been left in a most advantageous position in the center of the table. Which group do you choose?

To decide, you must establish a pattern before you shoot your first shot. Are there any problem areas on the table? First, notice that the 15-ball is tied up for the upper-right corner pocket because of the impeding 6-ball. Worse, the 9-ball can't be made in either corner, with the 6-ball blocking the right side and the 8-ball blocking the left. Because you can't see the 9-ball in any pocket, your most prudent move is to take the solids.

If you plan to run this rack, take the 6-ball early so you can pocket the 3-ball in the same pocket later. If you don't plan to run out, leave the 6-ball as a blocker for the 15 and 9 balls, creating problem areas for your opponent.

Let's assume you do plan to run out. The pattern is relatively simple: Pocket the 2-ball, then the 6-ball, and swing down table between the 6-ball and the rail to shoot the 1-ball in the corner. Then play the 4-ball in the other corner, and swing up to shoot the 7-ball straight in the side. This will give you a straight-in 5-ball in the corner, followed by the 3-ball in the other corner. When you play the 3-ball, use follow on the cue ball to roll up for a shot on the 8-ball in the left corner.

What happens if you absolutely cannot run out? Figure 7.6 illustrates a rack that can't be run. Though it's unlikely you'll face a rack quite this tough, you will see racks with two or three clusters involving your group of balls. This is when it's prudent to plan a safety pattern. The best safety for our rack in figure 7.6 is to send the cue ball into the 5-ball (allowing either the 5-ball or the cue ball to contact the cushion for a legal hit). With a gentle hit, this shot will still loosen the 15-ball from this cluster while leaving no good shot at either group of balls. Your opponent will be forced to counter with a safety of his or her own.

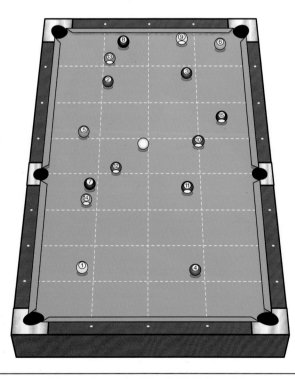

Figure 7.5   Which group would you choose in this Eight Ball rack?

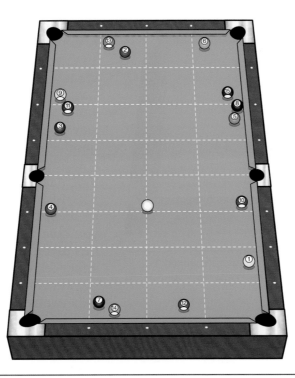

Figure 7.6 This rack is not likely to be run—look for an alternative.

Keep in mind that when you're forced to plan a safety or series of safeties, it helps to slowly break up clusters with each subsequent shot. In this way, you've given your safety play a plan, continuing to maneuver the object balls into a favorable position for the eventuality of an offensive opportunity.

If your opponent is knowledgeable about the game, you can assume he or she will be doing the same things, with the same intentions. In this case, you'll most likely engage in a safety battle in which the more patient player has the edge. Don't take a risky shot out of boredom or a misconception that you're not accomplishing anything proactive in the game. Continue to plan your eventual pattern and strategy. Far too many games are lost because a player tires of what seems like an interminable waiting game.

STRAIGHT POOL

The first rule of basic pattern play in Straight Pool is to try and cut your game down to a half-table game. This means simply that you'll do your best to play on the upper half of the table, keeping all object balls in this area. Use the upper-left and upper-right corner pockets, along with the side pockets, as your destinations for all or most of the object balls in your run. Avoid the two bottom corner pockets as much as possible. These pockets translate to longer shots and less cue ball control. The top Straight Pool players seldom use the lower corner pockets—perhaps only once or twice in a 100-ball run.

The other rule to remember is to open up the pack (the rack of 14 or 15 balls) a little at a time. Your goal is to make a ball and break out a ball or two before the next shot. Visualize continually whittling away at the rack and slowly spreading it open bit by bit, the way you'd work a piece of clay or dough from a small lump to a larger, more flexible shape. In the same way, your rack will slowly take on a more

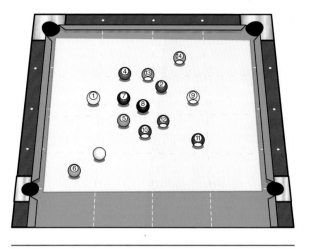

Figure 7.7 Begin slowly opening the balls in a Straight Pool rack, working them apart for your best chance at a run-out.

manageable shape, allowing you to continue your run and position an eventual break ball. Slow and steady rack management helps you keep the balls at the upper end of the table. This also prevents leaving a wide-open table for your opponent if you miss.

Figure 7.7 shows a typical rack that has been broken open and spread out a little. You'll want to open the balls a bit more as you continue your run. To begin this tactic, shoot the 1-ball in the upper-left corner pocket with low-right english to bring the cue ball in between the 7 and 5 balls. The low-right english will spin the cue ball to a point where it will throw the 7-ball and 5-ball away from the cue ball, freeing it up for another shot. This is a very good play because it leaves you with the 6-ball in the side as your safety ball. It's smart to have a safety ball in Straight Pool because even the most careful planning can sometimes result in the cue ball getting too close to other balls in the pack, leaving you little to shoot at.

As you practice your Straight Pool patterns, breaking up racks and setting up safety balls and break shots, you'll want to follow a certain order of attack that has served Straight Pool players well for generations. You'll first want to clear the corner pockets on the lower end of the table. If there are balls lying at or near the pockets, play them first, clearing the path for other balls closer to the center of the table to be pocketed. Then concentrate on breaking open troublesome clusters. If they can't be broken apart immediately, form a plan for when you'll attack them. Third, try to clear off balls that have become positioned near the rails. Unlike in Nine Ball or Eight Ball, thinking backward in Straight Pool won't come into play as often at the beginning of a rack. When you get to the final six or seven balls remaining on the table, this is the time to determine a break shot, and the key ball from the break

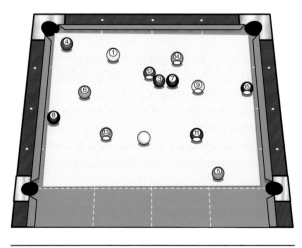

Figure 7.8 Completing a Straight Pool run using just four pockets.

shot, and then work backward from there. This sequence of steps makes it easier to develop proper patterns and continue your run.

Figure 7.8 shows another Straight Pool layout. As you can see, here the balls are a little more wide open. The 8 and 15 balls are on the rails and will soon need your attention. As you slowly pick off balls, work your pattern play toward the center of the table. Nudge balls as you pocket others, keeping them on one end of the table and allowing yourself to complete the run without using the two lower corner pockets.

Even if you're not normally a fan of Straight Pool, you might find that a short Straight Pool game with a partner makes a great warm-up for a set of Eight Ball or Nine Ball. This game focuses on key areas, including cue ball control and pattern and position play, along with the mental benefits of patience and proper planning. Straight Pool was quite an art of the legendary cueists—players like Willie Mosconi, Jimmy Caras, Irving Crane, and Steve Mizerak—as they ran effortlessly from ball to ball, well into the hundreds, while making the cue ball dance from one shot to another. Amateurs not well versed in the art might comment, "So what? Every shot they make is so easy, I could do that. . . ." The more astute player will smile knowingly and patiently explain that, in fact, making every subsequent shot simple is the art of the game.

ONE POCKET

The pattern-play options are endless in the game of One Pocket. The types of shots and layouts are limitless. This is a game in which there are very few hard and fast rules, and pattern play is anything but common. For this reason, One Pocket is definitely the game to play if you want to use your imagination and creativity to its fullest. One Pocket is also the most difficult game to play because every skill you will ever develop comes into play: shooting straight, controlling the cue ball, controlling object balls, safety play, kick shots, bank shots, caroms—you name it. Every conceivable type of shot can come into play at least once in a single game.

The rules we can outline for pattern play in One Pocket will thus focus on common threads that can run through any particular game. First, because of the unpredictable nature of the game, you'll never be able to think a full rack ahead. Too many situations change; the balls get moved around, and you never know what your last ball will be. Second, there's always one excellent place to leave the cue ball—and that's as near as possible to your opponent's pocket, shown by the shaded area in figure 7.9. In this case, your opponent has the left corner pocket, and you have the right corner. Whenever possible, you'll do your best to leave your cue ball in the shaded area. Leaving opponents here leaves them with no straight-in shot options. The best option they'll have is a bank, and they'll have to be able to bank very well. Consistently having to shoot from this area will be frustrating and counterproductive for them. It's also a great pattern play and strategic move to fall back on when you're not sure what your next move should be.

The intricacies and highly defensive characteristics of One Pocket make it analogous to a chess game. Like chess, One Pocket can be broken into three basic components: the beginning game, consisting of some typical and not so typical opening moves; the middle game, in which balls tend to get shifted to the other end of the table; and the end game, in which one or both opponents need just one ball for the win and play becomes extremely defensive.

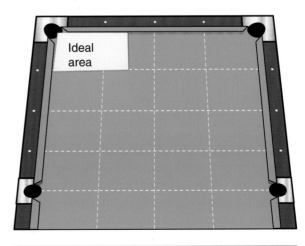

Figure 7.9 The best place to leave the cue ball for your opponent.

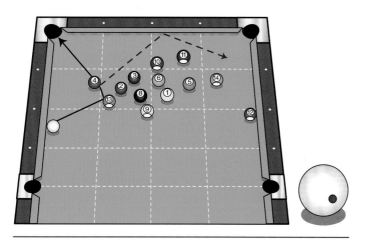

Figure 7.10   The beginning of a One Pocket game.

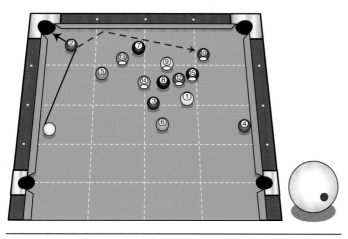

Figure 7.11   Practice your thin cuts—they occur often in One Pocket.

Figure 7.10 shows one example of the beginning of a One Pocket game. Your opponent has broken the balls and left you with a difficult layout. While no straight-in shot exists, a carom shot is available, indicative of the sort of shot for which you will always be on the lookout. Shoot the cue ball with right english off the 13-ball to pocket the 4-ball, spinning the cue ball with the english to get to your opponent's side of the table. As you can see, the rest of the object balls are then between your cue ball and your pocket. This is the kind of move you'll often try to make because you leave your opponent no shot if you miss. If you make the 4-ball, you have a better chance at another shot toward your pocket.

See figure 7.11 for another beginning game situation. Your opponent has broken well, but the 2-ball, which was the corner ball on the rack, leaked toward your corner pocket. As a result, you have been left with a very thin cut on the 2-ball. Extremely thin cuts on balls come up very often in the typical One Pocket game. This shot in particular is an important shot to practice.

After you get past the opening moves, you come to the middle of the game. The middle game occurs when you and your opponent begin a defensive battle that gradually moves the balls down table. When you start moving the balls down table, keep in mind that it's to your advantage to keep the object balls on your half (right or left side) of the table. In figure 7.12, notice that the balls were strategically played to the shaded area and the cue ball was left as close as possible to your opponent's pocket. As you might imagine while studying the layout, this makes it very difficult for your opponent to attempt a shot at his or her pocket, let alone make a shot. If he or she attempts a shot and doesn't make it, you'll likely have a shot to your own pocket.

At the end of the game, only a few balls will be left, and chances are good that either you or your opponent needs just one more ball pocketed for the win. An end-of-the-game situation is shown in figure 7.13. Your opponent has the upper-right corner pocket, and you have the upper left. You need all three balls to win the game, but your opponent needs only one. Your best play here is to bank the 5-ball two rails, following the 5-ball with the cue ball to send it down table and up off the bottom short rail, leaving an angle to the left of the 2-ball. This allows you a shot on the 2-ball and a natural angle to the right of the 2-ball to arrive in position for the 14-ball. Again, even if you miss any of these shots, you leave your opponent very

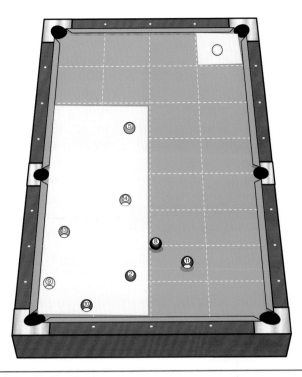

Figure 7.12   The middle of a One Pocket game.

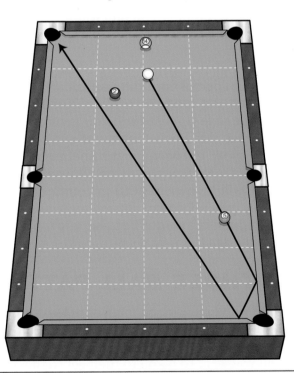

Figure 7.13   The end of a One Pocket game—a true test of will and patience.

little to shoot at by keeping the cue ball on his or her side of the table. The two-rail bank, like the thin cut, is a valuable One Pocket tool. In fact, the best offensive and defensive shots in One Pocket involve the multirail bank skills. Your knowledge of banking, banking systems, and natural tracks around the table will elevate your One Pocket game instantly.

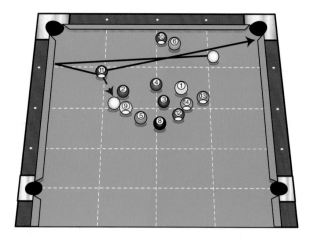

Figure 7.14   Using the critical kick shot in a game of One Pocket.

Besides thin cuts and multirail banks, kicking ability also quickly advances your skills in this game, allowing offensive shot selections that are quite defensive at the same time. Upper-echelon players take plenty of time to develop strong kicking skills for this very reason. Kicking at a ball in the game of One Pocket allows you to place an object ball close to your pocket and still place the cue ball quite near or frozen to other balls. For example, in figure 7.14, your opponent has wisely left you near your own pocket with little opportunity for a shot, and surely none with defensive results. You must counter his or her move. You kick into the rail first, sending the 11-ball toward your pocket and allowing the cue ball to glance off the 11-ball and nestle itself, ideally, between the 2-ball and the 9-ball. If the cue ball freezes between these balls, that's wonderful—your opponent won't have a shot. Keep in mind that you must hit this shot firm enough because you're going rail first to send the 11-ball to another rail or into the pocket to and avoid a foul. If you aim to hit the 11-ball thin, it will head toward the 6-ball and possibly break up this cluster, and will send the 6-ball to a rail for a legal shot.

The vast majority of your shots in One Pocket are strictly defensive, to the point where you're attempting to control both the cue ball and the object ball, or a multitude of object balls. You'll constantly be trying to send balls toward your half of the table while at the same time trying to snooker your opponent from making an offensive shot for his pocket. One Pocket is a move and countermove game; sometimes your focus will be more offensive, and sometimes more defensive. If your opponent is a very good One Pocket player, you'll need to play a more offensive game because he or she will be experienced in countering defensive moves and accomplishing shots that you might not immediately see. If you're the stronger player, a more defensive game is in order because you'll have the added luxury of forcing your opponent to make the mistakes.

THE THREE-BALL PATTERN

Throughout this chapter we've mentioned thinking at least three balls ahead during your pattern and position play. The reason this works is quite simple. If you are, for instance, looking at the 1-ball and trying to get to the 2-ball, it will help knowing which side of the 2-ball you want to be on to then get to the 3-ball. Once you're on the 2-ball, you'll be looking ahead to the 4-ball, and so on. Because angles come into the game of pool so often, thinking a minimum of three balls ahead keeps you safe from many poor pattern decisions.

The most common three-ball patterns come in one of three variations: working the three balls close together (usually at one end of the table or the other), working the balls from one end of the table to the other end, and working back and forth between the ends of the table. Each of these situations has been illustrated to show you how they're likely to appear, and how to tackle them when they do.

In figure 7.15, all three remaining balls in a rack of Nine Ball are at one end of the table. Typically, a three-ball pattern such as this allows the luxury of not having to move the cue ball very far. At the same time, the pressure is on you to stay on the right side of each ball, or else you'll have to send the cue ball all the way around the table to get back to your group of balls. If you shoot the 7-ball with straight follow, you can bring the cue ball off the short rail and back down toward the center of the table, as shown in shot A. If you're going away from the line of attack to make the 8-ball in the corner, you'll need to get the cue ball past the third diamond, as shown in shot B. Then a straight drag shot or center-ball hit will allow you to play the 9-ball in the left corner. If you come up short on shot A, you'll need to come back across the table to play the 9-ball in the right corner, as shown in shot C.

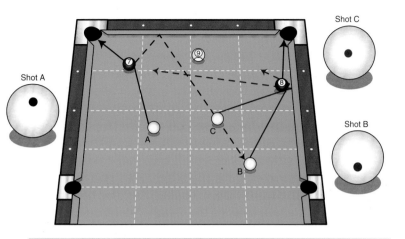

Figure 7.15   A three-ball pattern with all three balls at one end of the table.

In our next situation, shown in figure 7.16, you'll be working the balls from one end of the table to the other. The 7-ball stands at one end of the table, the 8-ball is in the center, and the 9-ball lies at the other end of the table. From where the cue ball is, your best angle into the 8-ball will result from using a touch of low-left english on the cue ball as you pocket the

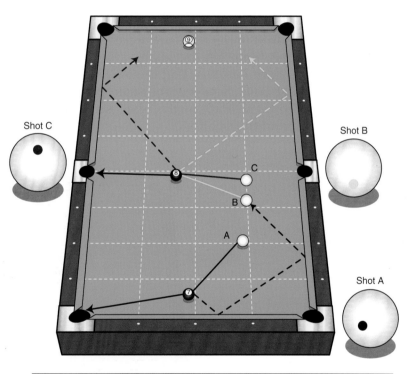

Figure 7.16   Working a three-ball pattern from one end of the table to the other.

7-ball, as shown in shot A. This allows you to use the short rail and the long rail to get an angle on the 8-ball. So long as you use the second rail, you'll get a great angle coming up the table.

Let's say you barely hit the second rail and come up a little short on the 8-ball. In this case, you can use straight draw to bring the cue ball to the right side and shoot the 9-ball in the left corner pocket, as shown in figure 7.16, shot B. If you come up a little farther, you'll have the natural angle to follow the cue ball up into the rail near the second diamond, and then off the rail again to shoot the 9-ball in the right corner pocket, as shown in shot C.

This brings us to moving back and forth down the table. In figure 7.17, the 7 and 9 balls are at one end of the table, and the 8-ball is at other end. This type of pattern forces you to move the cue ball a greater distance. Your speed control will have to be a little better, but planning a correct pattern play in advance should eliminate any problems. Hit center ball on the cue ball when you pocket the 7-ball to come down table, passing the angle of attack on the 8-ball in the corner. If you come down table short on the resulting position for the 8-ball, you could have a long straight-in shot, in which case you'd have to put more force into the cue ball and draw it the length of the table to get back to the 9-ball. As long as you come down table past the side pocket, you'll have an easy shot on the 8-ball, which will result in easy position play for the 9-ball. Play the 8-ball using low-left english, using the long rail on the right side, crossing over the table, then into the long rail on the left side, and out again toward the 9-ball. Now you can shoot the 9-ball in the upper-right corner pocket. The key shot in this pattern is on the 7-ball; use your speed control on the 7-ball for a good angle on the 8-ball.

The next series of three diagrams shows just how much thinking three balls ahead can affect your pattern-play decisions. In figure 7.18, you have a relatively easy shot on the 5-ball in the side pocket. Stopping the cue ball or rolling up would give you a fine shot on the 6-ball. However, looking ahead, you'll see that you want a bit of angle on your third ball in the pattern, your 7-ball. So instead, create an angle, using low ball, to pocket the 5-ball.

In figure 7.19, now that the 5-ball is gone, your three-ball pattern includes the 6, 7, and 8 balls. Note that the angle you gave yourself on the 6-ball gives you an easy way to get an angle on the 7-ball, so that you can draw back off the left long rail for a shot on the 8-ball.

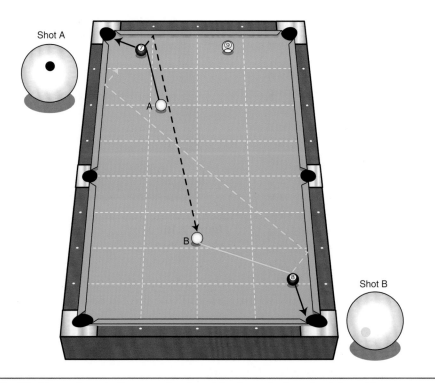

Figure 7.17   Working a three-ball pattern back and forth on the length of the table.

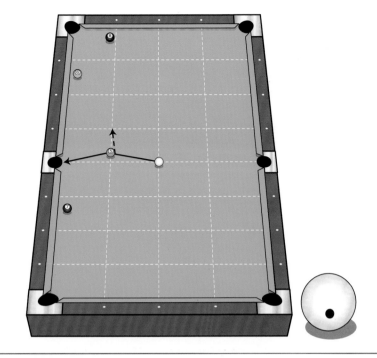

Figure 7.18 Thinking ahead keeps you ahead of the game in this three-ball pattern.

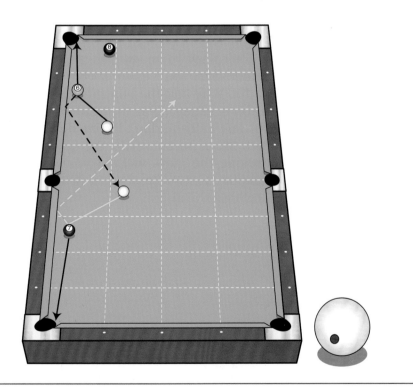

Figure 7.19 Getting an angle on the 7-ball allows an easier trip back to the 8-ball.

Once you pocket the 6-ball, your three-ball pattern includes the 7, 8, and 9 balls. Draw off the 7-ball (as shown in figure 7.20) for a simple shot on the 8-ball that leaves you in a perfect spot for the 9-ball.

But don't stop there. Despite the fact that your 9-ball is the last ball on the table, let's pretend you've pocketed the 7-ball. Play a three-ball pattern for the 8-, 9-, and

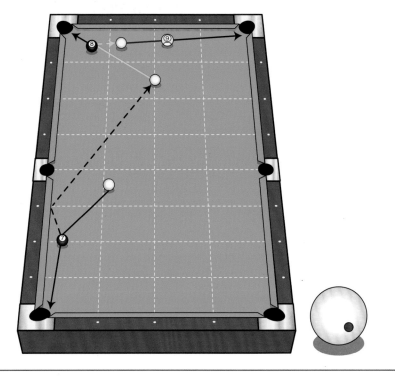

Figure 7.20   Once you've pocketed the 6-ball, the 7, 8, and 9 balls become your final three-ball pattern.

an imaginary 10-ball. You don't need to imagine anything crazy; just pretend the 10-ball is somewhere near the 9-ball. You'll either stop the cue ball on contact with the 9-ball, or roll up just a bit. Why add the imaginary ball? The reason so many players miss game-winning balls, especially in the games of Eight Ball and Nine Ball, is that they get down to the last ball and don't have a destination for the cue ball. This often causes too much focus on pocketing the object ball. The result—not stroking, or maybe overstroking, the shot—will give your opponent the game. This is a silent rule of thumb among most professionals: Always have a destination in mind for the cue ball. Learn from them!

Safety Play

In the movie *The Hustler*, Eddie Felson (Paul Newman) says to Minnesota Fats (Jackie Gleason), "You don't leave much when you miss." Fats retorts, "That's what the game is all about." That statement is truer than ever in today's most popular games.

Years ago, in games like Eight Ball and Nine Ball, the rule was two fouls, ball in hand, also commonly referred to as *one rollout*. That meant you could roll your cue ball to a more favorable position if you didn't have a clear shot at your ball. It was then your opponent's option to have you shoot again or to take control of the table. If you took the shot and didn't either send a ball to the rail or scratch the cue ball, your opponent then had cue ball in hand. In other words, the cue ball could be placed anywhere on the table for the incoming shot. Under these rules, players tended to play a more aggressive game and make more spectacular shots. In fact, before the jump cue was the norm, top players who could jump the ball with their regular playing cue would roll out to jump shots. If opponents couldn't jump over a ball, they had to give up the shot option.

The rules changed to one foul, cue ball in hand for television so games would play faster. As the rules of Eight Ball and Nine Ball have changed over the years to one foul ball in hand, a solid safety game has become more important for a winning pool game.

TYPES OF SAFETIES

Safeties can be sorted into a few categories, with the lay of the balls on the table dictating the best choice. Most safeties involve hiding either the cue ball or the object ball. It tends to be easier to hide the cue ball than to hide an object ball. Because the game of pool is all about controlling the cue ball, it's more natural to place the cue ball in an awkward place on the table for your opponent. Hiding an object ball is considered more difficult because few players practice controlling the speed of the object ball. They're usually thinking about pocketing the object ball, so they focus on speed that will get them to the pocket, not on the fine gradations in speed that can get them close to the pocket or close to another ball. Thus, safeties that involve object ball speed control are considered more difficult to execute.

In another type of safety you hide both the object ball and the cue ball, which requires excellent speed control on both balls. Again, you'll need to spend time practicing object ball speed control to become proficient at this kind of safety. Then there are safeties that appear to be aggressive shots and not safeties at all—what we call *two-way shots*. In the two-way shot, you attempt a difficult bank or combination and then hide the cue ball from your opponent's intended object ball in the process. Should you miss the difficult shot, you leave nothing for your opponent. These are also called *free shots*.

Finally, another form of safety play is to lock up balls, or create a cluster. This tends to be done when there's no way that you can hit the intended object ball. This kind of safety is explained in greater detail in chapter 10 on strategy and intentional fouls.

When the need to play safe arises, a vivid imagination and creativity can be your greatest assets. Imagine the cue ball exactly where you want it to be. Ideally, you'll attempt to freeze the cue ball to another ball or to a rail. If the cue ball is frozen behind another ball, it's very difficult to execute a simple one-rail kick at the hidden object ball. Your opponent will be faced, at best, with a multirail kick, which is a very tough shot. And when the cue ball is frozen to, or very near, a rail, your opponent has limited options because you've taken away any shot that's hit below center on the cue ball. A hit on the cue ball above center is harder to control, which increases your chances of getting back to the table.

You can enhance your safety game by practicing shots that are easy to execute and easy to see in regular game situations. When you learn each type of safety we've described, look for opportunities to play them every time you practice, even if you're playing by yourself. Looking for safety opportunities helps build your safety game through increased use of your creativity.

Controlling the Cue Ball

As mentioned, the most common safety option involves a light touch on the cue ball. Your intent is to move the cue ball a very short distance, while at the same time moving the object ball a short distance. Figure 8.1 shows a one-set shot. To accomplish this shot, begin by hitting the cue ball slightly below center with a touch of left english. You're attempting to drive the object ball forward, past the 9-ball, and send the cue ball behind the 9-ball. This is an excellent shot to practice because it gives you a feel for moving the cue ball only a short distance. This sort of light touch is a skill

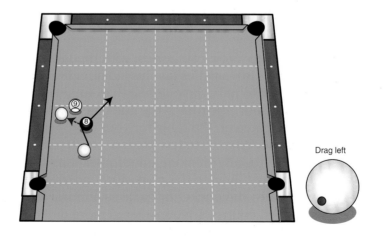

Figure 8.1 This safety requires a light touch on the cue ball, a key skill in safety play.

you won't use on most of your regular shots, but it's invaluable to be able to do it when needed, and the need arises most often in safety situations.

In figure 8.2 we have a similar shot in a Nine Ball game. To execute this shot, send the 2-ball down the table and squeeze the cue ball between the 6-ball and the 3-ball. Once you learn this shot, it's easy to execute and offers excellent results.

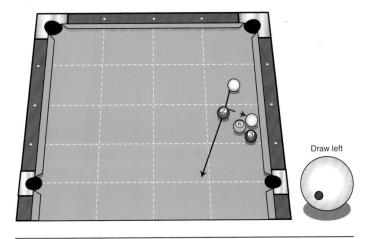

Figure 8.2   The use of the soft safety in a Nine Ball game.

Let's say you're playing a game of Eight Ball and your opponent has just scratched. You have cue ball in hand. As you'll notice in figure 8.3, your 3-ball and 6-ball are tied up. It's virtually impossible to break them up with the other balls on the opposite side of the table, and neither one has a clear path to a pocket. You're best off executing the safety as shown. You'll open the 6-ball and 3-ball, while placing your cue ball between the 6-ball and the cushion, giving your opponent a very difficult kick shot. Should he or she foul again, you'll have cue ball in hand with a much easier chance of running the table.

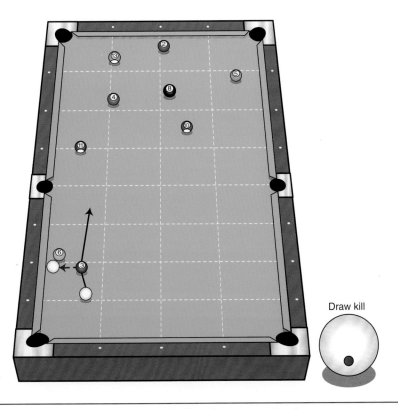

Figure 8.3   An Eight Ball safety play that puts the balls in better position for your next turn at the table.

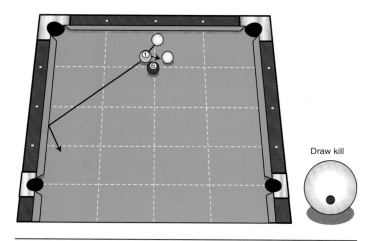

Draw kill

Figure 8.4   Stopping the cue ball while sending the object ball down table.

Another type of safety shot that comes up quite often is shown in figure 8.4. In this situation, the incoming player has cue ball in hand, but there's no open shot at the 1-ball to make it in any pocket because the 6-ball is blocking its path. Rather than try to bank the ball or take a high-risk shot, a safety is your best bet. To accomplish this shot, you'll need to stop the cue ball dead after it makes contact with the object ball, sending the 1-ball down table. The closer you leave your cue ball to the 6-ball, the better off you'll be.

The possibilities are endless for stopping the cue ball with cue ball in hand and trying to freeze it on a ball or stop it behind a row of balls. Look at figure 8.5, which shows another Eight Ball situation. Your opponent has just missed, and you have no open shot at the 1-, 2-, 3-, 5-, or 6-ball. Rather than take a flyer, simply shoot on the left side of the 6-ball with a touch of follow, using either straight high ball or a bit of left english. This sends the cue ball into the short rail and back into the 3–5 cluster. Hit the cue ball hard enough to barely glance off the 6-ball and open the 3–5 cluster just slightly, while leaving the cue ball behind these balls.

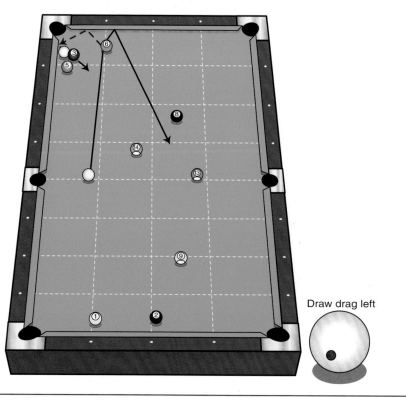

Draw drag left

Figure 8.5   Sending the cue ball into a cluster.

In figure 8.6, you'll be sending the 3-ball down table, but you have to hit it pretty firm to get it there. At the same time, you're trying not to let the cue ball travel too far once you hit the 3-ball. To control this, use a below-center shot with a thick (three-quarter) hit on the 3-ball. You'll need to take as much speed as possible off the cue ball to park it behind the 5 and 6 balls. This is a shot that comes up frequently, especially in Nine Ball.

In figure 8.7, you came up a little short for your position on the 9-ball. You're left with a decision. Should you take the flyer bank or play safe? Taking the bank probably isn't advisable for a couple of reasons. First, if you don't know conditions of the table, it could play short or long on you. Plus, you must know where your cue ball is going and how to get it out of the way. Finally, if you miss the bank, chances are you'll sell out, leaving your opponent an easy shot for the win. Better to play safe by cutting the 9-ball on the left side. Hit it very thin and send the cue ball two or three rails down table. If, for example, you want to come short on the second rail, you would use a little low-left english. If you want to come longer, you would hit the cue ball with high-left english, hoping to drive the cue ball at least three rails on its way to the other end of the table. This gives your opponent a very difficult shot, even to execute a safety of his or her own.

Being able to hit an object ball very thin is vital to great

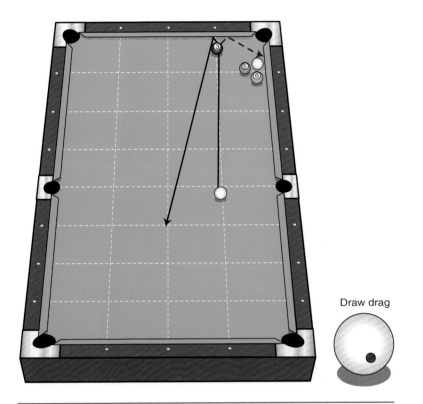

Draw drag

Figure 8.6 Stopping the cue ball behind blocking balls with a below-center hit.

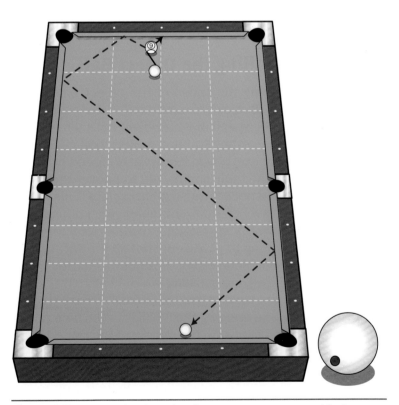

Figure 8.7 Opting for the safety leaves your opponent with the tough shot.

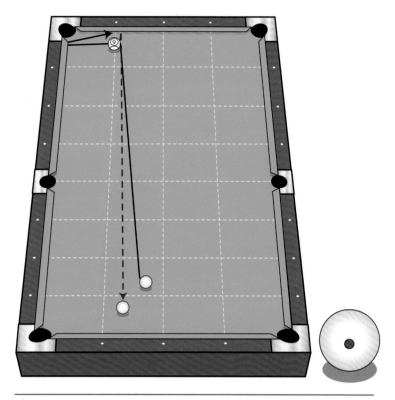

Figure 8.8   Attempting the shot on the 9-ball will still allow you a safety.

safety play, and definitely worth the practice time invested. There will be plenty of times when you're presented with a shot situation involving a length-of-the-table thin cut on a ball. You're better off trying to overcut the ball than to undercut it. The overcut shot will send your object ball to the long rail and then back into the short rail, leaving your opponent virtually the same shot. An undercut shot will hit the short rail first, bounce out in front of the pocket, and leave an easier shot for your opponent.

In figure 8.8 your opponent has left you an extremely tough shot on the 9-ball. Attempt to cut the ball in, but use a thin cut with a middle-ball hit (or a touch below center because it will have become middle ball by the time you get all the way down the table to the 9-ball). If you make the shot, great—you've won. If you don't, the cue ball has traveled back down table, leaving your opponent with an even tougher option.

Controlling the Object Ball

Controlling the speed of the object ball becomes a crucial part of playing good safeties. But, as we mentioned at the beginning of the chapter, because you seldom gauge the speed of your object balls when you're pocketing them, it will take some practice getting to know object ball speed in relation to cue ball speed. A great practice exercise in learning the speed of the object balls is to throw a rack of balls out on the table and try *not* to pocket them. Instead, attempt to lag each ball to its intended pocket without hitting it in. This will give you a feel for just how fast object balls travel on different tables, with different cloth, different hits, and so on.

Figure 8.9 shows an excellent example of using speed control on the 9-ball. Attempting to play a cut shot all the way up table on the 9-ball in this illustration is a low-percentage shot. Possible scenarios include leaving the object ball hanging in the pocket and allowing the cue ball to travel back and forth between the short rails, no doubt leaving your opponent an easy straight-in shot. Or you can try holding the angle and banking the 9-ball into the side pocket—but if you do that, you leave the cue ball almost in the middle of the table and sell out if you miss. The smart play is to bank the 9-ball into the long rail across to the opposite long rail to leave it in the middle of the short rail. At the same time, by using low-right english on the shot, you'll bring the cue ball roughly to the opposite side of the table on the other short rail. Practicing this shot will help you develop a feel for controlling the object ball.

This shot also plays very well in Eight Ball. Look at figure 8.10. You have one ball left on the table. The 8-ball is all the way up table, making it a low-percentage shot

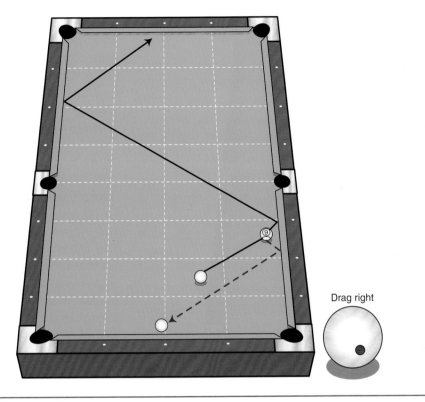

Figure 8.9   Controlling speed on the object ball requires practice.

to bank the 2-ball cross-side because you have to hold the angle. It's very difficult to bank cross-corner. Even if you do, you won't have a decent shot on the 8-ball. If you play a great shot and cut it up the corner, again, so what? You still won't have a shot on the 8-ball. You're much better off playing a two-rail safety, trying to bring the 2-ball just in front of the 8-ball. Hit this shot with low-right english, and remember to keep the cue ball near the center of the short rail.

Sometimes it's not possible, or quite difficult, to control the cue ball for a safety. In such cases, you can try controlling both balls, as shown in figures 8.9 and 8.10, but keep in mind that it's more important here to control the 9- and 2-ball in the diagrams than the cue ball.

Let's say you're executing a safety in which you've contacted the object ball and your cue ball is now approaching a blocker—that is, another object

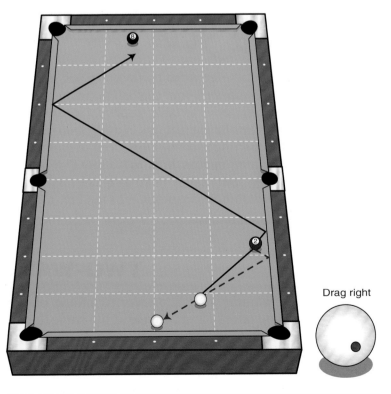

Figure 8.10   Controlling the speed of the object ball in Eight Ball.

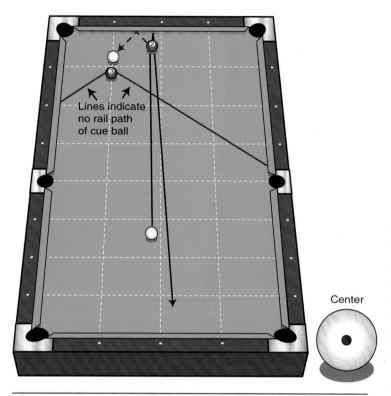

Lines indicate
no rail path
of cue ball

Center

Figure 8.11 The closer you can leave your cue ball to an impeding ball, the fewer options your opponent will have to kick at the ball.

ball on the table. You should keep in mind that the closer the cue ball comes to the blocking ball, the fewer options your opponent has to execute a good hit. Why? Because it takes away more and more of the table that the cue ball can directly hit. For example, in figure 8.11, the closer the cue ball gets to the 3-ball, the more difficult it will be for your opponent to hit the 2-ball. This is because the closer the cue ball comes to the 3-ball, the greater the area on the table is hidden from your opponent for a straight-in hit, no matter where on the other end of the table your 2-ball should land. It would now take a multirail shot to hit the 2-ball. Thus, it's more important in this situation to control the cue ball, and the more you want to control the cue ball, the more difficult it is to control the object ball. So remember where to keep your focus.

Put It in Practice

Here's an exercise to try for practicing safeties: Throw a few balls on the table and simply aim with your cue ball to cut an object ball as thinly as possible, sending the cue ball down the table. Your goal is twofold. First, you want to keep the object ball very close to where it was, moving it no more than an inch or two. At the same time, you're trying to control the speed of the cue ball. Very thin cuts often provide excellent safety options, but this is a shot that needs specific practice attention. Too many players see the shot, but they either hit the ball too full and sell out or try to hit it so thin that they completely miss the ball and give their opponent cue ball in hand.

TWO-WAY SHOT

The two-way shot is a favorite among players because of its efficiency—you're playing offense and defense at the same time. The offensive shot tends to be a low-percentage shot, but if you pocket it you can continue play. On the other hand, if you miss the shot, you have played a safety. In figure 8.12, the cue ball is placed in a situation in which you're almost straight in on the 1-ball. It would be very difficult to draw the ball straight back to get on the 2-ball. Instead, you'll attempt to bank the 1-ball cross-corner and, at the same time, send the cue ball down table to get position on the 2-ball. It's a much easier shot to execute, and you can hit it either way.

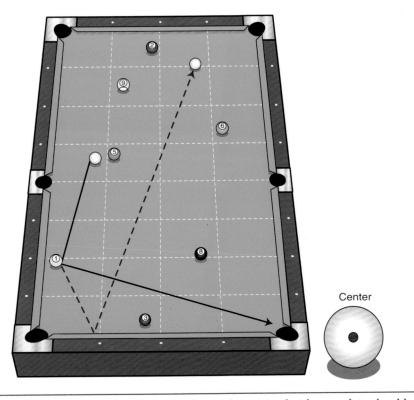

Figure 8.12   This two-way shot offers a chance to pocket with position but has a safety should you miss.

Whether overcut or undercut, you won't give your opponent a decent shot. You're more apt to overcut this one, but it doesn't matter—you still have the 6-ball as a blocker at the other end of the table. And, by banking it cross-corner, you'll wind up with a better shot on the 2-ball, and with an angle to get on the 3-ball to boot.

In figure 8.13, you're in a situation in which you have no straight-in shot on the 1-ball. However, it's a very easy shot to bank the 1-ball cross-side and hold the cue ball where it is, or to draw it back just a hair to have a shot on the 2-ball. Once more, if you do miss the 1-ball, you have the 5-ball and 6-ball as blockers. The bonus: If you go too far, you leave the 1-ball long and make it more difficult for your opponent to get back down table for the 2-ball. This requires executing only a simple stop shot and is an excellent two-way shot to have in your arsenal.

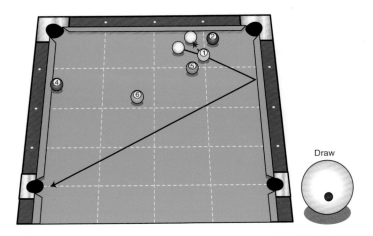

Figure 8.13   This two-way stop shot is a critical shot to have in your safety arsenal.

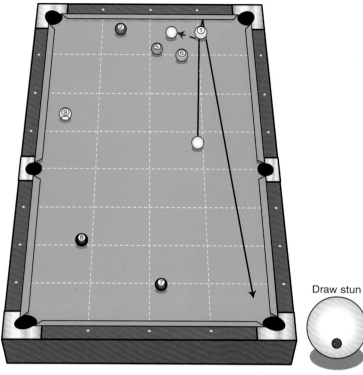

Draw stun

Figure 8.14   This long bank offers you safe cover if you miss.

Figure 8.14 shows basically the same situation. However, this shot requires a length-of-the-table bank. Once again you have two potential blockers, the 5-ball and 6-ball. All you have to concentrate on is getting the speed of the 1-ball down and swinging the cue ball behind the 2-ball. Some players have a tendency to overlook these shots. Beginners might try to cut the 1-ball thin on the right side and bring the cue ball down two rails, which is a difficult shot with which to hook your opponent.

Caroms and combinations (which come up more often in Nine Ball than in Eight Ball) also provide excellent two-way shot possibilities. Look at figure 8.15. You might be able to clear the 1-ball to the corner pocket, but it will be extremely difficult to get a shot on the 2-ball because it's clustered with the 5-ball on the rail. However, you can attempt the 1–9 combination while parking your cue ball by the 3 and 4 balls. If you pocket the 9-ball, you've won the game. If you don't, and if you've kept the cue ball very near or (better still) frozen to the 3-ball, your opponent will have a very difficult time getting a good hit on the 1-ball, likely resulting in cue ball in hand for you on your next turn at the table.

In figure 8.16 you have a low-percentage shot on the 5-ball, but the 9-ball is sitting close to the pocket. Pocket the 9-ball by caroming your cue ball off the 5-ball and into the 9-ball, while sending your 5-ball up toward the other end of the table. Again, this is a potential game winner, resulting in a safe shot should you miss. If you enjoy the game of Nine Ball, the opportunity to shoot a carom shot, involving the 9-ball or many other balls, will come into play quite often. It's definitely worth practicing.

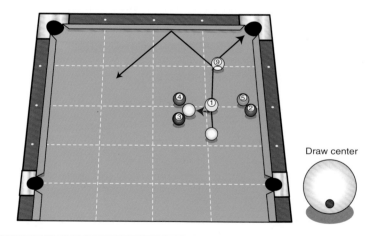

Draw center

Figure 8.15   A combination can make for an excellent two-way shot possibility.

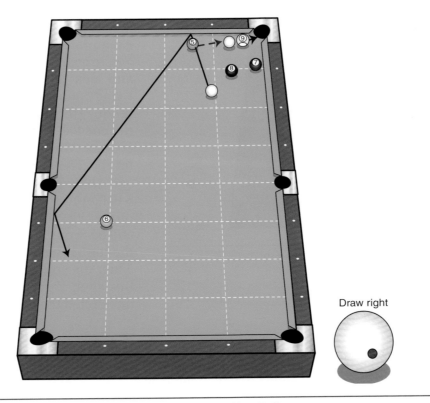

Draw right

Figure 8.16 The carom shot is a common two-way shot in Nine Ball.

COUNTERING SAFETIES WITH SAFETIES

Let's say your opponent is at the table. He shoots at a ball, misses, and leaves you hooked, or else he plays a safety and hooks you (meaning he's left you an obstructed path to your object ball). Now your only alternative is to try and kick at the ball to make a legal hit. Although you might think your opponent is now in control, in fact you have the edge in the safety battle, as long as you know the basic strategy of trying to control the cue ball after the kick. In other words, you'll often be aiming for one side of the object ball to enhance your possibilities of winning the game rather than just trying to get a hit and sit down again.

Too many players try to slam into the object ball by kicking it as hard as they can, hoping they can slop a ball in, create clusters down the table, or change the whole table layout. This is not the thing to do. Instead, try to control the cue ball. In the past 5 to 10 years, we've seen a real renaissance in kicking at balls. Many top players have become so proficient at kicking balls that they'll choose to roll out to a kick shot rather than leave their opponent a direct shot. They are hoping to have the push (or rollout) returned to them, so they can execute the shot by kicking at the blocked ball and leaving their opponent in a tough spot. If you're attempting a kick and there's a cluster of object balls around your target ball, it's much easier to hook your opponent just by hitting the correct side of the object ball.

As you start learning to kick at balls, practice trying to hit one side of the ball and then the other. Only in rare instances (such as when your object ball is hung in the pocket and you're kicking to play position off that ball) will you want to kick full into an object ball. In safety play, though, hitting one side or the other is often required to return a safe play to your opponent.

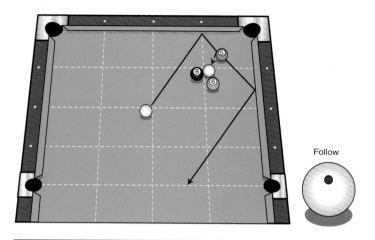

Figure 8.17   Your opponent has left you safe. Counter with a safety of your own.

Figure 8.17 shows an excellent example of an opponent's safety. You're going to use high ball (follow) and kick rail first into the 5-ball. Using follow on the cue ball will produce the reverse (draw effect) on the cue ball as it leaves the rail and contacts the 5-ball, allowing you to hit the 5-ball and park the cue ball somewhere between the 6-ball and 8-ball. And by contacting the 5-ball on the side, you'll send it into the rail and back out, leaving less chance of the cue ball having a clear path to the 5-ball for your opponent. Practice this shot. Variations of it come up more often than you might think.

PLANNING A SAFETY

In Nine Ball, the opportunity to plan a safety in advance comes up quite often. You'll recognize the chance most often when you have balls tied up that you just can't break up with earlier shots in the rack. For example, say you break the balls and notice that the 6-ball and 7-ball are tied up, but the rest of the balls are straight into the pocket. There's no way to break up these balls with the shots you have leading up to them. In this case, the best thing to do is run down to the 5-ball and make it easy

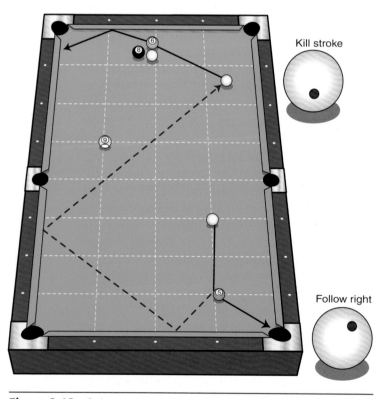

Figure 8.18   Safeties might not come up immediately, but with a tough rack it's wise to plan a creative safety in advance.

for yourself to play a safety on the 6-ball. You'll want to get the angle to kill the cue ball after hitting the 6-ball and freeze it to the 7-ball. With one-foul, ball-in-hand rules, you should always run up to your trouble balls and try to place the cue ball in position in which it's relatively easy to play a strong safety. Simply stated, if you can't bust up that cluster before you get to it, you're better off playing a safety from that cluster.

Figure 8.18 shows a situation in which the 6-ball and the 8-ball are tied up. You have no realistic way of breaking up the 6–8 cluster from the shot you have on the 5-ball. Make it easy on yourself by playing correct shape on the 5-ball. Go two rails on the cue ball after contact with the 5-ball (short rail, long rail, as shown), giving yourself a straight angle shot on the 6-ball. Now you can contact the 6-ball, sending it into the rail, while just sliding the cue ball over and freezing it on the 8-ball. If the cue ball is very close to the 8-ball, your opponent will have few options. If the cue ball is frozen on the 8-ball, so much the better.

WHEN TO PLAY SAFE

Over time, you'll become more proficient at these simple safeties, and your safety game will become more elaborate. You'll learn to immediately recognize a great safety opportunity and begin creating more imaginative safeties on your own. In fact, some of the most imaginative players actually prefer to play One Pocket. This game, when played well, is virtually all creative safety play until your opponent makes that one mistake that allows you to run out.

For today's most popular games, Eight Ball and Nine Ball, you'll want to keep a few simple safety rules in mind. If you can't make the shot you're presented with at least 75 to 80 percent of the time, try to find some place to play a safety. If you're playing an opponent whose game is far superior to your own, raise that percentage to 90 percent of the time. If the table looks impossible to run, but the shot in front of you is simple to execute and doesn't offer much of a safety opportunity, play the easy shot and have a plan to get shape on an eventual better safety. In this way, you take the least amount of risk in allowing your opponent a run-out and give yourself the best chance for an easier run-out when you get back to the table. It's always better to play the smart safety shot and let your opponent make the first mistake.

The more creative and imaginative you are, the better your safety game will become. It's in the creation and execution of safeties that your precision pool game will advance to a higher mental awareness. The intricacies and options available to you each time you play are endless, which is what makes the cue sports such a challenge. Add to this all the strategies and tactics involved in rules of game and match play and we can assure that you'll remain challenged for many years to come.

photo by Garry Hodges

World champion Xiaoting Pan of China is equally skilled at offensive and defensive strategy.

Challenging Safety Games

One of the most difficult tasks in safety play is figuring out a way to practice. Safeties might not come up often enough in your regular playing for you to really learn them, and drills just don't cut it in this area. Because the true secret to great safety play is imagination and creativity, you need to practice creating safeties where you don't naturally see them. Here are a few easy ways to make safety practice productive and interesting.

Practicing by Yourself

Start with a rack of six balls (the 4-ball through the 9-ball) racked in a small triangle with the 4-ball in front. Break the balls wide open. Now, whether or not you have a shot on the 4-ball, play safe instead. You can attempt to hide the 4-ball, or try to hide the cue ball. If the option exists, hide both balls. Even if the 4-ball is straight in the pocket, you must play a safety. Following your first safety, if you can't see the 4-ball, try to kick at it and leave it safe again. You continue to play safe on this ball until you leave yourself a shot on it. Then pocket the 4-ball and play safety on the 5-ball.

This exercise forces you to practice your cue ball and object ball speed as well as your tactical play. As you play, you'll soon realize that some places work better than others for *ducking*, or hiding the cue ball. You'll constantly have to create a safety where you don't automatically see one. Practice freezing the cue ball to other balls and leaving yourself absolutely no shot. We see a great many pro players doing this in warm-ups—testing the speed of the cloth and trying to knock an object ball to a rail while freezing the cue ball to another ball.

Once you get proficient at this, try a full rack of nine balls. Or, if Eight Ball is your game of choice, rack all 15 balls. In each safety attempt, try to hide yourself from all the balls in the other group. From here, expand to playing safe and then trying to maneuver your way out of your own safety.

Practicing With a Partner

You and a partner can play what's called Safety Nine Ball. Break the balls, and play safe on the 1-ball. If your opponent can see it, he or she can shoot it in but then must play safe on the 2-ball. If your opponent can't see it, he or she must try to kick it safe. If you can then see the ball, you may pocket it and then must play safe on the 2-ball, and so on. The better you both get at playing safe, the longer a single game will take you. You'll find that it can be quite difficult to play safe on each shot. As a result, you'll learn a great deal more about creating safeties than you would in ordinary game situations.

This is also an excellent exercise for developing your mental concentration and patience in your safety game. Having the mental determination to engage in a grueling safety battle not only protects your table territory but can also wear down your competition. When opponents become frustrated, you have a good chance of toughing it out for the first shot that offers a true offensive opportunity.

Situation-Specific Shots

Whether you're putting together critical shots in a pattern play or executing a well-played safety, it all comes together at game time. When things come together the right way, pool can be poetry. But when you look at the table and are overwhelmed by the number of choices you see, it won't seem poetic at all—it'll seem like a nightmare. Which way should you go? Should you go for the offensive move? The bank or the cut? The safety? There's no way to cover all the scenarios that will come up in each game you play, but there are plenty of situations that we've seen over our decades of playing and watching the best players compete that warrant some discussion. The more you know about pool, the more important it becomes to think critically and assess the pros and cons of options at the table.

SPECIFIC SHOT DECISIONS

These are the little tips and tricks that can keep you from the pitfalls and unforced errors we see amateurs make on a daily basis. Although you may never see the exact situations shown here, by practicing and studying these situations you'll increase your ability to diagnose the circumstances and prescribe a winning course of action.

Hitting Hangers: Full or Thin?

Hangers are those balls at or near the edge of the pocket. They seem easy enough, but they're some of the most misunderstood shots as regards to how to shoot them and still end up with the best resulting cue ball position. Figure 9.1 shows three ways to pocket a hanging ball, depending on where your cue ball might need to be. If you use a follow stroke, the cue ball will die along the short rail. If you use low-right draw, the cue ball will react as a follow shot coming off the first and second rail. The third shot, shown by the black line, is a rail-first shot. This is by far the toughest shot of the three to control the speed of the cue ball because the thickness of the hit on the 4-ball will determine how much energy is left on the cue ball. Practice hitting rail first and different parts of the 4-ball to get the feel for yourself.

Now let's say the hanger is part of a combination shot. You'll still want to choose the correct side, or else risk giving up a run caused by poor resulting position on the object ball after pocketing the hanger. Shot A in figure 9.2 allows the player to

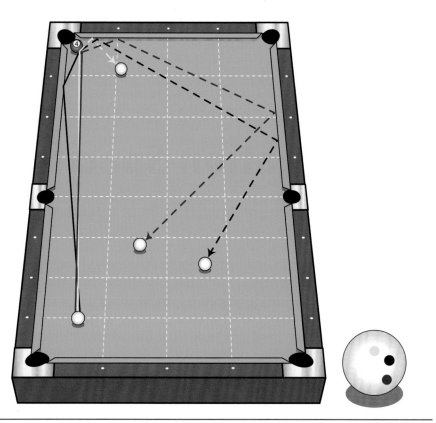

Figure 9.1 Getting position off a ball hanging in the pocket.

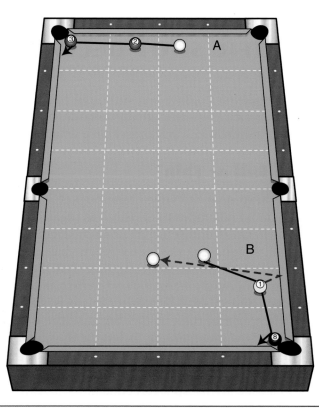

Figure 9.2 A hanging ball shot involving a combination.

shoot the 2-ball into the 3-ball on the left side, thus sending the 2-ball away from the pocket, resulting in poor position on the 2-ball. Hitting closer to the center or just right of center would keep this 2-ball in front of the pocket. Shot B illustrates a combination where it doesn't matter what side the 1-ball hits the 8-ball to pocket it because you'll still have a shot on the 1-ball—unless the 1-ball hits the 8-ball perfectly in the center and follows it in.

One Ball or Two?

This brings us neatly to whether you want to pocket two balls if you've got a hanging combination shot, or any combination shot that includes the luxury of pocketing both balls. In figure 9.3, the 5-ball is hanging in the hole; your object here is to pocket the 5-ball and 7-ball on the same shot. When the distance is greater than two or three feet (about half to a full meter), you won't need to put a special hit on the 7-ball; the ball will already be rolling forward on impact with the 5-ball. The crucial part of this shot is that the 7-ball must hit the 5-ball full in the face to follow it into the pocket. If the 7-ball hits either side of the 5-ball, it will pocket the 5-ball but then head toward one of the rails adjacent to the pocket. If there's less distance between the two target balls, hit low on the cue ball. This will have the opposite effect on the first target ball, allowing it to roll forward with more momentum into the hanging ball. There will be less energy remaining on the first ball but still enough to propel it into the pocket. You see this type of shot all the time in Eight Ball. When your opponent's ball is blocking a pocket that's in play for your run-out, this shot comes in very handy.

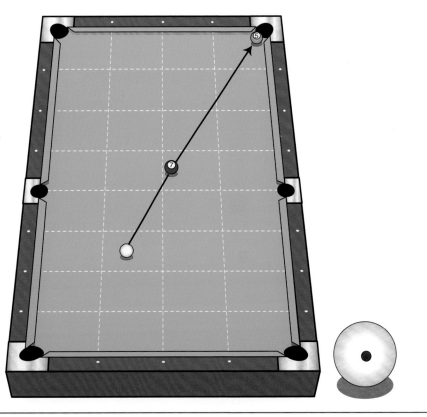

Figure 9.3   Pocketing two balls at once requires careful execution.

Straight In or Rail First?

Like those hangers, another shot that can look deceptively easy is the straight-in shot. It might be your favorite shot to execute (if you've practiced a straight swing), but position options are so limited that landing straight in requires you to do something funny with the cue ball. Sometimes hitting the rail first is the right decision to get out of the predicament.

See figure 9.4 for a pretty common long straight-in shot on the 2-ball, with great potential for a scratch because the cue ball is too close to the cushion for a level draw stroke. Instead of trying this shot, let the cue ball hit the long rail first and then pocket the 2-ball. By shooting the shot this way, you won't scratch and the cue ball will end up off the rail for your next shot. Keeping the cue ball off the rail allows more options to maneuver the cue ball around the table. With a little practice this shot becomes a reliable option (and will definitely impress your friends).

The rail-first option in figure 9.5 allows you resulting cue ball position off the rail, which is especially helpful if the cloth on the table is worn. (When this happens, a trough or gulley forms along the rail, and both object ball and cue ball seem to settle into the groove.) The shot appears tough, but it's not as difficult as you think. You need only to hit the cue ball with some inside english (center to slightly high works best). For the shot shown, you'd use left english with medium to soft speed.

Now say we end up straight in on that rail and need to get the cue ball back down table, as shown in figure 9.6. You see this occur often in Nine Ball when a player lands straight in on the 8-ball and must get back down table for the 9-ball (a classic example of thinking only one ball ahead). The trick to pocketing this shot and getting shape is to aim the cue ball with middle-left or low-left english and about a half-ball left of center on the 5-ball. Deflection will occur with the left english, and the rubber cushions will compress, spitting the cue ball back out at the angle you create.

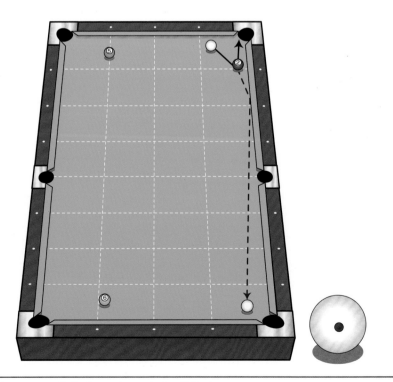

Figure 9.4　Pocketing a potentially hazardous shot rail first.

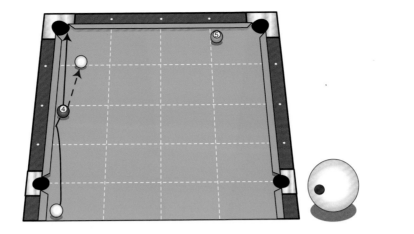

Figure 9.5   Hitting this ball rail first allows for better resulting position.

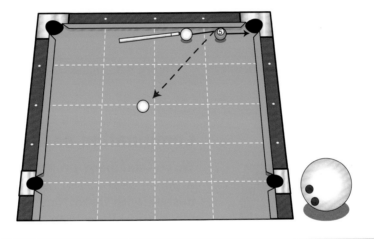

Figure 9.6   Getting all the way back to the other end of the table.

Jump or Kick?

What if the choice is between two difficult critical shots, such as a jump shot or a kick shot? Which shot you're more proficient at is a big part of the consideration. Some pro players never risk jumping a ball and losing control of the cue ball. They'll kick at a buried shot every time. Likewise, players who have mastered jump-shot skills will take to the air rather than risk sending the cue ball one, two, or three rails for the kick. If you're not proficient at either shot, kick at the ball (you're less likely to injure someone!). If you're lucky enough to be proficient at both, let the table dictate your decision.

As an example, the shot shown in figure 9.7 looks like a great opportunity for a jump shot, but look again. A well-struck kick shot not only gets you the hit but probably keeps you at the table. Likewise, in figure 9.8, what looks like a simple kick is better off jumped because you can probably pocket the ball and have your next shot waiting for you as well.

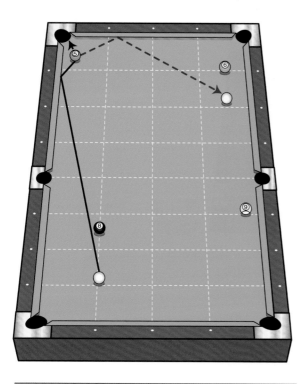

Figure 9.7 Kick or jump? In this case, a kick will do the trick.

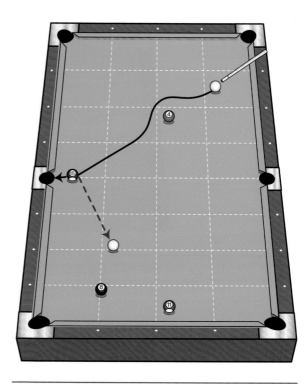

Figure 9.8 In this case, a jump shot is the better option.

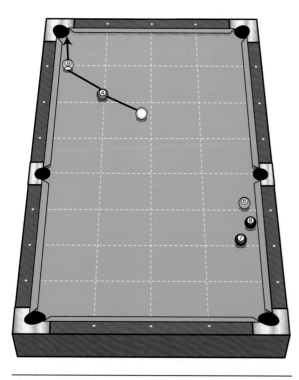

Figure 9.9 Go for the combo; it's the higher percentage shot.

Combination or Run-Out?

We've seen many pros go astray with this one. A player gets ball in hand after an opponent's mistake with three, four, or five balls left on the table, and rather than run the balls, he or she goes for a low-percentage combination shot on the 9-ball to try to win the game with one shot. Now there are times when that's the right play, such as when any of the remaining balls are laying funny or are tied up, or if the combination shows little distance between the two target balls and the pocket.

See figure 9.9 for a good option for a combination shot. Even with ball in hand there's no easy way to get a decent shot on the 6-ball, so a combination on the 4-ball and 9-ball looks pretty good for the win. A lower percentage option for a combination is shown in figure 9.10. With all the balls wide open, why go for the 6-ball–9-ball combo when an easy layout is ripe for the picking? The quick win is nice, but if the balls are wide open, exercise some patience and play for the run. Balls hanging in the pockets and easy combinations are the exception to the rule.

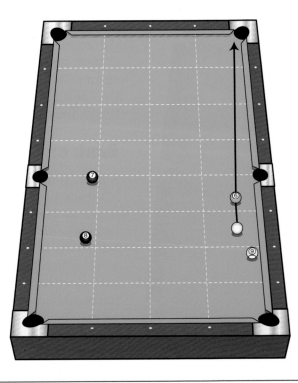

Figure 9.10 Don't risk a low-percentage combo when a run-out is the better option.

OFFENSE VERSUS DEFENSE

The trouble with becoming proficient at some critical shots is that we can become blind to the smarter play. When it's better to lay low and play safe, we try the low-percentage crowd pleaser. Like it or not (and we've come by the lesson the hard way), pool is more about what's probable than what's possible. Let's look at some more situations in which the decision depends on the higher percentage shot.

Combo, Carom, or Safety?

If you're a whiz at combination shots (some players are naturals at them), then by all means go for the shot. If the mere thought of adding a ball to the simple cue-ball-to-target-ball and target-ball-to-pocket theme gives you the willies, then the safety shown in figure 9.11 will have you giving up the table. But if you try it, you'll likely have a better chance to return to the table with ball in hand to play the rack your way.

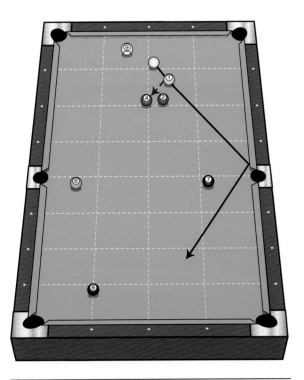

Figure 9.11 A well-played safety can get you back to a better table layout.

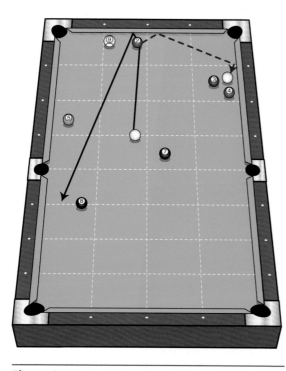

Figure 9.12 Safety or carom? That depends on your comfort zone.

Figure 9.12 demonstrates that a carom on the 9-ball is a pretty good choice, but if you're not proficient at carom shots, opt for a safety. Missing the carom likely gives your opponent the victory.

Bank or Cut?

Again, part of your decision on whether to cut or bank should be based on your strengths. If you have trouble with long cut shots but can bank balls all day long, then you have no dilemma. But if all things are equal, your decision will be made based on the resulting position of the cue ball to get to next shot or the resulting position of the cue ball should you miss. In figure 9.13 the ball can be cut, as shown with the red solid arrow, but doing so leaves you in tough shape for the 9-ball (see red dashed arrow).

Banking the ball, as shown with the black arrow, allows a stop shot for an easier shot on the game ball.

Conversely, figure 9.14 shows how the bank shot (red arrow) might be a sell-out shot, whereas the long cut (black arrow) offers a better resulting position (blue dashed arrow) and a tougher shot for your opponent should you miss. Nobody wants to think in terms of "what if I miss?" but playing the percentages on which shot will yield the most predictable results will keep you at the table.

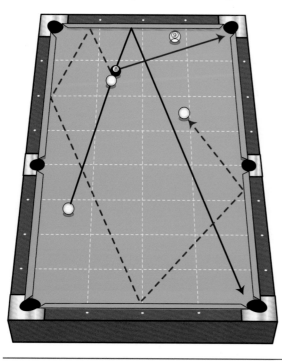

Figure 9.13 A thin cut is possible; a bank is better.

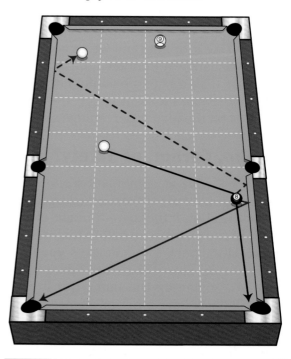

Figure 9.14 Play the percentages: Go for the thin cut.

Bank or Safety?

A bank shot is the more thrilling choice, but a safety might keep you in the game. Figure 9.15 shows a shot that comes up often. The bank just isn't feasible here (though too many players try it anyway, either selling out to the side or corner pocket), so it's much better to play a safety that puts the maximum distance between the 8-ball and the cue ball. Let the other player make the mistake.

The key to this safety is to control both balls, which requires that you practice this shot to get a feel for the right speed. Use a half-ball hit on the 8-ball with a touch of low-outside english. Move the object ball to different places on the long rail for additional prac-

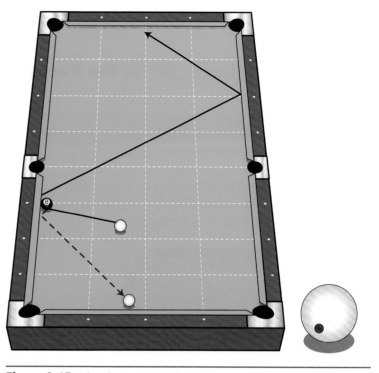

Figure 9.15 A safety is the safer bet.

tice, aiming always to have the cue ball land on the center of the short rail and the target ball on the opposite rail.

Safety Timing: Now or Later?

In Nine Ball the primary choices have been made for us—or have they? Say a rack, like the one shown in figure 9.16, looks like it's going to present later trouble. You know right after the break that a safety is the right move. Unfortunately, no such possibility exists on the 1-ball or 2-ball. Players tend to rush through these, or worse, optimistically think they can do something crazy once they get to the 3-ball. But the stealth move here is obvious. Shot A is to pocket the 1-ball in the low left corner pocket. Shot B is to pocket the 2-ball into the side pocket and send the cue ball toward the 3-ball. Your next shot will be to bury the cue ball behind the 5-ball and drive the 3-ball at least three rails. This leaves your opponent a very tough kick indeed. Safeties are always a good

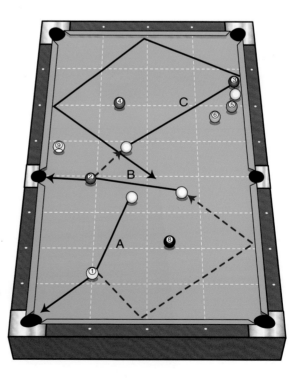

Figure 9.16 Patience is important: A well-timed safety will bring you back to a neater table.

decision if you can't get further through the rack—but only if you wait for the right opportunity.

Ball in Hand: Go for the Run or the Foul?

If you have the opportunity to three-foul a player, is this better than going for the run-out? (See chapter 10 for more on this dilemma.) This is where an honest assessment of your strengths versus your opponent's strengths comes into play. Many good players have made the mistake of playing a substandard safety with their opponent on two fouls, assuming they'll win or at least get another shot at the table. The thing is, they already have control of the table, so why give it up?

If your opponent is on two fouls, you should go for the three-foul win in situations like the one shown in figure 9.17. Here you can really bury the cue ball and send the target ball away from the pack. Even if your opponent gets a hit, you've now broken out a ball and likely made it easier to accomplish a run-out on your next turn. If not, you still have another safety option available to you.

Then there are those times when the balls just don't open up after the break. In figure 9.14 (page 172), your opponent broke the balls, and the cue ball flew into the side pocket. There's no possible way to run the rack, so you need to show patience here. Using the concept of controlling both balls, you would drive the 1-ball into the right edge of the 2-ball and park the cue ball behind the 6-ball. This simple shot, shown in figure 9.18, makes it difficult for your opponent to hit even the 1-ball and opens up the cluster for your next time at the table.

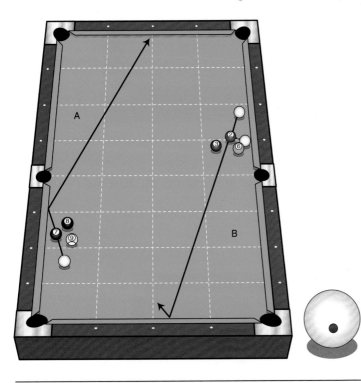

Figure 9.17   A safety is the better option.

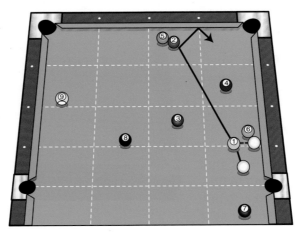

Figure 9.18   Controlling both balls when the balls are clustered.

POSITION DECISIONS

We told you in our earlier discussions of position and pattern play to let the table be your guide, and we stand by that. But, yes, there will be times when a decision seems like a toss-up and you're stymied on which way to execute a shot. Here are some situations that will keep you thinking critically in your decision making at the table.

Long or Short?

Watch a player like Allison Fisher and you'll learn something right away about playing patterns. Her matches against many of the rest of the top women (or men, for that matter) are nearly flawless because of one very simple principle: She never turns the cue ball loose. She always has a destination in mind.

Why is this important? Well, for one thing, there's less margin for error. Dragging the cue ball around the table prevents it from rolling, and as we know, a round object that's pushed or dragged is easier to control than one that's rolling. The choice, when you've got one, is always the shortest distance between two points. In figure 9.19, holding the cue ball close with a drag shot allows you position on the 6-ball that's actually perfect to get you to the 7-ball. The cue ball moves only a few inches, which makes for less chance to come up short or go too far on this shot.

Then again, longer can be better for optimal position, especially if you have one or two rails to take speed off the cue ball and the position to the shot is natural. In figure 9.20, trying to go one rail and back down for the 6-ball isn't nearly as effective as the more natural two- or three-rail option. Yes, it's twice the distance, but it comes into the angle of the next shot more naturally and allows a bigger margin for error.

photo by Garry Hodges

Multiple world champion Allison Fisher has broken every record thanks to careful position play.

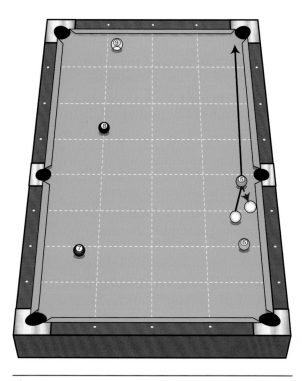

Figure 9.19 A drag shot keeps the cue ball close for optimal position.

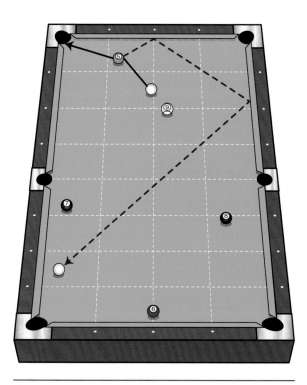

Figure 9.20 Here, sending the cue ball a longer distance is smart.

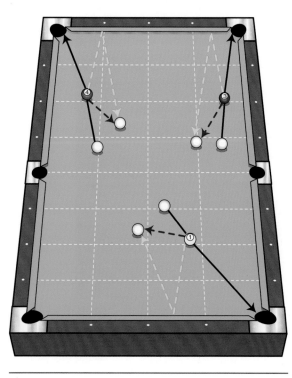

Figure 9.21 Moving the cue ball less distance.

Forward or Back?

This falls into the same category as questions like "high or low?" and "follow or draw?" When we can't use center ball, our first decision is usually whether to move the cue ball forward after contact with the object ball or move it backward.

Our long versus short discussion applies here. Most often, you'll want to go for the shot that sends the cue ball on the shortest path to its next destination. Many players repeat the same mistake, taking what they think will be the easier follow stroke route up and down the table rather than dragging the cue ball back a much shorter distance. Take a look at the examples in figure 9.21. These are three easy shots to learn that come up often. Note how you can get to the same spot using follow (yellow dashed arrows) or draw (blue dashed arrows), but the obvious choice is the one that moves the cue ball much less distance.

Players all too often take the longer route and risk losing cue ball control and position when they could have landed so easily in the right spot. Typically, this is caused by fear in controlling the speed of a draw shot. In figure 9.22 we show resulting positions for three target balls after pocketing the 1-ball with a draw shot. The blue dashed arrow shows ideal position on the 2-ball. The red dashed arrow is for the 3-ball, and the black dashed arrow is for the 8-ball. This illustration doubles as an effective exercise for your draw stroke to eliminate any fear you might have in controlling the speed of your cue ball. A little lower on the cue ball without any additional force generates more distance from your draw stroke. But remember to keep that stroke smooth and level for the best results with the least amount of effort.

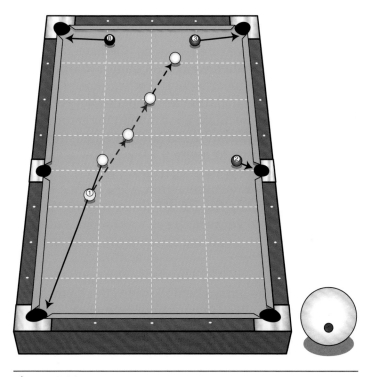

Figure 9.22   Controlling the speed of the cue ball is imperative to decision making.

Around or Through?

So many games are lost on poor decisions in this area, it's hard to know where to begin. Unfortunately, the right answer usually flies in the face of all we've talked about keeping the traveling distance of your cue ball to a minimum.

This is a time when common sense should prevail. A little math helps as well. Play the percentages. If you're looking at a shot like the one shown in figure 9.23, the option that moves the cue ball the least is shot A. However, the problem is that by just cinching the 1-ball into the side pocket, you're leaving yourself a bad angle on your 2-ball to get any kind of good shot on the 3-ball. That's why the best shot selection (shot B) is to drive the cue ball around three rails, going into the angle on the 2-ball that gives you the best way to get position on the 3-ball in the corner. Moving your cue ball around the traffic is sometimes your best option to continue your run-out, even if it means more distance.

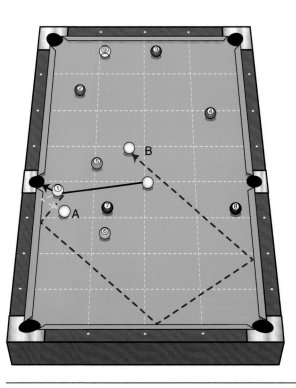

Figure 9.23   Sometimes you need to maneuver the cue ball around traffic.

Which Way to Miss?

As we've often said, no one likes to miss a shot or position. But it happens, especially when we're executing a low-percentage shot. We've discussed missing a ball to the safer side, but what about missed position? The most helpful hint we can give you in this case, especially if you're not yet confident with your speed control, is to calculate your margin for error before you shoot.

Again, we're not being pessimistic here, just trying to increase your chances for success. In figure 9.24, we show a shot in which coming too far with the cue ball will get you in big trouble, but coming up short is really OK. Pocket this 1-ball and land anywhere within a few inches of the rail coming out, and you'll be fine. But traveling too far will leave you buried. As you prepare to take this shot on, you'd say to yourself, "I can't go too far, but not far enough will be OK." That will prevent you from hitting the shot too hard and winding up with no shot on the 2-ball in the corner.

Figure 9.25 illustrates the opposite. If you come up short on this shot, you risk being buried behind traffic. But if you hit it a little harder than necessary, you'll still be right in line for your next shot. The red dashed arrow in the diagram indicates the danger area for the cue ball to land. The blue dashed arrow indicates the entire generous distance of the track you can land on and still be in good shape for the 3-ball in the side pocket, with the easiest subsequent position on the 4-ball.

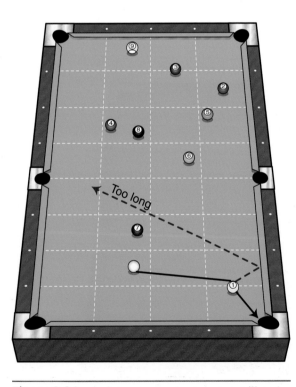

Figure 9.24 As long as you aim smart, you'll end up OK if you miss.

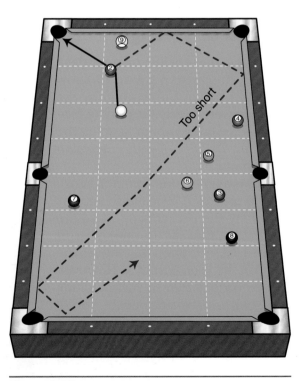

Figure 9.25 Planning ahead allows you to remain in line for the next shot.

WHICH WAY IS WHICH?

No matter how long we play or how much we practice or how much we love pool, we're never going to make the right decisions 100 percent of the time. Frankly, the game would quickly get boring if we did. Likewise, no one can possibly anticipate all the decisions that can be made for even a single match; it would take an entire book of these diagrams to outline all the possibilities. Yes, pool can be that creative. Here's where your practice comes in. Before you get into an actual competitive situation, you have the opportunity to practice all of these either-or situations to your heart's content.

Dodge the Bullet: Avoid the Sneaky Scratch

A costly scratch can lose a game or match. With six 4.5-inch pockets on a pool table, there's over two feet of cliff your cue ball can fall off at any time. Because you know the pockets will always be there, the best way to avoid accidentally falling into them is to keep the cue ball a safe distance away.

See figure 9.26 for a shot that comes up often. This shot can kill a run because while attempting to just cinch the ball you can easily scratch in the bottom right corner pocket. To avoid this, use a touch of inside english to bring the cue ball to the long right rail. Experiment with the speed you need to execute this shot. It might save you some games.

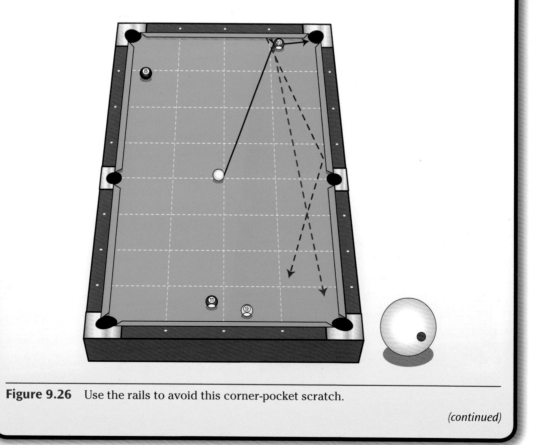

Figure 9.26 Use the rails to avoid this corner-pocket scratch.

(continued)

(continued)

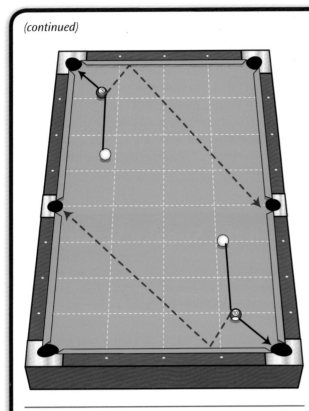

Figure 9.27 It's important to pay attention to the cue ball's angle coming off the short rail to avoid this common scratch.

The side-pocket scratch is another common way to kill a run, especially when you're shooting at the game ball and paying less attention to the cue ball's destination (although you should know better!).

In figure 9.27 we show the most common side-pocket scratch of all: the one-rail-into-the-side scratch. It's a heartbreaker. To avoid it, pay close attention to the cue ball's angle coming off the short rail. Choose a destination for the cue ball to hit the second rail instead of going in the side pocket. Visualize that spot and hit the cue ball accordingly.

Figure 9.28 illustrates an even sneakier scratch. You pocket a fairly easy shot into the side pocket, planning to come around the table for the 8-ball, and *bam!* You get nailed by the two-rail scratch. On this shot, instead of a center-ball hit, use a touch of inside english (in this case left english) to shorten the angle coming off the second rail and bring the cue ball down table.

If you can avoid these sneaky one- and two-rail scratches, you'll stay much longer at the table.

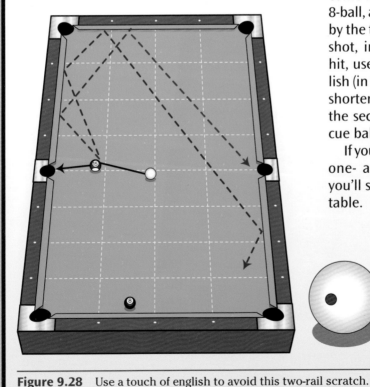

Figure 9.28 Use a touch of english to avoid this two-rail scratch.

When faced with an either-or decision in practice, make sure you take the opportunity to try the shot both ways and see which shot works better. For added fun, take a shot you think should be played only one way, and try something new—just to see what possibilities might exist that you'd otherwise overlook.

Practice for pool players isn't just about developing your physical talents. It's also about accumulating kernels of knowledge so that when tough situations arise in a match, you're ready for them. You have the confidence to make decisions because you've been there before and know what works for you. As you continue to practice you'll also find that fewer either-or situations come up. As you practice the keys and concepts we've presented in these chapters, your brain learns to critically think its way through patterns without having to consciously pick its way through so many choices. What once seemed a perplexing "what do I do here?" problem becomes a matter of applying what you've learned and heading in the most practical direction.

CHAPTER 10

Match Strategy and Tactics

Beyond the intricacies of pattern and safety play, beyond the myriad of decisions you're in charge of making on each turn at the table, hundreds of advanced game situations also exist, situations you should be prepared for if you plan on any sort of regular competition. Whether you're playing local, regional, or professional tournaments, or organized league play, the nature of competition changes the game from one of trying to play one's personal best, to trying to, as they say in the TV show *Survivor*, outplay, outwit, and outlast your opponent. In this chapter we cover little tricks of the trade that don't get much publicity but are imperative for a well-rounded pool game. These include knowing when to roll out or take an intentional foul, winning games via the three-foul rule, using an opponent's strengths and weaknesses to your best advantage, and employing team strategy.

In each case, the knowledge we're sharing with you is perfectly fair and legal. We're not proponents of shark moves or unsportsmanlike behavior at the pool table. A win is only a win if you've accomplished it on a level playing field. There's no voodoo here, no cheating, no shortcuts. However, advanced strategy and tactics might provide more of an edge in your competitive play than you ever thought possible. This can happen simply by knowing rules and key elements of the game that your opponents might not have taken the time to learn or incorporate into their games.

ASSESSING YOUR OPPONENT

Assessing the strengths and weaknesses of your opponent can influence your game plan as you prepare for a match. For example, in one women's pro tournament, Shari was preparing for a match against a player to whom she had recently lost. Her coach advised that the best strategy against this player was a game laden heavily with safety play. "If you don't have a shot, duck!"

Shari's coach had watched her opponent play a couple of other matches and noticed that, when confronted with a safety, she had very little talent kicking at balls, giving up ball in hand on virtually every kick attempt. The result? Despite less than stellar play, Shari defeated this player with a couple of ball-in-hand opportunities that she wouldn't have planned had she not known this player's weakness.

Now you might not have the advantage of a great coach, but you'll often have a chance to watch other players whom you will at some time be matched up against.

This is especially true if you play local events on a regular basis. Take the time to watch their games. Do they avoid long shots? Have problems kicking at balls? Trouble with banks? Once you start playing tournaments regularly, you might even want to keep a notebook to consult before each match.

Don't ever assume, however, that because your opponent has a certain weakness you will automatically win the match. We've seen otherwise excellent players focusing so much on what opponents are doing the first few games that they distract themselves from their own games. Worse, we've seen players underestimate opponents and subsequently take low-percentage shots, assuming they'll surely get another chance at the table. No matter who you're playing, never assume you'll get a reprieve inning at the table, unless of course you're playing a safety.

This leads us to a major rule in the cue games: Play the table! Always play the rack as if it's your one chance to win the game. This keeps you physically and mentally ready, no matter what the skill level of your next opponent. While it's to your advantage to know your opponent's game, once you step to the match, you'll need to focus on your game and play the table. When it's your turn at the table, nothing else matters—just you, that table, and the task at hand.

Because of the challenging nature of the sport, pool is probably one of the best games for bringing out competitive spirit in players. Excellence in pool requires tremendous physical control and mental discipline. Pool is an individual, noncontact sport, but at the same time you're playing the table, you are immersed in combat against your opponent. Yes, it's important both to assess your opponent and to play the table, but the most common mistake made by players is to incorrectly gauge the level of their competition and change their game accordingly. Remember there's a very fine line between an excellent player and an above-average player. If you take your opponent lightly, not giving him or her the respect deserved, even a player with far less skill can best you.

Assessing your opponent comes with another caution: Don't let the opposition change your game. All too often when playing against quick-firing offensive players, slower-paced, well-rounded players make the huge mistake of playing their opponents' game instead of their own, speeding up and taking chances they would never take in their usual play. Assess your opponents, but don't mimic them! Doing so will throw off your game plan, your rhythm, your timing, and the confidence you bring to the table with your own game. Similarly, we've seen players play very slow opponents and, without realizing it, speed up their own game to compensate for the time their subconscious perceives is being wasted in the match. Pace yourself at the speed of play you're comfortable with, regardless of your opponent's play.

FACING TOUGH COMPETITION

Let's change the scenario a bit. You're playing in a local tournament, and you have just discovered that your next match is against John, the club's house pro. John not only dominates the local scene but has fared well in several recent pro events also. You might be feeling a little doom and gloom because this is only your second tournament, and one more win would have put you into the money rounds. In such a case, be aware that you have a couple of advantages over your opponent—advantages that might even catapult you into the winner's circle.

First, you're an unknown quantity. You haven't played John before, and he doesn't know your game, though you've watched him play plenty of times. Plus, you have

Photo by Lustig/Matchroom Sport

The UK's Raj Hundal shows his focus and determination when facing tough competition.

nothing to lose. John does. John is expected to win. You're actually in a great spot because you can relax and just have fun. John might have a harder time doing this. If you win, great. If you don't, then appreciate the experience of playing a better player; you can measure how you fare against him and take away lessons to apply in your next match.

What happens when you're matched up against an opponent with a reputation? If you're like most people, you tend to give the player more credit than he or she deserves. When you place players above their ability level, it takes away from your own game. You begin anticipating what's going to happen, often predicting an unfavorable outcome. Now's a time when you have to play your game, play the table, and forget who your opponent is. We've all fallen into the trap of playing the opponent and not the table. But all players' games would improve if they concentrated on their own skills. When you compete, don't take a win over an opponent for granted, but also don't overestimate the talent of higher-echelon players. Find your even keel by playing the table.

Another great quality to develop when facing tough competition is tenacity. Be a bulldog. Never give up. You could be down 8–1 in a race to 9. It doesn't matter. We've seen countless matches in which players have been that far in the hole and come back to win. And we've seen players who, after being up 8–1, completely lost their mental toughness as their opponent came back on them. Some players fold, but players who are mentally tough never fold. They want to defeat their opponents as quickly as possible. This attitude comes from developing mental toughness through practice and experience.

Try to remain focused on the game better than your opponents do. It doesn't matter what they do, or what they leave you with, or if they run five straight racks. Stay focused. Play your own game when it's your turn. This can be difficult to do at first. Most matches contain at least a small degree of psychological warfare. The toughest part of the game is to watch while your opponent runs racks and gets great rolls. You're sitting in the chair and can do nothing about it. But rather than get frustrated or throw a tantrum (which too many players do), you're better off showing no emotion at all. This will get into your opponents' heads. They'll wonder, *what's he thinking about?* or *isn't she worried?* A tough mental attitude wears opponents done and gives you the edge.

That's the mental side of it. Now what can you do physically to improve your chances? Eight Ball is an excellent game from which to draw examples of physical changes you might make in your game depending on the skill level of your opponent. The game of Eight Ball so often comes down to timing, which is nothing more than knowing when to try to run out. If you're playing a weaker player, chances are good that he or she won't run out but will clear off three or four balls and leave you a wide-open table.

The stiffer the competition, the sooner you must attempt to run out because the better player will be doing the same thing. In most league Eight Ball competition today, organizers have made it crucial for players to run out as early as possible because the number of balls opponents leave on the table dictates the score. Though it's probably better to play for the game win than ball by ball, the rules have evolved for the sake of saving time. Scoring strictly by game wins and losses means a lot more games go into overtime as players get accustomed to winning via long and tedious safety battles. With the evolved rules, every ball counts. So when you're playing a skilled opponent, you must take maximum advantage of your inning at the table.

All things being equal, if two players are evenly matched, the outcome usually comes down to who's psychologically stronger. The player who plays the strategically sound game is in a better position to win. For example, if it's prudent to play a safety in a match situation, the person with better strategy *will* play the safety. A player with weaker strategic skills might take the flyer or try something off the wall in a desperate attempt to create something that isn't there. These are the decisions that come back to haunt you.

You'll develop sound strategy most quickly by facing tough competition over and over again. Building mental toughness and becoming aware of certain shots and situations is a process that takes time. The more you play, the tougher you become. The tougher you become, the more matches you'll win. You'll develop mental calluses that enable you to shake off tense situations, surrounding distractions, and the pressure of knowing what's at stake.

USING ROLLOUTS TO YOUR ADVANTAGE

The rollout refers to an option after the break in Nine Ball. Its use or misuse can vastly change the outcome of a game. The reasoning for implementing the rollout rule was that the first shot after the break was the one shot that both players could be unwittingly penalized by. For example, the player breaking the balls pockets nothing on the break, but the balls come to rest in such a way that the opponent has no shot at the lowest numbered ball on the table. The breaking player is unfairly rewarded for a poor break. A player could break badly, make no balls, sit down, and watch his opponent suffer with absolutely no shot. At the same time, the player could accomplish a great break, pocket two balls, and suddenly the cue ball is kissed to a point on the table where the designated object ball can't be hit.

Putting the Rollout to Work

To avoid situations like the one just described, on the first shot after the break, either player (depending on who's at the table) can roll the cue ball to another position without hitting the lowest-numbered ball and without committing a foul. You may hit a rail, but you don't have to. You may pocket a ball. You may use the shot to tie up other balls.

For example, let's say you're at the table and it's your break. You break the balls and make a ball but wind up with a very difficult shot on the 1-ball. You now have the option to roll out (i.e., shoot the cue ball) to a spot where you think you would have the advantage over your opponent. Your opponent then has the choice to take the shot you've left, invent a safety of his or her own, or hand the shot back to you, in which case you must shoot again. In either case, whether the opponent elects to take the shot or hands it back, a legal shot must now be hit.

Many players are unfamiliar with the full impact the rollout can have on a game and its most effective strategic uses. In fact, the rollout is an incredibly useful tactic to set up a shot that you're more capable of making than your opponent is. If he or she banks poorly, simply roll out to a bank. If he or she has a miserable time with long shots, roll out a shot long. If you're playing a better player, you'll usually find that there's more safety play early in the rack, whereas against a weaker player, more safeties occur later in the rack. This makes the rollout very important when you're playing a strong player. Make one crucial mistake in the beginning of the rack, and your opponent will run out; or he or she will turn the tables on you to a point where you'll be kicking two or three rails to get a hit on the object ball. In this case, your best bet might be to roll out with a safety in mind should your opponent pass the shot back.

If you wish to roll out to a safety, you need to use your imagination and visualize what you want to accomplish before you roll out. Know where to put the cue ball, and know what you'll do with the shot if your opponent gives it back to you. Never just bump the cue ball to where you can see the object ball. Without a plan, your careless rollout could prove disastrous.

A good rollout at the beginning of the game is like a well-executed move in chess. It involves strategy, predicting what your opponent will do, and alternative plans should he or she do the unexpected. If your opponent has the shot and rolls out to a certain area of the table, you have several quick considerations:

1. What is your opponent trying to do?
2. Does he or she have the ability to execute the shot that has been left?
3. Can he or she execute the shot with efficiency and proceed through the rack?

If the answer to questions 2 and 3 is yes, then you're forced to play the shot.

Rollout Tricks of the Trade

It's important to know how to roll out to your best advantage, and it's equally important to know how to react to a rollout shot that's left for you. We've seen the following techniques used to great advantage.

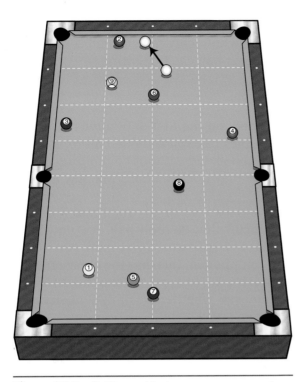

Figure 10.1 Rolling out to leave your opponent a longer shot.

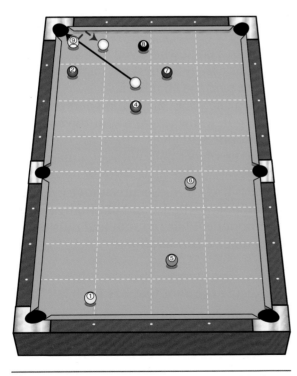

Figure 10.2 Best move here? Pocket the 9-ball with your rollout.

Adding Distance

First, if all else is equal, the longer the distance you put between the cue ball and the object ball, the greater the degree of difficulty. A difficult long shot, with the added limitation of having little control over the cue ball for the next shot, will make things tricky for your opponent. If he or she takes the flyer, so much the better for you. If he or she passes it back, make sure you have a safety attempt already in mind. Figure 10.1 shows such an example. By rolling the cue ball near the rail, you've left your opponent long and nearly straight on the 1-ball. (Try never to freeze the cue ball to a rail.) This is a difficult shot, but your opponent might try it anyway. Even if the shot is made, what's he or she going to do with the 2-ball?

Looking Ahead

Let's say your opponent decides to roll out to the straight-in shot. These happen to be your favorite shots, so you jump up to attack. Again, the problem here is that your next object ball is at the other end of the table. You always need to ascertain exactly where the balls are on the table and if the shot you have confidence in making actually has any future in it. In this particular situation, it doesn't. There's no way to get back on the next ball. You're much better off playing a safety off the object ball (in this case, the 1-ball), rather than attempting to pocket the ball and draw the cue ball the length of the table or cheat the pocket and follow the length of the table. By taking the safety, you can maintain control of the table without passing the shot back. Focus on giving your opponent a miserable situation to contend with. Because there's no longer a choice involved—he or she must shoot.

In our next situation, shown in figure 10.2, you break the rack, make a ball, and nearly pocket the 9-ball, leaving it hanging precariously on the lip. Worse still, you can't see the 1-ball, and there's no place to roll out to that won't result in your opponent banking the 1-ball into the 9-ball, or making the 1-ball and then a 2-ball–9-ball combination. You'd be surprised how often such situations come up; players execute a poor rollout, hoping they'll get back to the table. That seldom happens. Your best maneuver here is to pocket the 9-ball and roll the cue ball to a spot where you can see the 1-ball. In Nine Ball, all balls stay down except the 9-ball, which will be brought back to the foot spot. This move might be even better if there are other balls near the spot to create a difficult cluster for your opponent.

Creating Clusters

This brings us to another good rollout maneuver: creating clusters with other balls. When creating a cluster, you always want to put the lowest-numbered ball of the group closer to the pocket (see figure 10.3). You're playing from the right corner pocket, and there are a couple of balls in the vicinity. You can tie up the 3-ball and 5-ball, with the 3-ball closer to the right corner pocket than the 5-ball. This creates all kinds of problems for your opponent. If you put the 5-ball closer to the pocket, he or she might have a carom or combination shot, or a safety opportunity that can also open the cluster. Remember, too, to have a safety option in mind for the 1-ball because you might be asked to shoot again.

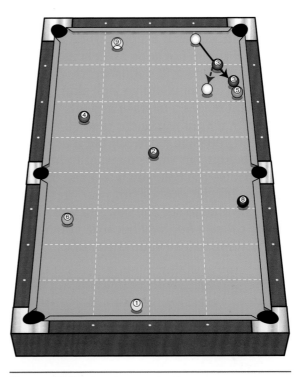

Figure 10.3 Another good rollout maneuver: creating clusters.

Speed Control

Speed control is an important factor in your rollout skills. Careless speed control can leave your opponent a run-out opportunity or leave you in an even less desirable position should the shot be handed back to you. Creating clusters is one example of this because careful speed control results in a cluster, whereas too hard a hit can break up the balls and make a run easier for your opponent. Another example is when you're trying just to roll the cue ball a few inches to a certain spot on the table near a cushion. In this case you're not trying to freeze the cue ball on the cushion. If you do land the cue ball too close to the rail, your opponent will likely give you the shot. It's much harder to execute a shot with the cue ball frozen on the cushion.

Rolling Out to a Jump Shot

As you learned in chapter 5 on critical shots, the jump shot was once a rare shot and a very strong move for those players who could do it well. These players could roll out to a jump shot, and their opponents were usually glad to hand the shot back to them. With the advent of today's jump cues, this maneuver no longer works. Many players can jump balls quite proficiently. Nevertheless, if the jump shot is one of your strong areas, it's worth a try. If your opponent opts to give the shot back, you've learned that you can use the move again in the match because he or she is clearly not fond of the shot. If your opponent does elect to take the shot, and fails, you still have the option of using the move. The next time it comes up, your opponent, now lacking confidence in the shot, might opt to give it back to you, which would be to your advantage.

Rolling Out to a Kick Shot

Rolling out to a kick shot presents a similar scenario. Many of today's players are quite adept at kicking at balls. If opponents are strong in this area, chances are they won't just kick to legally hit the ball. They'll attempt to hit the hidden ball on one side or the other, driving it away from the cue ball and leaving you with a safety in return. Those same accomplished kicking artists will roll out to kick shots themselves. If you're not good at kicking balls, you're going to have to give up that shot to your opponent. It's thus worthwhile to improve your skills in this area. If you can't execute an effective kick shot, you'll have to give up the shot, hoping your opponent makes a mistake and lets you back to the table.

Finally, if your opponent is weak in the rollout game and rolls out to a position in which you have a difficult but makeable shot, take the option to do so. The shot might be tougher than you want to handle, but plan ahead. Play the shot so that if you do miss the ball, you won't sell out the rack. If you make it, great. If not, you'll leave a difficult shot or put your opponent in a tough position in which he or she won't be able to see the ball and will have to play a miraculous shot. This is commonly called a *free shot* because you have a great deal to gain if you make the shot and nothing to lose should you miss.

photo by Jerry Forsyth

BCA Hall of Famer Efren "The Magician" Reyes is world renowned for the accuracy of his kick shots.

USING FOULS TO YOUR ADVANTAGE

A foul means scratching the cue ball or not contacting the proper ball or group of balls first. In Nine Ball and some Eight Ball league rules, a foul by your opponent allows you to place the cue ball anywhere on the table when you take over the table. It's a great advantage, to be sure, but even greater are the tactics behind fouls: how to cause them and how to capitalize on them, even if no run-out opportunity exists.

Three-Foul Rules

Like the rollout, another rule more players should take advantage of is the three-foul rule. Three consecutive fouls by the same player loses the game. This occurs most often in Nine Ball, though you also see it in Eight Ball in many sanctioned leagues and tournaments. The rule also applies in One Pocket. To take advantage of the three-foul rule, you must pay attention to the game situation at all times. In pro competition you're required to tell opponents they're on two fouls in order to have the third foul result in a loss. Local and regional tournaments sometimes don't have this rule in place. In these instances it's considered proper etiquette to inform opponents that they're on two fouls before they approach the table for their next attempt at a legal hit. Because your opponent might not return the same measure of courtesy to you, pay attention to your own game to avoid being put in this position. For example, you won't want to take an intentional foul if you know you're already on one foul—especially if there are plenty of places your opponent can hide the cue ball to make you foul a third time and lose the game.

Now that we've explained the defensive aspect of the three-foul rule, we'll focus on ways you can capitalize on the offensive strategies involved in the game. Let's begin with the break. If your opponent scratches on the break, or the cue ball leaves the bed of the table during the break, you'll have ball in hand. A scratch on the break usually gives you one of three excellent options. First and most obvious is a run-out. If the balls have spread well and you have the advantage of cue ball in hand to plan the ideal run, by all means do so. Second, having ball in hand might present you with a combination situation, if the lowest numbered ball on the table is close to the 9-ball and in reasonable proximity to a pocket. Third, if neither of these two options looks promising, you have the three-foul option. With most or all of the balls still on the table, it should be pretty easy to play an excellent safety and cause your opponent to foul again. Now he or she is on two fouls and feeling the pressure, and there are still plenty of places to hide. Again, remember to tell opponents that they're on two fouls before they approach the table for their third attempt at a legal hit. Figures 10.4 and 10.5 show an example of a ball-in-hand situation after the break and the two consecutive safeties that will most likely result in a three-foul game win. In the first illustration, you're sending the 1-ball toward the right corner pocket (near the 3-ball and 8-ball), while hiding the cue ball in the 5–6 cluster. If the player gets no hit, you simply send the 1-ball back toward the 5–6 cluster, hiding your cue ball in the 3–8 cluster. By planning your safeties ahead of time, you're better able to capitalize on the three-foul rule.

By now, you understand that having ball in hand gives you no guarantee of running the table. If you have two or three clusters on the table, even with ball in hand you won't be able to tackle them all. It's usually wise in such cases, especially with your opponent already on one foul, to play another safety and let him or her try the kick shot. Even better, with ball in hand, you can often strategically place the

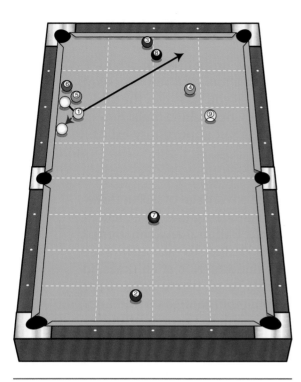

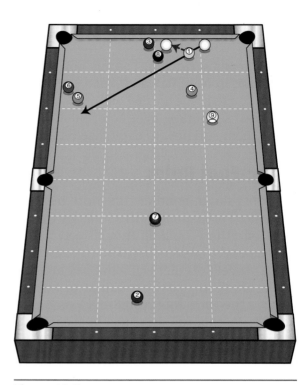

Figure 10.4 The first safety in the three-foul strategy.

Figure 10.5 The second safety in the three-foul strategy.

ball your opponent will be kicking at near one of your problem clusters. Whether or not he or she makes a legal hit, one of the clusters is bound to be broken up, making a run-out more likely for you.

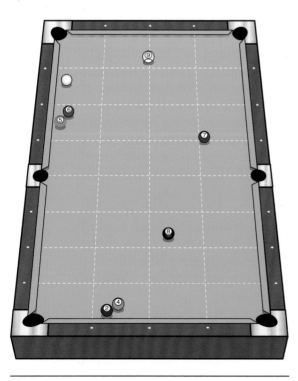

Figure 10.6 Taking an intentional foul.

Intentional Fouls

Sometimes you're better off taking an intentional foul of your own. If the lay of the balls already looks problematic for your opponent, it's probably not prudent to try an impossible kick and risk loosening up the table layout. See figure 10.6 for an example in Nine Ball. The 2-ball and 4-ball are tied up, along with the 5-ball and 6-ball. Even with ball in hand, your opponent won't be able to win the game in the next inning. He or she will have to open up two clusters and leave you safe at the same time. In this situation, strategy dictates that you give your opponent cue ball in hand by simply shooting away, or picking up the cue ball and handing it over.

Resort to the intentional foul only when there's no legitimate shot present to allow you to open up the balls and still get a decent shot on the next ball. Only in such cases will you want to give your opponent ball in hand instead of trying to do something difficult. Trying the

Entering the Competitive Arena

So you've practiced long and hard and are having success against some very tough opponents. You feel you're ready for league and tournament competition. Where do you begin? If your preference is for competition in your local bar, you'll more than likely be playing Eight Ball. If your favorite bar is not already involved in a local league, you have a couple of options. You can try another establishment. Or you can find out what leagues exist in the area and convince the owner of your favorite location to get involved.

Eight Ball leagues come in two basic flavors: independent local leagues and leagues affiliated with a national organization. Independent local leagues are owned and operated by an area player, enthusiast, or club owner. They typically feature a 5- to 7-dollar weekly fee to participate, and tavern owners also pay a fee to host a team. Funds collected are put toward administration (scorekeeping, scheduling, and so on), season-end celebrations, trophies, and sometimes purse money for the highest finishing team. The money is a bonus—if you're looking to make a score, independent leagues won't make you rich quick. But if you're looking for camaraderie, competition, team spirit, and the chance to play competitively on a weekly basis, an independent league might be for you.

Then there are those leagues affiliated with national organizations, such as the BCA Pool Leagues, the Valley National Eightball Association (VNEA), or the American Poolplayers Association (APA). If your local league is affiliated, your team's success could take you on to regional or national competition. These organizations host annual national championships with six-figure purses and feature competition by hundreds of teams who travel to Las Vegas and other destinations to meet up with other teams from across the nation. Events usually contain masters and regular divisions, and some include scotch doubles teams, seniors, juniors, and wheelchair divisions.

If tournament competition better suits your game, most billiard clubs offer some form of weekly (or monthly) scratch or handicap tournaments. Formats will vary, as will the games. Typically, Nine Ball and Eight Ball tournaments are the norm at most clubs, though some host Straight Pool and Three-Cushion billiard tournaments. Many clubs also offer in-house or traveling Eight Ball and Nine Ball leagues, giving patrons the best of both worlds. Our recommendation is round-robin tournaments, which give you the chance to play several different opponents for your entry fee. These run anywhere from $5 to $25, depending on the club. If round-robin tournaments are not available, the next best thing is the double-elimination format. In this type of tournament, you proceed through the winner's bracket until you lose, then move to the one-loss bracket. Two losses and you're out. The eventual winner of the one-loss bracket plays the winner of the winner's bracket for the title. Finally, there are single-elimination events in which you lose once and you're out.

Promotionally minded clubs also host events that are part of larger regional tours, open to amateur and professional players, along with state championships and sometimes even professional events. If you have the opportunity to play in a regional tour or state championship event, take it. You'll get to see quite a few accomplished players, and many of these events are qualifiers for bigger pro status tournaments. Some of the regional tours also offer point formats and rankings, with rewards and recognition to top scorers at season's end. These tournaments occur less regularly (every two to six weeks) and require entry fees from $25 to $65, but they tend to be well operated and offer purse money in excess of what has been put up by the players.

difficult shot likely gives your opponent cue ball in hand anyway, but you risk disturbing the balls and allowing an easier run-out.

Here's yet another way to prevent opponents from running out. Let's say you're left with a very difficult safety; you're well hooked, and you have little or no chance to hit the ball. Apply what you've learned about creating clusters. Attempt to create a cluster with another group of balls so that even if your opponent gets ball in hand, he or she won't be able to run the table in the next inning. Remember to try to place the lowest-numbered ball of the group you're tying up closest to the pocket, making it more difficult for your opponent to break up the cluster.

TEAM STRATEGY

Hundreds of thousands of players compete in sanctioned league competition each year, in addition to hundreds of independent leagues operating across the nation. Team league competition is a huge part of today's recreational cue sports, yet very little has been written about team play or team strategy. The teams who win the big-purse amateur competitions aren't always the best players, but they are the best teams. They know how to capitalize on their strengths and minimize their weaknesses. Careful strategy goes into making them winners, just as in any professional franchised team sport.

The first things to consider in team strategy are the number of players you compete with on a team, what game you're playing, the format of the league, and whom you'll be playing against. Typically, teams are made up of three, four, or five players. In most cases, you may list additional players on your team roster, though they often must be declared when your team signs up. Before the season begins, establish an understanding among teammates that each of you will remain committed to completing the league season. It's frustrating, especially in sanctioned league competition, to lose a key player before qualifying for larger-purse regional and national events.

The majority of league play is Eight Ball, though Nine Ball leagues are picking up steam in some areas of the country. In Eight Ball leagues, because of the strategy involved, if you're trying to put together a winning team, you'll want good strategy players, not just great shot makers. Remember, though, that your first consideration should be to have fun as a team. Picking up a good player who doesn't normally associate with the rest of your team socially will sometimes deflate team morale rather than improve the team as a whole.

OK, so say it's league night, and you're in charge of your team's lineup. Most often, lineups are dictated by who the opponents are in each individual match. There are two schools of thought for creating a lineup. Some believe your stronger players should start, guaranteeing that they'll play more games. The remaining players are ordered according to decreasing skill, with weaker players playing last.

Others believe your stronger players should play last, figuring that when it's crunch time they will have a much better chance of winning the match, particularly if it comes down to the last one or two games. We'd tend to side with those who believe that it's wiser to put the stronger players first, simply because you don't want to take the cue out of their hands. In other words, if you're playing on a five-person team and are down to three or four games left and already far behind, your better players become useless to the point that even their wins can't pull you out. If both teams are packed full of great players, it really doesn't matter what you do. Just keep in mind that the skills of your players often determines the best team strategy.

Warm Up for the Win

Warming up for a big game or match can be one of the most important things you do to ready yourself for play, yet few players know how to really warm up. Warming up is not about practicing (you should have done that before the match). It's not about banging balls around the table, which won't do much to prepare you for the game ahead. It is about preparing to turn in your best performance. Here are four fun drills that we like to use as warm-ups. Some players use these as practice drills between matches as well, so don't be afraid to incorporate them into your regular routine.

Find Center Ball

In chapter 3 we mentioned the importance of finding center ball. Center ball is the baseline against which you gauge all other shots. A fun way to check your hit is shown in figure 10.7. Place an object ball just off the long rail, as shown in shot A, and place the cue ball directly in front of it near the center diamond. Hit the object ball full in the face. If you're using center ball, the result will be a double-kiss, and the cue ball will carom straight back into your cue tip while the object ball stays about where it began. Be sure to stay down on the shot to see where in relation to your cue tip the cue ball rebounds. Once you have mastered the long-rail shot, move to the short-rail shot and then increase the distance between the object ball and the cue ball (see shot B). Once you're comfortable that your body and cue are aligned, move on.

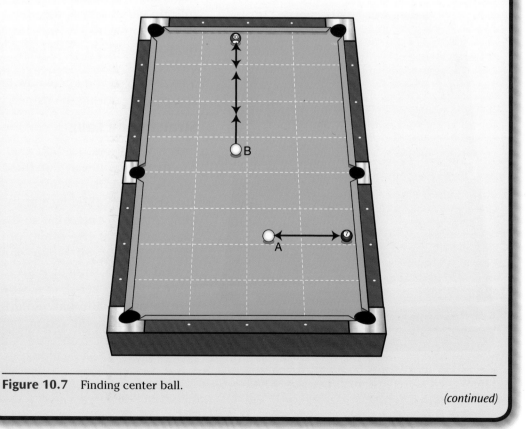

Figure 10.7   Finding center ball.

(continued)

(continued)

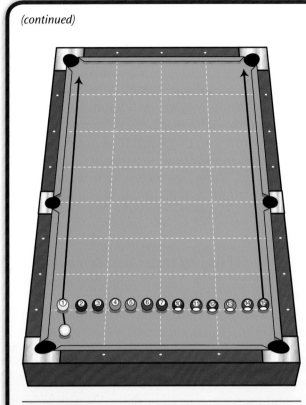

Figure 10.8 Practice pocketing long shots to get a feel for the table.

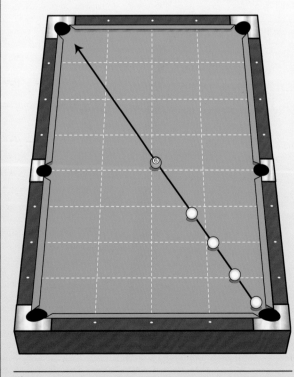

Figure 10.9 Warming up with these straight-in shots will give you instant feed back on your stroke.

Pocket Long Shots

The farther the object ball is from the pocket and the farther the cue ball is from the object ball, the harder the shot becomes. Get a feel for the table you're playing on right from the start with these quick warm-ups. As shown in figure 10.8, you'll place a line of object balls across the first diamond and put the cue ball behind the 1-ball on the end (if you have less warm-up time, include just a few from each side to get a feel for the table). Shoot each ball into the corner pocket, and then take ball in hand and place the cue ball behind the next ball in line for the next shot. Hit center ball with medium speed to keep the object ball on its truest path. This also informs you quickly if the table has bad rolls on either side. If the object ball veers toward or away from the pocket and displays a bad roll on the table, you'll want to shoot a few more so you know how to compensate during the game.

Straight and Long

Figure 10.9 shows a simple exercise that lets you warm up those tough, straight-in shots and increase your confidence at the table. Place an object ball in the exact center of the table; put the cue ball about a diamond behind it on a straight path to the corner pocket. Use a stop shot to pocket the ball. Return the object ball to the center, but each time position the cue ball farther away, a ball's width or so, until the last shot has you deep into the opposite corner pocket.

Remember to avoid the peeking temptation imposed by long shots; stay down on the shot until you hear the ball drop in the pocket. This warm-up offers instant feedback on which way your stroke is moving, allowing you to make subtle adjustments before the game begins.

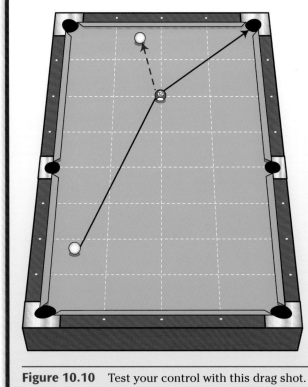

It's a Drag

You saw in chapter 5 how valuable the drag shot can be to good position play, so make sure to dust it off and have it ready for your match. Figure 10.10 provides a great exercise featuring a simple stop shot to help you get in stroke. Place an object ball on the foot spot and the cue ball just behind the headstring about a half a diamond out from the rail. Pocket the ball in the corner using a solid drag shot, and try to keep the cue ball from hitting the bottom rail.

Figure 10.10   Test your control with this drag shot.

As you've seen, there are plenty of tactics and strategies involved in the cue sports, especially at the competitive level. Extensive knowledge of these requires practice and keen attention when you do compete. Always ask yourself if there's a better option than the obvious first choice, especially when you're in a tough spot. The more you experiment, the more tactics you'll develop to improve your game, and more options will become second nature to you.

CHAPTER 11

Mind–Body Toughness

Think for a moment about why you want to play better. The reasons might be many and varied, but chances are they center on one of three primary motivations. You might play for the competition aspect, because you enjoy defeating opponents. You might play for financial gain in tournament or league competitions. Or you might play to play the table; in other words, you play for the sheer beauty of the game and its intricacies.

Option three is clearly the best reason to play and compete. Playing the table makes you the best player you can be. If there's any one concept about the cue sports that should be ingrained into the brain of newcomers to the sport, this would be it. If you continually learn and exceed your goals at the pool table, everything else naturally follows. The game of pool should be enjoyed. If you have somehow lost the enjoyment, try taking a break from the game for a while. We're confident it will return.

In this chapter we'll deal with attaining and exceeding your goals of high-performance pool playing through mental and physical training. You'll learn to concentrate, to develop your skills of mental imaging (crucial to position play), and to improve your physical skills with increased power and coordination. In the words of the Dalai Lama, "To train the mind, you must exercise the patience and determination it takes to shape that steel."

MENTAL TRAINING TECHNIQUES

Playing great pool involves a complex web of mental and physical coordination. Dr. Robert M. Nideffer, in his classic *Athletes' Guide to Mental Training* (1985), has this to say on the subject:

> As a sport, billiards is much like archery in terms of both attention demands and the demands for control over muscle tension and coordination. A typical attentional sequence involves assessing the situation, including position of the balls on the table, game score, skill level of the opponent. Then, information is analyzed and a shot is planned. Next, attention is directed internally as the shot is rehearsed and as tension levels are adjusted and breathing controlled. Finally, attention narrows and becomes focused on the point that allows the player to stroke the ball in the desired manner. The athlete's analysis must allow the ability to think several shots ahead. (p. 139)

All the mental and physical control required for the cue sports demands attention, concentration, and the use of mental imaging to produce the best performances. Haphazardly swatting at balls without a plan or attention to detail will prove suicidal in competition.

But overfocusing can be equally damaging. You might have heard a player say after a match, "I thought too much" or "I overthought that shot." Overthinking produces mechanical body actions, unnatural rhythm, and second-guessing in your pattern play and shot selection. You need to allow your body to let go and play the game. Think of picking up the phone and dialing a well-known number. You do it automatically, without conscious effort. Yet if someone asks you for the number, you might stare at the keypad, dumbfounded. So it goes with pool. As your skills increase, your body develops muscle memory. When faced with a particular shot, your mind can successfully "dial the number" as it's done a hundred times before.

Your focus, then, shouldn't be on every little detail but rather on letting your mind and body flow naturally through a game or match, while shutting off outside distractions.

Concentration

So how, you ask, can you concentrate and not concentrate at the same time? Well, if there were a magic formula for this, athletes would pay for it in spades. Think of concentration as a narrowed focus. In pool, you need to narrow your focus to the task at hand—that is, the game or match you're playing. You focus on each shot; you don't focus on the crowd or on the tip of your cue. You also don't focus on self-reminders about stroking through the ball or not hitting a shot too softly. Letting these thoughts in can wreck your concentration on the task at hand.

Maybe you've witnessed a match in which a player plays an unbelievable game or series of games, seemingly effortless in their execution. Afterward, the player could honestly not tell you much about the match, or the crowd, or the room he or she just played in, let alone any particular shot. This kind of mental zone is something like a trancelike state. The player's concentration was so honed, his or her attention to the task at hand so focused, that outside distractions virtually disappeared, allowing the player to completely use the knowledge built up through practice without conscious thought or analysis. If you haven't yet experienced this in pool, or doubt that such a state exists, consider an example you've probably encountered in your day-to-day life, such as driving home from work. Your mind can wander, and yet you arrive at your destination just fine, often not remembering how you got there. Your subconscious mind took over while your conscious mind attended to other details.

Here are more wise words from Dr. Nideffer:

> You are reacting so automatically that you do not have to consciously direct your body; you are simply letting it do what it has been trained to do. . . . Masters of karate and aikido refer to the special state of concentration where everything occurs automatically as "making your mind like water." When you are in complete control of your mind, you are able to keep your own anxiety as well as external distractors from interfering with concentration. (pp. 6-7)

Think back to a time when you played a match, maybe in a tournament or a league, after not having played for a time. Chances are you started out playing well; your mind forgot all the little commands and reminders that could interfere with your concentration. As the match progressed, you likely began to think more. Self-doubts started to creep into your head, and you fought them off with extra effort that you in fact needed for your focus on the game. Toward the end of the match, you became uncomfortable; your rhythm was off; you were having a more difficult time concentrating on the task at hand. Your mind began telling you all the things you should be doing and second guessing all your moves. Your play was no longer natural or flowing; it became a series of little steps and actions, diametrically opposed to the ideal flow of an athletic performance.

Total concentration requires freedom from both internal and external, distractions. If your mental and physical response to the task at hand is not automatic, your attention will scatter. Your brain will begin a search for an answer to what you should do next; your attention will turn from the match to inward thoughts, including self-doubt.

Preparation

Now that you understand what concentration is, we can work on a few methods to improve it. First, you must come to your practice session, tournament match, or league night prepared. Part of this is making sure you're comfortable. Wear clothes and shoes that make you feel comfortable and confident; this gives you one less thing to think about during your match. This is not the time to try out a new pair of shoes or to wear a shirt that might draw attention to you. Go with what has worked for you in the past. You don't want to be thinking about how you look as you bend over the table for a shot.

Another part of preparation is stretching your muscles to promote relaxation and ease in movement. (See page 210 about stretching target areas for the pool player.) Also be sure to eat a light, healthy meal before your match. Don't think that because pool is less physically strenuous than some other sports that you can blow off breakfast. You might not work up a sweat during a long pool match, but you'll exert a tremendous amount of physical and mental energy. If your body hasn't been fueled, your energy will run low. Conversely, a huge meal will weigh you down and make you uncomfortable at the table. Using your common sense in your preparation will help you relax and maximize your concentration.

Relaxation

The second step is relaxation. In pool, if you are keyed up or anxious, you are sunk. Because of your natural flight/fight reaction to tense situations, your body will produce extra adrenaline to physically prepare it for the battle at hand. While this may be a nice feature for sprinting or bullfighting, the touch and finesse required in pool will surely suffer from too much power in your stroke! And, across the board, coaches in virtually every sport promote relaxation for their athletes through deep-breathing exercises. Various martial arts even demand its use, and for good reason. Deep breathing clears both the mind and the body, allowing calm focus on the task at hand.

Deep-breathing methods are recommended by almost every authority on mental training in sport. One of our favorites, Steven Ungerleider, devotes an entire chapter of his book *Mental Training for Peak Performance* (2005) to breathing exercises. According to Ungerleider, "The most important single aspect to staying focused in sport is breathing. Without proper breathing, even the best-conditioned athletes can get easily winded and fatigued and perform poorly."

This is good news for us pool players. Deep breathing is something we can do not only before a match but each time we're sitting and waiting for our next opportunity at the table. The anxiety normally caused by waiting for your opponent to miss can be conquered by concentrating on your breathing while in your chair. Try this exercise. Take a deep breath through your nose, visualizing as you inhale that the air is being drawn into the very center of your body. Do this for 8 counts. Hold the breath for 2 counts, then slowly release it for 16 counts through your mouth, visualizing as you do that all the tension, anxiety, and self-doubt is exiting with that breath. Some people add to this visualization by using colors. When breathing in, visualize the color blue. When breathing out, visualize the color red. Blue is said to be a relaxing color, whereas red equates with anxiety. Thus you're taking in relaxation and releasing anxiety. Players will often tell you that a few minutes of a breathing exercise before they play lets them feel lighter, more focused, ready to play, and that the table and balls even seem clearer and brighter in their vision.

Once you're prepared and relaxed, your focus and concentration will allow you to make your own mind like water and turn in a peak performance. But one further step is necessary, and that's shutting down those external, or outside, distractions. Though pool is often compared to an activity like chess, or to a sport like golf, the crowds and patrons of tournaments, billiard clubs, and lounges usually don't know or respect the kind of concentration required of our sport. It's rude, but not uncommon, for a server or customer to walk in front of your line of sight as you pull the trigger, and only the most focused players can ignore these kinds of distractions. On the other hand, athletes in many sports must conquer the same distractions. Picture the gymnast, who, while competing on the balance beam, must deal with the sudden burst of applause directed toward a performance on the uneven parallel bars mere feet from where he or she is completing a routine. In other words, you're not alone; we all experience challenges to our focus, and you can make use of advice given to other athletes in similar situations.

First, relaxation is paramount and, again, best achieved through deep breathing. Second, chances are good that your concentration is deteriorating while you're not actually playing but waiting for your next match or your next turn at the table. You begin to hear the voice of the rather boisterous fan behind you cheering on your opponent. You notice the waiter who seems determined to walk in front of players as they shoot, and you anticipate he'll do the same to you. You notice someone kicking her leg back and forth off the edge of her stool. The music is too loud, someone just dropped a glass—the list goes on and on. By the time you reach the table, your nerves are frayed. The least little movement caught from the corner of your eye might cause you to jump off your shot. Your concentration has shifted from the game to everything else but the game.

Professional players are well aware of the potential hazards of outside distractions and have come up with several tricks to keep them dialed in. Here are a few of our favorites:

- Keep your eye on the cue ball while you're sitting in the chair. Don't watch how your opponent is playing or try to predict what he or she will do next. Don't try to anticipate what shot you might have to take next. Just watch the cue ball. This keeps your mind and attention on the table. The last thing you want is to lose your focus by watching your opponent or by guessing what your next move will be, only to be disappointed when your guess is way off. Keeping your eye on the cue ball allows you to be ready to shoot when it's your turn. Your attention won't have to shift—you're already zoned in to where you need to be.

- Develop a rhythm or tempo in your mind. Establish your own rhythm for your shot execution at the table. For example, if you bend, execute two regular warm-up strokes, then a short stroke, and then move back and into your execution, your beat or rhythm might be *bum, bum, bum, be, bum, buuum*. Once you establish your rhythm, repeat it over and over in your mind, even when you're not shooting. Think of how a chant or mantra during meditation takes precedence over anything else occurring nearby. Focusing on your own internal rhythm can work a similar way.

- A variation is to pick a favorite tune, one that matches the rhythm of your playing style (hard rock not advised!), and hum it to yourself throughout your match. Many players find they play better with music in the background because they can lose themselves in the sound and ignore other distractions.

Thorsten "The Hitman" Hohmann is the embodiment of mind–body toughness. His unflappable mental focus and strict physical regimen have helped him become a world champion.

- Distance yourself emotionally from distractions. They are what they are. That waitress and waiter are just doing their jobs, probably not even realizing they're in your way. If you get caught up in the question, *why is this happening to me?* your focus will surely unravel.

Mental Imaging

Once you reach a certain point in your physical pool game, your mental game will make the difference between winning and losing. By mental game, we refer not only to the memory of run-outs and proper strategy but to three key mental elements used extensively in athlete training today: visualization, mental practice, and mental imagery. Though they sound like the same thing and the terms often become interchangeable, you should know a bit about each, how they differ, and how you can use these concepts to develop your pool game. From visualizing your shot and position-play selection, to mentally rehearsing shots, games, matches, or even entire events, to using complete mental imagery, honing your mental imagination and focus is valuable to any player. Entire volumes are devoted to the practices and execution of different forms of mental imaging. A few of our favorite resources are listed in the references section on page 239.

Visualization

You're probably already using visualization in one way or another in your pool game. Players first learn to use visualization to pocket balls. Then they learn to expand their visualization techniques to position play. Thinking three balls ahead is a great example of this. If you're thinking three balls ahead (as we've encouraged you to do), you're already visualizing where the cue ball will have to be on the next ball to get a visualized spot on the table for the third ball.

Here's a suggested sequence for using your visualization skills. First, set up a sample Nine Ball run-out on your table. Now look at your first shot. Visualize the object ball to be pocketed. See it in your mind's eye rolling cleanly into the corner pocket. Then look for the position, or the angle, you want on the next object ball to get to the third object ball. As you visualize the shot in its entirety, narrow your focus to just the ball in the pocket and the resulting cue ball position. Now step into your stance and execute the shot, allowing your mind to calculate all the things you have already taught it: cue ball speed, direction, spin, and so on. As you try this the first few times, keep in mind two "do nots": *Do not* consciously think of all the processes the cue ball must go through to get to the next ball. *Do not* jump down on the shot after you visualize the object ball going into the hole. In other words, don't even step into your stance until you see the cue ball coming to a stop on the table. This promotes visualizing the entire shot, not just pocketing the ball, which is really a job only half done.

Now let's see if you can take your visualization skills a couple of steps further. We've already mentioned how important it is to always have in mind a destination for your cue ball. But what happens when you're shooting at the game ball, such as the 9-ball in a game of Nine Ball? Visualization can be a powerful tool in these instances. Say you're shooting the 9-ball into the corner pocket. You know the cue ball can stop anywhere, as long as you don't scratch, and you'll win the game. The danger in this thinking is that your mind can actually stop at the edge of that last ball. There's no extension or natural progression to the next ball, and your mind has a tendency to just stop at contacting that ball. This is a big reason you see so many game balls missed in competition. If you always have a destination for the cue ball, your mind can't stop or become lazy; it must complete the shot. Try visualizing a 10-ball an arm's length away from your game 9-ball. Visualize the entire shot—pocketing the 9-ball and arriving in the position for the imaginary 10-ball— before executing. You don't have to imagine difficult position on the imaginary 10-ball. Locate it near the 9-ball; that shape on the 10-ball will help you shoot a crisp, firm stop shot.

Visualization might also improve your break shot. First visualize an ideal position for your cue ball before you break. Then visualize a ball (e.g., the corner ball in the Nine Ball rack) flying into a pocket. Finally, visualize the ideal position you want to shoot at the next ball. When you get strong enough mentally, you'll be able to visualize all the various scenarios in your pool game and confidently picture yourself straight to victory.

Mental Practice

Mental practice is the next step after visualization. Whereas visualizing involves seeing a shot situation at the table, mental practice helps you visualize a series of shots, games, or even an entire match without being at the table. Many professionals will tell you they knew they were first hooked on pool when they began seeing run-outs in their sleep, in their daydreams, even while driving or watching TV. Some of them don't recognize this as a first step toward mental practice. Fewer still realize that you can indeed practice your pool game even when a table is nowhere to be found. Mental practice can be achieved through using your memory, recalling your own performances and practice situations, and through the memory of external experiences, recalling the talents and moves of others to improve your own skills.

Jean Houston, the director of the Foundation for Mind Research (Pomona, New York), has authored several books, including *Mind Games*, *Listening to the Body*, and *The Possible Human*. The latter discusses at length the concept of kinesthetic body imaging—that is, using the mind to practice body movements without actually moving the body. This is a good reference, offering actual training for exercises for developing your mental imaging. Such exercises can then be transferred to your pool game. Say, for instance, you're sick for a few days and can't practice. You can still imagine playing a game or match—imagining shots, run-outs, pattern plays, and so on. Through body imaging, you can imagine the feel of stepping into your perfect stance, swinging the cue smoothly, making contact with the cue ball, and cleanly pocketing the object ball.

Houston (1982) refers to drawing on the talents of other athletes to optimize the use of your kinesthetic body for rehearsing sport skills. She uses a tennis example, suggesting that young players imagine themselves as such players as Venus Williams or Roger Federer and then going through the motions of their own games in their mind. Of course this can work for pool as well.

> With kinesthetic rehearsal we can make the identification between these ideal images and our own movement . . . allowing the expression of our stored imagery of more optimal performance. (p. 20)

Author Steve Ungerleider (2005) also refers to drawing on the talents of other athletes, citing how skills might be improved by taking mental pictures of the flawless performance of others: "[O]ur minds take snapshots of the skills and record them in a specific region of our brains. . . . Imagery is based on memory and we constantly reinforce the internal process by a flood of new pictures from external experiences to out minds."

Perhaps this has happened to you. Have you ever watched a performance by a great player on TV and later that day turned in a performance exceeding your usual capabilities? It can happen. This makes a great case for watching professional players in competition, be it live, on TV, on the Internet, or on DVDs for sale at billiard clubs and supply stores. If you haven't tried this yet, it's time to give it a try. Pick a player who matches you as closely as possible in body type to make it easier for you to imagine yourself performing his or her style of play. Watch the player on DVD (so you can go back and watch certain sequences again and again), and then go out to play.

Mental Imagery

Steve Ungerleider explains the concept of mental imagery and its relation to visualization this way: "Imagery can be described as an exercise that uses all of the senses to create an experience in the mind. . . . Visualization is just one part of this imagery experience. We can also feel, smell, taste, hear and touch in our imagery experience" (2005, p. 32).

In other words, mental imagery differs from mental practice in that it involves all the senses to create a more complete mental picture. By using all your senses in the focused mental rehearsal of your pool game, you can simulate competitive conditions to the point of eliciting natural physical reactions from your body, such as increased adrenaline and heart rate. Try this. Picture yourself in an important match playing against the best player you know. Visualize the crowd watching the two of you compete. Hear the crowd and ambient noise in the background, the sound of each shot as your cue contacts the cue ball, and the cue ball sending an object ball crisply into a pocket. Feel the cue stick between your fingers and the fabric of the table beneath your hand. Most important, visualize a positive outcome to the match. Top athletes, even when they're not in actual physical practice, continually rehearse and use mental imagery to project positive reinforcements in their mental performances that will translate to eventual physical performance. This kind of reinforcement allows you to practice while you're not at the table; it builds confidence in your game that carries over when you do play a match.

You can also use mental imaging to practice ideal emotional states surrounding your physical performance. Mentally image the postmatch emotions of winning. Mentally create the win in your mind; accept congratulations from fans, and feel the adrenaline in your body slowly dissipate as the competitive rush slows down. Enjoy the positive response of your mind and body to these mental images and make it easier to re-create them in competition.

PLAY WITH CONFIDENCE

Knowledge is power—in both the mind and the body. Knowledge of the body might be described as a developed skill honed through practice. In pool, there's a great deal of integration between mind and body knowledge; practicing a skill until it's second nature for your mind and your body will significantly increase your confidence. The more you play, the more shots you'll begin to let go of and just shoot the ball, without conscious thought or calculation. This allows you to shoot with authority, knowing you'll make the ball and that your cue ball will go where you want it to.

You've felt this way before: absolutely sure you're going to make a shot. Now we want you to transfer that feeling to *every* shot. Constant mental imaging within your game will further develop your tempo. If you can begin to shoot every shot with the same tempo and rhythm, projecting the same confidence and executing with the same sense of authority, knowing you'll make the ball and where the cue ball will go, more difficult shots will begin to find their way into the pocket. Little by little, more shots, more safeties, and more game situations will become second nature for you.

In pool, as in most athletic endeavors, fear is your greatest enemy. Henry Ford might have never held a cue stick, but he was on to something when he said, "Whether you think you can or you can't, you're right." Why waste any energy thinking we can't do something? There's no upside. A friend once told us that she was concerned about her son playing football and cautioned him endlessly, "Be careful, don't get hurt, protect yourself." The coach found out and told her this was probably the worst thing she could say. Fear of getting hurt could make her son overly cautious, hesitant in his actions, and more likely to injure himself. You're not going to hurt yourself too badly playing pool, but you get the point: Fear-based play can have devastating results. Too much hesitation, too much caution, babying shots that need to be stroked with authority—this kind of fear causes errors that can be avoided.

If you're afraid of the shot in front of you, the situation, the score, your opponent, or people watching you, how can you possibly make a shot? With fear, your fight-or-flight instincts kick in, which is precisely what you don't want to happen at the pool table. Extra adrenaline produces unneeded strength and reduces your sense of feel and timing.

Replace fear with confidence. If you have faith in your ability and confidence in the outcome of each shot, you can't simultaneously fear the outcome. Confidence and fear can't coexist. Have confidence in your ability to get out of a tough situation. Have confidence that the crowd will appreciate your prowess at the table. Have faith that you can reverse a score that's not in your favor.

Once you have built a base of confidence through practice and faith in your ability, you can move on to fine-tuning your confidence and self-image with effortless play—and occasional self-analysis to make sure you're having fun!

Effort Versus Effortlessness

Pool is often called a thinking man's sport because of the extensive strategy involved. The sport is even compared to chess in terms of strategic maneuvers and offensive and defensive moves. Unfortunately, too many pool players extend their thinking to a dangerous degree during a match. Remember that pool is still a sport. Too much thinking won't let your body do what it's supposed to.

So how can concentration and focus be so important? In pool, these concepts become very easy to confuse. You must strike a delicate balance. Thinking too much about your execution is no good. What your concentration skills must focus on is allowing the body to do what you have trained it to do. Once you have analyzed a shot situation, your body must take over to effortlessly make the shot. This can be difficult during a pool match because pool is a nonreactive sport; there are no automatic reactions to a ball coming your way as occurs in other sports. The nonreactive nature of the game allows time for the untrained mind to wander.

To combat this and to increase your confidence, play your matches with an air of effortlessness. If you're putting forth too much effort, you're not playing naturally, letting your mind and body flow through the game. Relax; enjoy what you're doing. You have already put forth enough effort through long hours of practice. Now it's time to show off a little and let your body do what it's been trained to do.

Have Fun

In any sport at which you choose to excel, you have to be enjoying yourself. Mike Veeck, owner of several minor league baseball clubs and son of legendary major league owner Bill Veeck, based an entire motivational business philosophy around the concept "Fun Is Good" (and wrote a book with that title, which we recommend). It's a simple idea—if you're grateful for the progress you're making and enjoying every step you take toward improvement, you're bound to improve. Conversely, with an attitude that says, "This is work" or "This is so hard," you don't get as much out of playing, you won't have any fun, and you won't learn much. Why bother?

Try to take something with you from each practice session and each match you play. Don't focus on what went wrong or what shot you should have practiced more. Ask yourself what went right. What shots were you proud of? What shot, technique, or safety did you develop a little more confidence in? If you obsess over every missed shot, every ball roll, or every lucky roll your opponent got, you'll have gained nothing but a headache. Your head will be filled with negative thoughts about everything that can (and thus will) go wrong, and you'll become a complete mess, lacking self-confidence and unable to shoot even easy shots with any kind of authority. Some refer to negative thinking as placing an order with the universe. If you think, speak, and act as if you'll fail, that's the order you place, and chances are that's the order you'll receive. If you think, speak, and act positively, that's what you'll draw to yourself, and to your pool game.

We're sure not suggesting that you shouldn't acknowledge your weaker areas or try to improve what doesn't work in your game. Just do it in a way that reflects a positive attitude. Think this way: *I can draw the ball 6 inches (15 cm) very well; now I'd like to practice drawing it 12 inches (30 cm) farther.* Look at assessing your performance as a fun way to learn. Once you've reviewed the good things about a match or practice session (even try writing them down sometimes), you can make a list of the shots you might have played differently. Allowing yourself plenty of praise and appreciation first will make you more eager to attack more challenging areas. You can then work on each of them to develop better abilities that translate to more self-confidence the next time you play.

PHYSICAL TRAINING TECHNIQUES

Here's a quick list of the ideal physical qualities every pool player would like to possess:

1. Good cardiovascular health for optimal breathing and physical and mental endurance
2. Good balance and posture for proper stance and execution at the table
3. Excellent eye–hand coordination
4. Flexibility to allow proper bending and stretching at the table and avoid muscle tension
5. Strength

Happily, these are desirable characteristics to possess in most aspects of your life; so if you're not already engaging in activities to improve in each of these areas, you should be—and not just for your pool game. Let's look at each of these characteristics individually and target some immediate improvement to your pool game.

Cardiovascular Health

If you're already in good physical shape, this will be easy for you. If not, it's time to get off the couch. Endurance in pool is critical in long matches. Though you might not feel the immediate effects of your body tiring, a body in poor health quickly becomes mentally soft, too. Poor cardiovascular health also leads to shallow breathing, which is counterproductive during a match; you need to be breathing deeply to shed off that excess adrenaline and remain physically focused at the table.

Best bets: cardiovascular activities such as brisk walking, jogging, swimming, jumping rope, aerobics, or the use of rowing machines, exercise bikes, stair-climbing machines, treadmills, and the like. These cardiovascular activities promote good circulation and build muscle tone. The added benefits include increased oxygen flow to the brain and disbursement of excess adrenaline in your system. Breathing and relaxation exercise become effortless with a regular program of cardiovascular activity. All of these activities have the bonus benefit of building a stronger core to strengthen your physical game as well.

Balance and Posture

At the pool table or away from it, poor balance and posture can cause all kinds of problems, including poor spine alignment; sore, tense, or cramped muscles; pinched nerves in your back, neck, or shoulders; and even poor digestion. Fencing, a sport in which balance and posture are critical, requires athletes to strengthen the back, abdomen, butt, and upper thighs—the center or the core of the body. Increased strength and tone at the core allow you to center properly, thus creating excellent balance. It might be no coincidence that one of today's top female pool players, Austrian Gerda Hofstatter, was a European junior fencing champion before she traded her foil for a cue stick.

Besides fencing, other sports that work your target areas as well as improve balance and posture include martial arts, bike riding, and in-line skating. More unique sport activities include apparatus such as the trapeze and the trampoline, each of which benefits both balance and cardiovascular health. If you're really adventurous, you can try tightrope walking, but for most of us, conditioning activities that keep us rooted firmly to the ground work just as well.

Eye–Hand Coordination

There are plenty of theories about eye–hand coordination out there, and many of them have been proven wrong as medical and brain research produces new findings. Eye–hand coordination was once thought to be predominantly a genetic characteristic (either you're born with it or you're not), but newer studies have shown that much of it is learned in the early stages of life, along with a great many other physical and cognitive abilities. Depending on your age, most of you probably don't have parents who were aware of these recent research findings when you were growing up. Don't despair. This doesn't mean you're stuck at your current level of eye–hand coordination.

As you learned in our section on vision enhancement in chapter 2, eye–hand coordination can be improved, no matter what your age. Juggling, archery, martial arts, and tennis all help develop eye–hand coordination—and so does pool. Some claim that video games are also excellent exercises, but we would argue that they tend to be nonrelaxing activities that don't engage much of your body beyond your fingers, and they strain your eyes.

Flexibility

Like eye–hand coordination, flexibility can be improved at any age with proper stretching techniques. We advise anyone who participates in any physical activity to learn and practice good stretching techniques. If muscles are not properly and regularly stretched, muscle tension can ensue. This can result in muscle soreness, pinched nerves, pulled muscles, and sometimes serious physical injury.

The benefits of flexibility to pool players, especially in the neck, back, and legs, are enormous. On larger tables, many shots require stretching across the table.

Almost every shot requires bending at the waist, and then raising the head up from this bent position to see the table. Inflexibility causes errors in your game and will likely result in physical discomfort.

Most aerobics and floor exercise classes teach excellent stretching techniques to promote better muscle movement and flexibility, as do the various forms of martial arts and yoga, which teach the added benefits of proper breathing and concentration. Swimming is also an excellent activity for the pool player, providing nonimpact exercise for your entire body. All good strength training incorporates stretching as well.

Most players assume they can execute a solid swing without any form of warm-up. We disagree. You should engage in some form of stretching before picking up your stick. Stretching increases your mental and physical relaxation, reduces tension in your muscles that can lead to soreness and injury, helps you develop better body awareness, and optimizes your practice and performance sessions.

Here are a few of our own favorite pregame stretches. Ease, don't bounce, into each stretch. Bouncing increases rather than decreases tension and can cause injury.

- Toe touches: These are good for stretching the back muscles and hamstrings. Spread your legs shoulder-width apart and slowly touch your fingertips to the floor. Bend your knees if you want to, working toward a straight-leg position and bending merely from the waist.

- Finger Push-Ups: These are excellent for stretching out the tendons in your fingers and wrist. Simply put your hands together, spreading your fingers apart as wide as you can. Use pressure to push against your opposite hand, stretching the fingers backward. This is particularly helpful when playing pool because your grip hand is always in a cupped inward position. By stretching this seldom-worked area, your grip hand won't lock up or tighten in tense situations, which might otherwise cause you to punch (with no follow through) or overstroke a shot.

- Neck Stretch: These stretches gently work your neck, shoulder, and arm muscles and can be done even while playing in a match to relax your body and your nerves. Sit straight on your chair or a low stool with feet in front of you touching the floor. Hold onto the edge of the chair with your left hand. Gently allow your body to pull away from your left arm, tilting your head to the right side of the maximum stretch in your neck and shoulder area. Hold the stretch for a few seconds; then switch arms and repeat.

- Neck Rolls: In a sitting or standing position, roll your neck clockwise four times around, stretching it in all directions. Repeat this exercise counterclockwise. Do these often to relieve neck tension, whether you're playing pool or working in an office. The first few times you might hear a crackling sound, which indicates that you could use a good stretch.

Make a point to refer to other books or classes on stretching. Our favorite book is *Sport Stretch* by Michael J. Alter (1998). Our preferred stretches are those that target possible problem areas for the pool player—knees, hamstrings, quadriceps, abdomen and hip flexors, lower back, posterior neck, lateral neck, anterior neck, triceps, and forearm flexors.

The Stretch Deck (Miller and Kaufman, 2002) from Chronicle Books is another favorite. It features a 50-card deck of stretches that you might want to incorporate in your routine. For more ideas, you might watch how some of your favorite professional players warm up before their matches.

Strength

Personal trainers Alex Chumley and Christina Yates head up trainer coordination at Pivotal Fitness outside Charleston, South Carolina. The two have trained many athletes for peak performance in their sports, including pool players. They advise that even the most talented and knowledgeable player at the table can benefit from the extra edge gained through increased strength and physical conditioning. The Eight Ball break, for example, is easier and more effective if you have some strength to support your fundamentals.

Look at today's stats of men and women playing the game and you'll note that the greater strength of men results in better breaks; on average, men pocket at least one more ball per break. This is evidence that strength can improve your game. Today's pros are working out more than ever before, with routines that build up their strength and endurance as well as keep their muscles stretched and toned.

What follows is a breakdown of target areas you'd be wise to attend to in your physical regimen. We do recommend consulting a trainer or physician before beginning a rigorous training routine. They can assess what your body should and shouldn't be doing. If you're out of shape, don't take on too much at once; pulling a pool muscle will surely sideline your practice sessions. Note that each of the moves we present targets pool-specific muscle groups and can be done with minimal equipment. Barbells (8 to 10 pounds are good for starters), bands, stability balls, and half Bosu balls are available at sporting good stores. Where specified, moves will double up to work more than one key area. If you frequent a local gym, a trainer there can also point you to machines that target the areas on which you want to focus.

For each exercise, begin with three sets of 8 reps. (Yes, it should get tougher at the end of your reps.) You can slowly work up to three sets of 12 reps before moving up in weight (when weights are required). We don't recommend doing any of these exercises more than a few times a week. Of course your trainer might override us on this based on your individual strengths, fitness level, and goals. If you're not sure of an exercise, seek the advise of a professional before trying it. We don't want an injury to keep you from the table.

Neck and Shoulders

You're looking for flexibility in this region. Shoulder strength supports arms that are bending, stretching, and stroking shots. This area is also where tension tends to collect during a match, so when you're not engaging these muscles, practice relaxing them. Drop your shoulders, move your head side to side, and keep things moving.

The first move shown in figure 11.1, *a* and *b*, demonstrates a modified dumbbell raise, which works the upper back, neck, triceps, and shoulders. Don't round your back; and rather than bringing the arm straight up with the dumbbell as in a traditional raise, swing it back and up in a pendulum motion as shown. Then hold the move at the top for an isometric contraction. Though this exercise is meant to work your stroking arm, make sure to work both sides to build overall shoulder resilience.

Figure 11.1   A modified dumbbell raise in action.

Upper Arms

Though we don't encourage overbuilding the muscles of the wrist and forearm (which might restrict stroke motion), we do endorse building up your triceps and biceps to generate more power on those shots that require the added punch, including long draw power shots and offensive break shots. In addition to the dumbbell raise, which works the triceps muscles, you can do hammer curls, as shown in figure 11.2, *a* and *b*, to work the biceps. Sitting on a stability ball, as shown, and working first one arm and then the other will maximize the biceps move (again, hold the move at the top of the raise for an extra second to isolate the movement) and work to stabilize your core balance, which is so important to a pool player's posture and solid foundation.

Core and Abdominals

Every workout should include an exercise that works both your upper and lower abdomen. If you're doing crunches, make sure you're focusing on lifting your body from its center and using your abs, not your back. Visualize drawing the bottom of your rib cage down to your pelvis to crunch your body. Use a stability ball, as shown in figure 11.3. To increase the stability strengthening features of this move, bring your feet closer together. The closer together your feet, the more you must work to keep the ball stable beneath your body.

Figure 11.2 Hammer curls offer the biceps a boost.

Figure 11.3 Using a stability ball to work your core.

Core and Back

Many athletes tend to ignore their backs in strength training because they don't see them much, and out of sight, out of mind. But a pool player's back takes quite a beating. We constantly bend over the table, stand up, and then bend again. Picture a coat hanger bending back and forth repeatedly; eventually it will snap. Without strong, pliable muscles to support your back and hips, you might snap too.

To keep your back strong, focus on working your core from the back each time you work on your abs in front. Strong back muscles will better support your spine, promote proper alignment, and let you enjoy hours at the table, no matter how many times you bend and stand up again. Figure 11.4, *a* and *b*, shows back raises that strengthen your back. Like ab-building crunches, these torso lifts are easier begun with the feet farther apart. Bring them closer together as you become proficient at these raises. This exercise also works the gluteals and hamstrings, where we'll be heading next. Note that if your back becomes sore you should seek professional help and give your back a rest to avoid a back injury. Bad backs are tough to live with, tough to fix, and, with all the bending in pool, tough to overcome at the table.

Figure 11.4   Use these back raises to strengthen your back and firm your core.

Gluteals

Bend over the pool table with your legs bent a few times and you'll feel those butt muscles contributing to hold you steady. Beyond that, all pool players want a good butt, considering it's sticking out from the table every time you bend over a shot. There's no substitute here for good old-fashioned squats and lunges. Figure 11.5 shows the proper down position for a squat (keep your body balanced behind your knees to avoid overstressing this area). Figure 11.6 shows the proper down position for a lunge. You can lunge repeatedly from the same leg or switch legs in a walking lunge across the room. Holding a stability ball in front of you for these exercises, as shown, increases the difficulty and helps isolate the muscles you're working.

Figure 11.5 The proper down position of a squat.

Figure 11.6 The proper down position of a lunge, using a stability ball.

Hamstrings and Thighs

As an athlete you already know the value of strengthening those upper thighs and hamstrings. Strain them or overstretch them, and you've got one painful version of a snapped rubber band. These muscles contribute to supporting your lower body, which will keep you strong and well toned at the table. To stretch and strengthen quadriceps, stand as shown in figure 11.7 and raise your lower leg behind you, holding at the top of the movement to isolate it. Use bands, as shown, to intensify the effectiveness of this exercise. Simple leg raises (figure 11.8) work the hamstrings and benefit the glutes as well.

Figure 11.7 Isolate quadriceps muscles with bands to intensify the move.

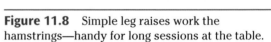

Figure 11.8 Simple leg raises work the hamstrings—handy for long sessions at the table.

Knees and Calves

Just as a strong core and legs are necessary to keep you standing there, don't ignore the muscles supporting the knees (often bending and flexing for shots, especially power break shots) and calves, which are most prone to painful cramping if you don't keep them stretched and toned.

To strengthen all those muscles supporting your bending and flexing knees, use the Bosu ball, as shown in figure 11.9, to do lunges and squats. These will work those knee muscles as well as your glutes and hamstrings, while still engaging your core to keep your balance through the moves.

To keep your calves stretched and toned, do single-calve raises on each leg by hooking one foot around the opposite ankle, as shown in figure 11.10, and rolling up onto your big toe. This requires balancing on one foot and will engage your core as you work the calves.

Our expert trainers warn that building flexible tone is easiest accomplished beginning with weights or moves that are comfortable for you. Work up to three sets of 12 to 15 reps before increasing the weight or difficulty of the move.

Figure 11.9   A Bosu ball increases the balance benefits of *(a)* the squat and *(b)* the lunge, keying in on muscles most strained by long sessions at the table.

Figure 11.10   Calf raises keep you from cramping in practice.

A Word About Water

No matter which workout, physical activity, or pool practice session you're enjoying, the importance of staying hydrated must be emphasized. Your body needs water, lots of it, even when you're just playing pool and think you're fine because you're not sweating. Personal trainer Alex Chumley explains, "When you feel thirst, you're already dehydrated, and when you're dehydrated, the first thing to go is your concentration, which is deadly to the pool player. Sweating or not, you're still losing fluids, and a poorly hydrated body will function poorly." In addition to losing mental focus, your eyes will tire, your strength will wane, and your endurance will fail. Our trainers recommend that you keep that water bottle next to you at all times; drink up and drink often, even when you don't think you need to. During a match, make sure you take a few sips whenever your opponent is at the table.

Stay strong, stay toned, and stay hydrated—you'll be in peak performance for your next match.

WORKING THROUGH SLUMPS

Now that you know a little about what's optimal for your physical attributes as a pool player, you can work toward goals of improved physical health, strength, and agility. However, even the most athletic and strongest pool players encounter an occasional physical slump. Usually, this slump can be accounted for by bad body position of some sort, whether after a layoff from the game, an injury, or simply a quirk in your stance or stroke. New equipment can result in physical changes, as can learning new concepts or skills. Your concentration on a new skill development might allow your body to lapse in a certain area. Perhaps you've even become lazy, and your swing or mechanics have changed to a point where they throw off your entire game.

There's nothing more frustrating than a physical slump, especially when you don't know its origin. When this happens to you, immediately check your fundamentals. If you have the advantage of playing with a teacher, coach, or good friend who knows your game well, have them watch you to see if they notice differences in how you approach your shot, stand, or swing a cue. If you don't have someone to watch your game, try videotaping yourself practicing. You might notice something you haven't caught at the table. If this doesn't help, you'll need to go through a step-by-step analysis of your physical game. Reread chapter 1, and, as you attempt different shots, try to feel what's different or uncomfortable.

Whatever the difficulty is, there's a solution. Avoid rushing into correcting something that doesn't need fixing, or you might makes things worse. In the sections that follow we'll run through typical problems encountered by pool players, along with their symptoms. You can use these sections as a checklist to analyze your physical game.

Foot Placement

Incorrect placement of the feet, predominantly the back foot, is a common problem, especially for players forced to play in smaller spaces or clubs with insufficient room around the table. If you're not properly spaced from the edge of the table, your eye–hand coordination will be thrown off kilter. Standing too close throws off your aiming ability because you don't have enough room for a free swing. When the swinging arm is cramped into too tight a space, the cue stick will naturally cross over through your shot, caused by your subconscious trying to make the ball even though you're not on it correctly. The crossover stroke results in mis-hits and unwanted english.

The reverse is also true. If you're standing too far away from your shots, you might be stretching too much. Your posture and balance will suffer, and your arm will be trying too hard to push through the shot rather than swinging naturally from the proper distance. In either case, go back to your fundamentals and check on the placement of your back foot.

Finally, check to see that your feet are not too close together. This results in awkward posture and bending and will affect your balance and your swing. Chances are, if your feet are too close together, you're either crowding your swing or standing to the side too much. Keep your stance open and comfortable.

Grip Position

Poor position of your back hand or grip hand can cause many difficulties. Let's begin with a grip that's too far forward. The simple mechanics of a too-forward grip prevent you from following through completely. You run out of cue on your follow-through, causing you to bring your entire shoulder into play. The shoulder and elbow drop farther than normal to compensate for the short, punchy stroke. Not only will you have swing problems, but the extra body movement will cause excessive difficulties in your delivery and aiming ability.

If your grip has slid too far back from its natural position, your timing will be thrown off. When your grip is back too far, you'll hit the cue ball before you're supposed to. The distance won't be what you anticipate, and you might end up with an unnatural hesitation in your swing. You can be lined up perfectly and won't understand why you're missing balls.

Bridge Difficulties

The bridge is the focal point of your swing. If your bridge hand is not in the right position, or if you've changed to a closed bridge, this could definitely throw off your stroke. Bridging too far back from the cue ball allows less control. Bridging too far forward results in more control but less follow-through and power. Also make sure that your bridge hand is in alignment with the rest of your body and not too far to the right or left of your shot. This is one reason we recommend the open bridge, although it's more difficult to achieve control over it in the beginning. Even a slight margin of bridge placement error in the closed bridge results in poor aiming ability and crossing over the shot in your swing as your body tries to compensate for the poor placement.

Too High, Too Low

If you're not getting down low enough over your shot, you might be having balance, swing, or follow-through difficulties because you're not allowing the arm its natural path for a swing (much like standing back too far from the shot). A head or back position that's too high will likely cause physical discomfort because you're forcing your body into an unnatural position.

If you're too far down over your shot, you might be hampering your swing and, consequently, your ability to follow through and achieve pinpoint position. When you stand too low, your body will have to rise up in your follow-through to allow the arm to stroke through the shot. Remember that moving any part of the body besides the arm is a big no-no.

Jumping Up

Another common problem among pool players is jumping up off the shot. Its causes include trying to watch the result of your shot, taking your eye off the object ball, and rushing your game. Some causes are mental, others physical, but the result is the same. To combat this, exaggerate the time you spend down on the shot after contact. Stay down on your shot until the cue ball comes to a complete stop, or until you count to three.

Improper Head Alignment

Perhaps you've picked up the bad habit of moving your head to one side or the other, or tilting your head in your stance. Some players can get away with this (and indeed, some must because of vision limitations). But for most of us, poor alignment only offers an improper perspective of the shot in front of you, and your aiming will suffer. The proper head placement, especially for anyone who doesn't play four or more hours a day, should be directly over the cue stick—chin over cue.

Finally, if you do find yourself in a slump, don't panic. Run through your checklist; go back and check your fundamentals. Experiment. Give yourself time to sort it out. It happens to the best of players. The worst thing you can do is try to change everything at once; you'll work yourself into a state of anxiety that tightens up every muscle in your body.

You're now mentally ready to excel. You're physically ready to win. The only thing left standing between you and pool excellence is a bit of time and energy devoted to practice. Yes, that sounds like work. But as you'll see in the next chapter, practice *can* be fun and interesting, especially with the help of several creative practice games and a routine you can customize to your own needs and abilities.

Practice Made Fun

Hall of Famer and world champion in multiple disciplines (Nine Ball, Straight Pool, and Trick Shots) Ewa Laurance has a favorite quote she offers to aspiring players: "When you're not practicing, remember that someone somewhere is . . . and when you meet him, he will win."

Ewa's not alone. This has been a favorite quote of savvy athletes for the past century, attributed originally to Hall of Fame basketball player Ed MacAuley back in 1928. Some quotes live on. One of the first quotes that many athletes hear is that "practice makes perfect." You've heard that one before. We all know we're supposed to practice. But what makes practice perfect? Anyone can bang balls around the table for an hour. Will we learn anything? A little over the long haul, maybe.

We're including a chapter specifically devoted to practice because we believe that practice is what separates the pros from the wannabes. With proper practice, you'll enjoy the keys to more efficient, more interesting, and more enjoyable sessions at the pool table. The primary reason most players don't achieve better results in their games is a lack of practice. Yes, practice can be boring in any sport. Pool, when practiced alone, can get tedious quickly if you don't vary your routine. Even though practice implies doing something repetitively until you learn the skill, you want to keep it fresh, mix it up a little, and make the best use of your skills in the time that you have to hone them.

We can work together to make the most of your practice sessions, integrating the knowledge you've taken from other chapters to get you up and running in record time. In this chapter we include details about goal setting, interesting sample practice menus, and practice games. Use this information as a springboard. Blend in your own ideas to develop practice routines tailored to your needs. As any professional player will tell you, a solid practice routine is all that's standing between you and your quest for peak performance at the pool table.

GOAL SETTING

Infomercial king Charles J. Givens once said, "Achieve success in any area of life by identifying the optimum strategies and repeating them until they become habits." Goal setting is where we identify those strategies, so we know that each bit of practice will be invested in their achievement.

BCA Hall of Famer Ewa Laurance is the first to credit a sound practice regimen for her long and illustrious career.

photo by Garry Hodges

As in any activity, in your desire to be a better pool player, you can set short-term goals and long-range goals, monitor your performance, and build consistently toward a better game. How much you progress and how fast is up to you.

The only constant we can guarantee you is this: You will *always* have something new to learn in the cue sports. That's the real beauty of the sport; no matter your age or knowledge of the game, you'll always enjoy a surprise around the corner. Visit a pro event with players who have been competing and winning for years, and you'll still see them in the practice room, sharing new shots or approaches they've recently picked up. Pro practice partners discuss shots and shot alternatives on a regular basis.

Let's begin with your primary (or long-range) goal for your game. What do you want out of pool? Do you want to

- Get good enough to win world championships?
- Compete on the pro tour?
- Win money in local or regional tournaments?
- Be the best player in your club?
- Play well enough to beat a few of your friends?
- Be able to make a few balls on your home table?

Answer honestly. It doesn't matter to us; one goal is no better than another. You just need to decide what you want from the game. Once you do, write it down in a practice notebook. This is goal number one.

Once you've chosen your primary goal, assess your current skill level with the same degree of honesty. This information will allow you to gauge the distance you'll need to travel from where you are to where you want to be.

Reaching Past Frustrating Plateaus

It can be frustrating when your game hits a brick wall. Suddenly, after measured improvement in your pool game over time, you seem to be running in place. Sometimes it feels as if skills have even deteriorated. You don't know if it's physical or mental. You don't know if you even want to play anymore.

Don't panic. This happens to everyone, even the pros. The first step toward getting past a plateau in your game is simply to take a break. Take a week or two off from your game—entirely off. Try doing different things during the times you normally play: a round of golf, video games, bowling, a movie. Pool is a sport that requires time to learn and patience to improve. We all get so much into learning and wanting to progress more quickly that impatience itself can hamper our progress. Forget about pool during your break. When you come back to the table for the first time, play just for fun. Put no pressure on yourself to perform.

What most players find is that even a short break gives them a fresh perspective and heightens their desire to play the game. Often this alone will get you over the hump and even provide a minor breakthrough as you play fresh, with no pressure.

Step two is to go back to the basics and work on your mechanics. Review your swing and your delivery; check your head and foot placement; adjust your grip. Focus on feeling what you're doing as you're doing it. You might simply need to get your body and your mind in tune again. Whether or not you're experiencing a plateau, this is something all players should do now and then to keep their games at a peak and avoid slipping into bad physical habits.

You might also want to change your choice of game for a while. If you play Nine Ball consistently, maybe your routine has become stagnant. Try Eight Ball, Banks, or One Pocket. Some establishments have billiards or snooker tables. If your club has either, try one of these games for a change. Playing new games can help you see different shots, tracks around the table, ball reactions, and other things you might have become anesthetized to in your regular routine. While searching out new games, maybe also take the opportunity to visit a new location. Sometimes a change of venue can restore lost interest.

Finally, you might want to alter your routine itself. If you're used to playing with a partner, try playing alone for a while. Maybe you need time to work on your game and your thought processes without interruption. Practice different areas of your game on different days: kicks on one day, banks and caroms on another. Sometimes getting the basic concept of a new shot down works wonders for your game and your confidence. If you already play alone, fine a partner to play with on occasion.

Above all, don't take your game too seriously. You might find that when you can't execute a particular shot you become frustrated, feeling that your game is slipping away. It's not. Your base of knowledge and experience will always be with you; it might just need a little prodding to resurface. Play the table and have fun. If you're not having any fun, you've probably lost sight of why you took up pool in the first place.

Your primary goal determines the length of time you'll invest in your short-range goals, which fall into three main categories:

1. Improving your mental skills (concentration, confidence, mental imagery)
2. Improving your physical skills (approach, swing, touch, critical shots)
3. Improving your knowledge (pattern play, decision making, strategic skills)

Once you've determined your practice schedule, divide your time (daily or weekly) to attend equally to these three areas. This will ensure your progress as a well-rounded player. If you concentrate on just one area, you'll end up with weaknesses in your game that affect the area in which you excel.

If you're a beginning player, start slowly and build your practice sessions. You'll find it's easier to give 100 percent to three one-hour sessions than to one three-hour session, at least until you build up your mental and physical endurance for the game.

PRACTICE GAMES

Practice routines with static drills and setup shots will get stale very quickly (though never discount their use for your game). To help you avoid boredom, we'll present over a dozen games to play and unique exercises in which you can practice your skills under gamelike conditions.

Three Ball

Objective: To consistently run the 7, 8, and 9 balls after your "break"

Skills Worked: Cue ball control, position play, safeties

Line up the 7, 8, and 9 balls in a triangle on the head spot. Break open the balls, paying particular attention to controlling your cue ball on the break. You may not take ball in hand after the break, so you'll really want to try to keep your cue ball close to the center of the table. If desired, beginners may take ball in hand on the 7-ball after breaking and work up to controlling the cue ball on the break. (For more details, refer to the Power Breaks section beginning on page 67.) Attempt to run the three balls.

If you don't get a decent shot on the 7-ball, try to execute an imaginative safety to hook your "opponent" or leave a difficult shot. Once you become fairly proficient at this exercise, change the game to Four Ball. Add the 6-ball and rack the balls in the shape of a small diamond. Three- and four-ball pattern practice will quickly have you recognizing patterns valuable to your Nine Ball game. (For more on pattern play, refer to chapter 7 beginning on page 135.)

Phantom Eight Ball

Objective: To consistently run the stripes or solids in a phantom game of Eight Ball

Skills Worked: Eight Ball power break, cue ball control, pattern play

Begin by racking all the balls as if you were going to play a real game of Eight Ball. Break open the balls. Look at the resulting table layout and decide which group (stripes or solids) you prefer. Remove the other group of balls from the table. This will help you see your patterns for Eight Ball. It's easier to visualize the lay of the table without the clutter of seven extra balls. Phantom Eight Ball will speed development of your pattern-play knowledge. Again, beginners may choose to take cue ball in hand after the break.

No Rails

Objective: To run the balls without the cue ball contacting any cushion on the table

Skills Worked: Cue ball control, speed control, pattern play

Toss six or seven balls out randomly onto the table; then place each at least 6 to 10 inches (15 to 25 cm) from a rail; no balls should touch each other or be close together. Study your resulting table layout and, with cue ball in hand, run the balls without letting any object ball or the cue ball contact a cushion.

There are many ways to run the balls without hitting a rail. This exercise is an overall great skill developer for pattern play, stop shots, and tightening up your cue ball control. It works both your mental and physical skills.

Safety Nine Ball or Eight Ball

Objective: To hook your (imaginary) opponent on every shot

Skills Worked: Cue ball control, speed control, safety play, kicking

Begin with a Nine Ball rack. Break the balls and take cue ball in hand on the first ball. Play safe by either hiding the cue ball from the object ball, or vice versa, or hide both balls. If you're successful, then try to kick at the 1-ball. If you're not, you may pocket this ball and play another safety, or, if you think you can, run out. If playing with a partner, the partner typically must play safe unless he or she has a clear shot to a pocket, in which case he or she can pocket this ball and play safe on the next ball.

For variation, try playing Eight Ball the same way. If you're shooting first at the striped balls, try to hide your cue ball from any clear shot on a solid ball, and so on.

Frozen Six Ball

Objective: To pocket all six balls without banking or combinations

Skills Worked: Frozen-to-the-cushion shots, speed control, pattern play

Set up the balls as shown in figure 12.1. Place the cue ball in the area shown, and attempt to run all six balls. Shoot them straight into the pockets with no caroms or combinations. Attempt to run them all without taking the cue ball in hand. This exercise is an excellent test of your speed control and pattern-play decision making; it will hone your ability to make balls frozen to the rail.

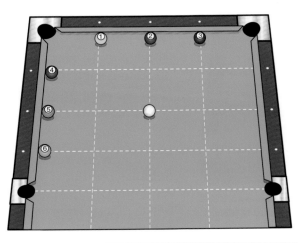

Figure 12.1 Attempt to run all six balls after setting up as shown.

Olympic Nine Ball

Objective: To achieve a 10-frame score, as in bowling, with 10 games of Nine Ball

Skills Worked: Developing a run-out mentality, cue ball control, pattern play, power breaking

Rack the balls as shown in figure 12.2. Initially, rack them the same way each time. Doing so helps you to recognize what's happening with your Nine Ball break in 10 consecutive racks. Later you can rack them like any Nine Ball rack, making sure just the 1-ball is at the head and the 9-ball is in the center.

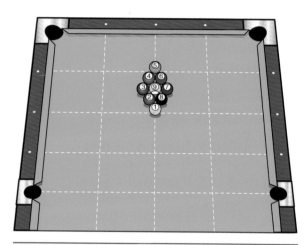

Break the balls. Whatever balls you pocketed stay down, as in a real Nine Ball game. With ball in hand (after the break only), attempt to run the table. Each ball you make is worth 1 point. Make a Nine Ball combination at any time during the frame and score 9 points. Break and run all nine balls to earn a bonus point, making the frame worth 10 points. Play 10 consecutive racks this way. The maximum score is 100 points. This is also a great practice game to play with a partner: you shoot a frame, rack for your partner, he or she shoots a frame and racks for you, and so on).

Figure 12.2 Rack the balls as shown to learn more about your break.

This exercise helps you develop a run-out mentality. You'll quickly see whether a run-out is possible and recognize how to go about getting there. It's also great for keeping track of your progress because you walk away with a score that you can compare to your performance in subsequent practice sessions. Keep in mind that as fun and addictive as this game might be, it works only on your offensive game, with no focus on strategy or defensive (safety) skills. It works as an excellent counterpart to Safety Nine Ball.

Philadelphia

Objective: To run the rack of object balls, pocketing each ball off the cue ball

Skills Worked: Cue ball control, speed control of both the cue ball and the object balls, caroms, angle knowledge

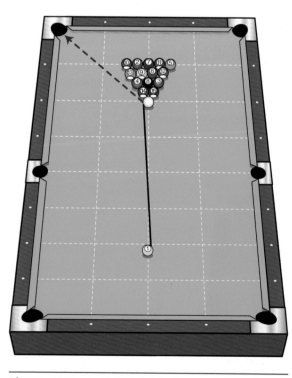

Figure 12.3 In Philadelphia, the cue ball is placed in the rack, and you break with an object ball.

For more information on the game of Philadelphia, see Put It in Practice on page 110. Rack the balls as shown in figure 12.3. The cue ball is placed where the 1-ball would be, and you may use the 1-ball as your cue ball. Break the balls, attempting to pocket the 1-ball by caroming it off the cue ball. After the opening shot you may use any object ball as your cue ball throughout the game. This helps you see angles of balls as they come off other balls and develops your judgment of where to hit a ball to have it carom correctly off the cue ball into any pocket. This is also an excellent exercise for controlling both the cue ball and the object ball. Note that stringing together runs of balls in this game requires patience and creativity. You should notice immediately that a carom off the cue ball into a pocket is made easier when the cue ball is closer to the pocket. In other words, it's in your best interest to pay attention to the speed of the cue ball. If it gets away from you, it might be several shots before you can maneuver it back toward a pocket. You can play this game yourself or with a partner. You can play for who takes a majority of the rack or to a set number of points.

Zigzag

Objective: To play a rack of 15 balls without shooting any ball straight in

Skills Worked: Cue ball control, banks, kicks, caroms, combinations

You can play this game alone or with an opponent. Rack all 15 balls and execute a power break to spread the balls as much as possible. You may shoot at any ball on the table, but you can't shoot it directly into a pocket. You can bank it in, carom it in off another ball, kick it in, or play a combination. This is an excellent game for working on your critical shot skills.

Make Tracks

Objective: To pocket a series of balls using only two-rail banks

Skills Worked: Aiming, banking

Place the balls along the right side of the foot spot out to the long rail, as shown in figure 12.4. You'll be attempting to pocket each of the object balls into the corner indicated. This is an excellent shot for your repertoire and is especially valuable in the intricate game of One Pocket. Begin by taking cue ball in hand and placing it behind the 2-ball, then the 5-ball, and so on; try to stop the cue ball on contact. Once you become proficient at this—when you can see the tracks to the pocket and know where to aim on the first rail to get you there—increase the difficulty of the game. Change the angle of the cue ball as it attacks the angle of the object ball. You'll notice right away how this alters the path of the object ball. This game is challenging.

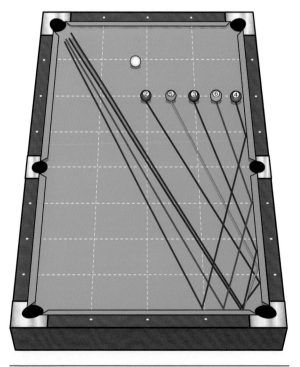

Figure 12.4 Set up the table as shown and attempt to bank the object balls two rails in the corner.

Expand Your Limits

Objectives: To discover just how many places your cue ball can arrive after pocketing an object ball; to be able to visualize a shot and have your cue ball arrive on the spot you have predicted

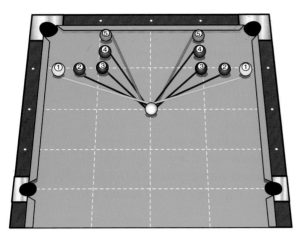

Figure 12.5 Before shooting each shot, visualize exactly where your cue ball should arrive.

Skills Worked: Cue ball control, speed control, follow, draw, english, visualization

This is a never-ending exercise because there are few limits to where your cue ball can travel on any given shot. Set up the balls as shown in figure 12.5. Place your cue ball on the foot spot. You'll execute your first shot with a center-ball hit at medium speed. Before you shoot at the first ball, however, visualize exactly where your cue ball will arrive. How did you do? Did the cue ball come short or long of where you visualized it would? Try the shot again. Once you've mastered the shot and resulting position with a medium hit, center ball, play it with draw and then with follow. Now add spin—low right, high right, low left, high left. If you like, add and reduce speed. Just remember that in each case you must first visualize where you'll be placing the cue ball.

Once you become proficient at the combinations of shots for each of the five balls, move the exercise to work the right corner pocket. Place the cue ball back on the spot each time so that you're working with a constant.

This exercise teaches you better than any other the wide variety of position plays you can execute, depending on the shot you're faced with. By visualizing both making the ball and your resulting cue ball position, you'll quickly develop a feel for where the cue ball is going and just what you need to do to get it there.

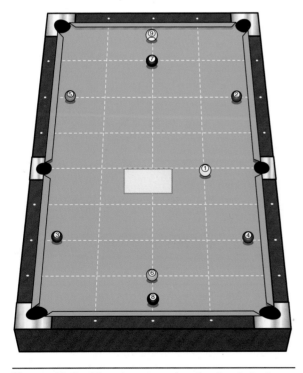

Figure 12.6 This exercise is harder than it looks and requires advanced planning and working the cue ball back and forth.

Mississippi Nine Ball

Objective: To run a predetermined pattern in a Nine Ball rack

Skills Worked: Cue ball control, pattern play, using the entire table

Place the balls as shown in figure 12.6. Balls near the rail should be about a ball's width from the cushion. Take the cue ball in hand anywhere in the shaded area shown. Now run the rack. Sounds simple, but this rack has been specially designed to make you travel back and forth without coming too far one way or the other. Get out of line once and you'll see just how difficult it is to finish the rack.

This is an excellent practice game for seeing patterns and honing your cue ball control. Miss, and you must start over. Through trial and error you'll soon learn on which side you must be for each subsequent object ball to get shape on (arrive in position for) the next. Unless you're an accomplished player, don't expect to get this one right on the first attempt.

Rotation

Objective: To run all 15 balls in order

Skills Worked: Advanced pattern and position play, cue ball control, critical shots, banks, caroms and combinations, power breaking

There's simply no better way to work all your skills than a game of Rotation. Rack all 15 balls as shown in figure 12.7, smash them open, and attempt to run all the balls in sequence. This is great training for Nine Ball. Once you're proficient at pocketing 15 balls in order, 9 balls seems like child's play. This game also works your advanced Eight Ball skills; when you run the first 8 balls, you will in fact be playing the solids, in rotation! This exercise is not for the faint of heart. If you're a beginner, achieve some proficiency at the other games before attempting this one.

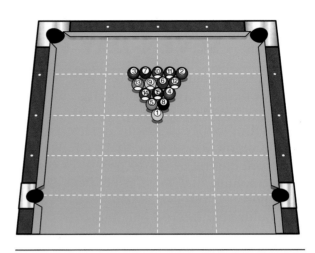

Figure 12.7 The Rotation rack. This game allows you to work all of your cue skills.

Get Centered

Objective: To get your cue ball back to the center of the table

Skills Worked: Cue ball control, position play

In chapter 6 we told you how important it is to get your cue ball to the center of the table. Doing so effectively reduces the size of the table because no shot is longer than half the table's length. It also keeps the cue ball off the rails and gives you the most options in shot selection. This game helps program your mind and muscles in how to get centered.

Place an object ball in each of the four corner pockets and one in front of each side pocket about a ball's distance away from the pocket. Place the cue ball on the head spot. Your opponent gets to choose which ball you must pocket for the opening shot as well as each subsequent shot each time you successfully pocket the target ball. If you run all six balls, you win; if you don't, you lose. A foul of any kind is an instant loss of game.

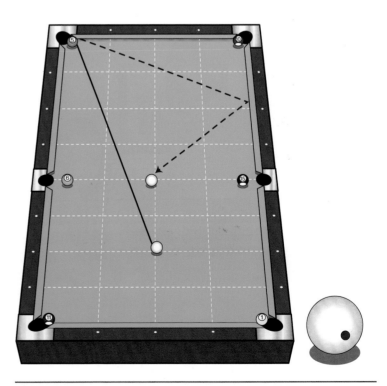

Figure 12.8 Try to get the cue ball back to the center of the table after each shot.

Rotate turns at the table. Figure 12.8 illustrates the opening setup. Try it. It's not as easy as it first appears. The best strategy is to keep the cue ball in the center of the table. If, for example, on the opening shot the cue ball lands on the long rail between the 11-ball and 15-ball, your opponent could call the 1-ball as your next shot and you would have to kick at it. Instead, be sure you hit this opening shot with a medium firm hit and low-right english to bring you right back to the center.

SEVEN-DAY POOL WORKOUT

Finally, to set you well on your way, what follows is a sample one-week practice menu, offering variety and interest to your practice routine. Where applicable, we've indicated the chapters you can reference for further discussion or explanation of the practice technique or shot listed. If you don't have time to include every part of a practice session, that's OK. We've presented a great deal of information crammed into one week to provide a complete selection. This program is meant only as a guide that includes all the areas of the game you'll want to enhance. Pick and choose as you like as you work toward developing an individualized program that holds your interest and improves your skills. Prepare your practice schedule as a teacher or coach might prepare homework assignments. Write your schedule down, and have a place where you can record your progress. Note what's practical and what's not. If you have only an hour to play, don't expect to work on seven areas of your game. If you can or want to play only three days a week, that's fine too. Again, this program is only a sample. If you do practice seven days a week and

Improving your skills with a casual group game makes practice more fun.

find that such a routine frustrates you, taper off to four or five days or fewer. The main objective is to have fun while you improve.

Don't be afraid to revise and update your schedule as often as needed. For example, if you begin with a lot of work on a proper stance and follow-through, these skills will eventually become second nature. You'll then want to replace some of the time spent on those skills with time practicing another skill or technique. Keep your plan fluid, and your game will progress naturally.

Note that each day's schedule assumes some form of stretching before your pool practice. Refer to page 210 for areas of the body to stretch before practice. You should also move toward incorporating eye exercises into your routine; these are found in chapter 2 and can be done at practice time or any time during the day.

We've designed each day of practice to work multiple areas of your game. Each day's practice session begins with a warm-up, followed by three exercises, followed by a cool-down period during which you'll work on your mental imaging skills. The practice session can take anywhere from 45 minutes to a couple of hours, depending on the time you have and how long you can maintain your focus.

Seven-Day Pool and Billiard Practice Routine

Every athlete works with a training regimen that seeks to develop the "whole athlete," whether it's a gymnast, a football player, or a pool player. We all have our favorite (and least favorite) things to practice, so it's important to develop a plan that keys on each area of our game if we're going to achieve well-rounded skills and strategies. What follows is a sample practice schedule over a one-week period that incorporates skill-building exercises found throughout this book. You can use this schedule or create one of your own; along with your exercises, just be sure to include a warm-up and a mental cool-down that lets you leave your session on a high note. Change your program as often as necessary to keep your time at the table fresh and interesting.

MONDAY

Warm-Up: Throw out a few racks of balls and play with your eyes closed to get a feel for your stroke and follow through. Play two or three racks this way.

Exercise 1: Throw a rack of nine balls out on the table. Shoot them with a closed bridge. Throw another rack out, shooting each shot with an open bridge. On the third rack, take the cue ball in hand on each ball to set up a shot in which the cue ball is on the rail. Use a rail bridge to execute. Throw out a fourth rack and take the cue ball in hand to make each shot difficult enough to reach so that you must use the mechanical bridge.

Exercise 2: Play two or three games of Philadelphia (see pages 110 and 226).

Exercise 3: Break at least five racks of Nine Ball and, no matter what the resulting lay of the table, roll out to a position in which your imaginary opponent has no shot but from which you can play a safety to hide the opponent. Play the safety, rerack the balls, and repeat the exercise.

Cool-Down: Sit quietly. Breathe deeply a few times while imagining yourself running a rack of Nine Ball (or Eight Ball, if you prefer). Begin with the break. See all the balls as they come to rest on the table. Plan your strategy, and mentally run the rack. This exercise should take about 10 minutes.

TUESDAY

Warm-Up: Perform the center-ball chalk exercise (see chapter 3, page 50).

Exercise 1: Play a few games of Olympic Nine Ball (see page 226).

Exercise 2: Play a few games of Safety Nine Ball (see page 225).

Exercise 3: Tighten up your game with a few rounds of Frozen Six Ball (see page 225).

Cool-Down: As on Monday, sit quietly, breathe deeply, and mentally image two racks of Nine Ball or Eight Ball.

WEDNESDAY

Warm-Up: Throw out a few racks of ball, executing each shot as a stop shot (see chapter 5, page 85).

Exercise 1: Play a few rounds of Make Tracks.

Exercise 2: Follow this up with a few racks of Zigzag.

Exercise 3: Tighten up your game with a few racks of No Rails.

Cool-Down: Imagine you're in a match and the score is hill-hill, meaning you and your opponent each need one game to win. Watch your opponent shoot and miss the first ball of the rack. Step to the table and find yourself hidden on the 1-ball. Execute a kick or safety to leave your opponent hooked. Watch him or her kick at the ball and leave you a shot. Then run out the table.

THURSDAY

Warm-Up: Throw out a couple of racks and play each shot to bring your cue ball back to the center of the table (see chapter 6, page 133).

Exercise 1: Play a few racks of Phantom Eight Ball.

Exercise 2: Play at least five rounds of Four Ball.

Exercise 3: Tighten up your game with an attempt at Mississippi Nine Ball; or play Get Centered to exercise your cue ball control.

Cool-Down: Mentally image a run of at least 16 balls in Straight Pool. Imagine the table is open and you've chosen your break shot. Run the rack leading up to the break shot, shoot this, and spread a few of the balls from the rack as you do so, enabling you to continue your run. You may mentally continue the run as long as you can without losing the mental picture.

FRIDAY

Warm-Up: Throw out a couple of racks of balls. Attempt to shoot each ball toward a pocket without actually sinking the ball. This works your object ball speed-control skills.

Exercise 1: This is the only exercise you'll focus on today. Play Expand Your Limits using only the left corner pocket.

Exercise 2: If time allows, repeat exercise 1, this time using the right corner pocket.

Cool-Down: The above exercise has trained your powers of visualization. Rather than mentally imaging something new, sit quietly and review the exercise in your mind, seeing all the resulting cue ball positions as you played them.

SATURDAY

Warm-Up: Throw out a few racks of balls and try to execute each shot with your resulting cue ball position at least 6 inches (15 cm) from any cushion on the table (see Shrink Your Table, page 132).

Exercise 1: Play five rounds of Three Ball.

Exercise 2: Expand your practice with a round of Olympic Nine Ball.

Exercise 3: Challenge your run-out abilities with a game or two of Rotation, attempting to run all 15 balls in order.

Cool-Down: Imagine running a rack of Rotation from the break to the 15-ball.

SUNDAY

Pick any exercise for warm-up, followed by three of your favorite game or drill exercises, followed by a half-hour of mental imaging sessions. Imagine any game situation you'd like, even if it's playing the best player on the planet in the world championships.

SHOOT STRAIGHT, HAVE FUN!

Congratulations! You now have all the blocks you need to build a solid foundation for a precision pool game. As with all endeavors, there will undoubtedly be a few stumbles along the way. Have patience. If you're tired of playing, take a break. The most important aspect to developing your pool game is to have the *desire* to become an accomplished player. Without it, you simply go through the motions of banging the balls around the table. If you find your desire waning, take some time away.

Take special care to check your physical fundamentals often because this is where players most often falter. When you do learn a new skill, enjoy your mastery. The more skills you learn and make your own, the more you'll want to learn. Experiment with the ideas we've given you. The possibilities for shot situations, creative safeties, and position and pattern plays are endless. Spend time on both your mental and physical skills; the integration of these is so important in the cue sports.

And, of course, in keeping with the spirit of the sport we love, we leave you with the two most important words: Have fun!

Glossary

bad hit: When a player fouls the cue ball by not making a legal hit on the intended object ball. Typically, the incoming player is awarded ball in hand.

ball in hand: When a player fouls, the opposing player may pick up the cue ball and place it anywhere on the table for his or her first shot.

bank shot: Refers to an object ball contacting one or more cushions before being pocketed.

bar box: Nickname for a coin-operated pool table, typically a model measuring 3.5 by 7 feet (1.4 by 2.7 m) found in taverns and lounges.

billiard: A shot in which the cue ball contacts an object ball before contacting and pocketing the intended object ball.

break: The opening shot of any pool game.

bridge: The support formed by the front hand on which (or in which) the front of the cue stick rests.

butt: The lower half of a cue stick (in a two-piece cue, from the joint down to the bumper).

carom shot: Shooting an intended object ball off an object ball to pocket the intended object ball.

cinch shot: When emphasis is placed on making a shot without regard to resulting position of the cue ball. This can be a difficult shot, used when you must focus complete attention on pocketing the ball, or when the next shot is so close to a pocket it doesn't matter much where the cue ball comes to rest.

combination shot: Shooting an object ball into an intended object ball to pocket the intended object ball.

deflection: The altering of the path of the cue ball when english is used, as the cue ball deflects to the opposite side of the hit. Sometimes called *squirt*.

double elimination: A tournament format in which players are paired on a chart and must continue to win each match to progress through the winner's side of the chart. The first loss a player incurs results in being moved to the loser's side of the bracket. Another loss results in elimination. The winner of each bracket plays in the final match.

draw: Achieved by hitting below center on the cue ball. Causes the cue ball to reverse its forward roll after impact with an object ball.

duck: A slang term for hiding the cue ball or intended object ball with a safety shot.

english: Putting left or right spin on the cue ball to change its path after contacting a rail.

ferrule: Usually made of hard plastic or ivory, the ferrule is found at the front end of the cue shaft. The cue tip is glued to the ferrule.

follow: Achieved by hitting above center on the cue ball. Causes the cue ball to roll forward after contact with the object ball.

foot spot: The spot midway between the long rails and two diamonds up from the short rail. Used as a reference for racking the balls. The front ball in any rack, or an object ball returned to the table after a foul, is always placed on the foot spot.

free shot: When you attempt a difficult shot, often a bank or combination, and then hide the cue ball from your opponent's intended object ball in the process. Should you miss the difficult shot, you leave nothing for your opponent. This is also called a *two-way shot*.

grip: Refers to the back hand's position on the cue stick.

hanger: A ball at or near the edge of the pocket.

head spot: Opposite the foot spot, the head spot is usually not marked by a spot but falls midway between the long rails and two diamonds up from the head (breaking) end of the table.

hooked: When the direct path between the cue ball and object ball is blocked by impeding balls (or, in the case of corner or side hooked, by the edge of the rail cushion). *Hooked* is the same as *snookered*.

inside english: This can be right or left english placed on the cue ball, depending on the angle of the shot. When cutting a ball to the right, inside english refers to right english. When cutting a ball to the left, inside english refers to left english.

joint: In a two-piece cue, the joint is where the butt and shaft screw together. Joint materials are usually composed of steel, plastic, or ivory.

jump shot: Accomplished by elevating the butt end of the cue stick and shooting down on the cue ball. The jump shot forces the cue ball to bounce into the table bed and over an obstructing ball or balls.

kick shot: When a direct path to the intended object ball is obstructed by another ball or balls, the cue ball can be shot (kicked) into one or more rails in an attempt to make a legal hit.

lag: Used to determine who will break, players each shoot an object ball from behind the headstring toward the opposite end of the table and back. The object ball that comes to rest closest to the head rail wins. The player winning the lag can elect to break or pass the break to the opponent.

legal hit: The intended object ball must be contacted by the cue ball, and either the cue ball or the object ball must then contact a cushion. In a frozen ball shot, the cue ball must contact the cushion after contacting the frozen object ball, or the object ball must be driven to another rail.

massé: An extremely elevated stroke of the cue stick on the cue ball (the cue stick is usually perpendicular or nearly perpendicular to the table surface). A massé shot allows you to send the cue ball forward, whereupon it will grab the cloth and come straight back.

mechanical bridge: The mechanical bridge has the appearance of a cue stick with a stable, grooved attachment at the end on which the front end of a cue stick can be placed to guide its path. A bridge is used when a shot is too far away to bridge with the hand. Also called a rake.

miscue: When the cue tip slides off the cue ball on attempted contact. Often caused by lack of chalk, lack of a scuffed tip, or a poorly stroked shot.

outside english: The opposite of inside english. Outside english can be right or left english placed on the cue ball, depending on the angle of the shot. If cutting a ball to the right, outside english refers to left english. When cutting a ball to the left, outside english refers to right english. Also called running english.

pilling: When bits of fabric fibers loosen from the fabric on the table bed. Usually occurs when the cloth is newer. Pilling causes erratic movement of balls across an otherwise smooth surface.

position: The place the cue ball should arrive, following any shot, to be in the best spot to execute the next shot.

rollout: Also called a pushout. This shot occurs when a player elects not to attempt contact on an intended ball and shoots the cue ball to a different position on the table. The incoming player may elect to shoot the shot left by the player rolling out or ask the player to shoot again, at which point the player must make a legal hit.

round robin: A tournament format in which a player plays every other player in the tournament, or every other player in a bracket. Players with the best win–loss record in each bracket often advance to a single- or double-elimination playoff.

running english: *See* outside english.

safety: A defensive shot in which the goal is to leave the incoming player a tough shot or no shot.

scotch doubles: A two-person team format, usually male and female. Scotch doubles often feature alternating shots at the table rather than alternating turns.

scratch: Pocketing the cue ball or jumping it from the bed of the table. A scratch is a foul, with the incoming player receiving ball in hand or the appropriate penalty for the game being played.

scuffers: A variety of tools used to scuff the cue tip, providing a rougher surface to which chalk may adhere, increasing friction between the smooth leather tip and the surface of the cue ball.

shape: Synonymous with *position*; you play position for the next shot or to get shape on the next shot.

shaft: The upper half of the cue stick (in two-piece cues, from the joint to the cue tip).

single elimination: A tournament format in which players are paired on a chart and must continue to win each match to progress through the chart. A single loss eliminates the player.

snooker: A cue game using a larger table (full-size models are 6 by 12 feet [1.8 by 3.6 m]) but smaller pockets and smaller balls. This game is popular in England and British Commonwealth countries, garnering hundreds of hours of live television coverage each year.

snookered: *See* hooked.

squirt: Same as *deflection*. Altering the path of the cue ball with english. The cue ball deflects, or squirts, away from the opposite side of the hit.

stroke: The motion of the arm that causes the cue stick to contact the cue ball. Same as *swing*.

stun: Shortening the distance the cue ball will travel on any given shot with the use of appropriate english.

tangent line: The line 90 degrees from the target line that your cue ball will normally glance off a ball after a center-ball hit.

throw: Refers to the altering of the path of an object ball struck by a cue ball traveling with english imparted.

tip tapper: A tool tapped against the cue tip to form a rough surface to which chalk will adhere, increasing friction between the smooth leather tip and the surface of the cue ball.

two-way shot: *See* free shot.

wrap: Found on the butt of a cue stick, the wrap is usually nylon, linen, leather, or cork. Partly decorative, partly functional, the wrap provides a less slippery surface than polished wood for which to grip the cue.

References

Alter, Michael J. 1998. *Sport Stretch* (2nd ed.). Champaign, IL: Human Kinetics.

Billiard Congress of America. 2007. *Billiards: The Official Rules & Records Book*. Denver, CO: Billiard Congress of America.

Chaney, Earlene. 1991. *The Eyes Have It: A Self-Help Manual for Better Vision*. New York: Instant Improvement.

Franklin, Eric. 1996. *Dynamic Alignment Through Imagery*. Champaign, IL: Human Kinetics.

Grandcolas, Lauren Catuzzi. 2005. *You Can Do It*. San Francisco: Chronicle Books.

Houston, Jean. 1982. *The Possible Human: A Course in Enhancing Your Physical, Mental and Creative Abilities*. New York: Putnam.

Koehler, Jack H. 1989. *Science of Pocket Billiards*. Marinette, WI: Sportology.

Kubistant, Tom. 1986. *Performing Your Best: A Guide to Psychological Skills for High Achievers*. Champaign, IL: Leisure Press.

Miller, Olivia H., and Nicole Kaufman. 2002. *The Stretch Deck: 50 Stretches*. San Francisco, CA: Chronicle Books.

Nideffer, Robert M. 1985. *Athletes' Guide to Mental Training*. Champaign, IL: Human Kinetics.

Stauch, Shari J. 2007. Editor's Desk. *Pool & Billiard Magazine*, Vol. 25, No. 3, March.

Ungerleider, Steven. 2005. *Mental Training for Peak Performance* (2nd ed.). Emmaus, PA: Rodale Press.

Veeck, Mike, and Pete Williams. 2005. *Fun Is Good: How to Create Joy & Passion in Your Workplace & Career*. New York: Rodale Press.

Index

Note: An italicized *f* following a page number indicates a figure.

About the Authors

Gerry "The Ghost" Kanov and **Shari "The Shark" Stauch** combine an unprecedented wealth of professional pool experience and talent to create this book. Both are staff members of *Pool & Billiard Magazine*, the top publication for the sport. They have played and worked with virtually every top professional pool player and instructor in the world.

Kanov has been playing professional and amateur pool since 1968. He has dozens of local and national top 3 finishes and championships, including two national team championships as a player and coach. He is an instructional editor and technical advisor for *Pool & Billiard Magazine* and has written dozens of instruction articles, including the popular "Ghost" and "Eight Ball Ernie" columns, *P&B* reader favorites.

Kanov was a touring professional on the Camel Pro Billiard Series and a coach for several top players. He also has a screen credit: He portrayed a referee in the motion picture *The Color of Money*. Kanov and his wife make their home in Nashville, Tennessee.

Stauch was a touring pro on the Women's Pro Billiard Tour from 1980 to 2004, when she retired to pursue promotion of the sport full time. She was consistently ranked in the top 32 players in the world, even while serving as executive editor of *Pool & Billiard Magazine* and handling publicity for the Women's Pro Billiard Tour. She has performed dozens of exhibitions for clients, including Gordon's Gin and ESPN.

Stauch was the founding president of the Billiard Education Foundation, which conducts youth billiard national championships and scholarship programs. Stauch was also a consultant for *The Color of Money*. In 2003 she was selected as the billiard mentor for *You Can Do It*, a book conceived by United Flight 93 heroine Lauren Catuzzi Grandcolas to inspire women to try new sports and hobbies. Shari resides with her husband and two children outside Charleston, South Carolina.

Together, Kanov and Stauch authored the first edition of *Precision Pool* as well as *Pool Player's Edge: Advanced Skills, Shots, and Strategies for 8-Ball and 9-Ball*. For more on the authors, including archived articles, visit www.poolmag.com.